FOSTERING KINSHIP

To my daughter Catherine

Fostering Kinship

An international perspective on kinship foster care

Edited by
Roger Greeff

Ashgate
ARENA

Aldershot • Brookfield USA • Singapore • Sydney

Published by
Ashgate Publishing Limited
Gower House
Croft Road
Aldershot
Hants GU11 3HR
England

Ashgate Publishing Company
Old Post Road
Brookfield
Vermont 05036
USA

British Library Cataloguing in Publication Data
Fostering kinship : an international perspective on kinship
  foster care
  1. Kinship care
  I. Greeff, Roger
  363.7'33

Library of Congress Cataloging-in-Publication Data
Fostering kinship : an international perspective on kinship foster
  care / edited by Roger Greeff; consulting editor, Jo Campling.
      p.   cm.
  Includes bibliographical references.
  ISBN 1–85742–410–7
  1. Kinship care.   2. Foster home care.   I. Greeff, Roger. 1946–
  II. Campling, Jo.
  HV873.F67   1999
  362.73'3—dc21   98-40534
                                                                                    CIP

ISBN 1 85742 410 7

Printed and bound by Athenaeum Press, Ltd.,
Gateshead, Tyne & Wear.

Contents

v

Acknowledgements

Above all, I would want to thank the other contributors for their persistence in producing their chapters. During the time we have been doing this work, two have obtained higher degrees, one has a new baby, and several have experienced personal or family illness or other tragedies. Through all this, the work has been rekindled and has finally come to bear fruit.

I should make clear that the final form of the book is my own responsibility. I apologise if any of the contributors feel I have misunderstood or misrepresented their views: I am grateful especially to those who wrote in English as a second or third language. I should also say that the views are those of the contributors, not their employers, with the exception of the two chapters which present research sponsored by the National Foster Care Association.

I must express my thanks to the International Foster Care Organisation for the excellent international conferences which it runs; they provide an outstanding opportunity for foster carers, young people, social workers and academics to meet, and to hold open and fruitful debate. It is in the context of these conferences that several of the contributors to this book have met, and discovered a common interest in kinship fostering.

It is a sign of the times that e-mail played a very important role in keeping this book moving forward. I must express my appreciation for the support given by John Dixon and Ray Beatson here at Sheffield Hallam University, and to numerous IT colleagues in other organisations around the globe for finding mutually compatible formats!

Like many other writers in the field of social work and social policy, I would like to thank Jo Campling for her encouragement in getting the project off the ground.

And finally, my thanks to the friends, colleagues and family members who have offered so much interest and encouragement, and in particular to my partner Viv who has shown so much patience when quality time seemed a distant memory!

As a small attempt to redress the operation of sexism, I have opted to use the female gender throughout, unless this would otherwise be inappropriate or confusing.

Notes on Contributors

Eddie Brocklesby has many years' experience in adoption and fostering, in statutory and voluntary sectors. An experienced Guardian *ad litem* and former chair of NAGALRO, she has researched and acted as expert witness on contact within adoption. She was development consultant on two Department of Health funded projects promoting the Children Act 1989.

Janet Foulds works as a manager of a child sexual abuse unit in Derby City Social Services department, prior to which she spent many years in social work with children. Her primary commitment is to helping children to recover from the traumas of sexual abuse.

Roger Greeff worked as a social worker with children and families in Social Services. He now teaches social work at Sheffield Hallam University, in the UK. He has interests in children's rights, social work with children and families, and in anti-discriminatory social work, especially in the area of racism.

Hermien Marchand is a social worker. Originally she worked as an educator with children with learning disabilities and with deaf children. For the last eight years she has worked in foster care, currently as team co-ordinator with Open Thuis. She has a great interest in relationships between family members, and in working in partnership with the natural parents and foster parents.

Wilfried Meulenbergs is a social worker with a career spanning more than twenty years in foster care. He has specialised in supporting children with learning disabilities and in foster families, and in organising selection programmes and day-release courses for foster families.

Bart van der Neut started as a social worker in a child protection agency and later in a youth care institute. He has specialised in systems theory and family treatment and has always worked extensively with foster families. For the last four years he has been director of the Foster Care Institute in Amsterdam.

Dr Valerie O'Brien works in University College Dublin (Dept of Social Work and Social Policy), and has recently completed her PhD in the area of relative foster care. She is a qualified social worker and family therapist and worked for many years in social work with children and families. She is a member of the Irish Adoption Board.

Riet Portengen worked for ten years in child protection social work. She then specialised in foster care with the Foundation of Intercultural Youth Care in Amsterdam, designing and implementing new methods, one of which is foster care in family or social networks. She has an international Masters degree in Managing Learning and Development.

Dierdre Pemberton has worked in child protection, in the probation service and in fostering services for 'hard to place' teenagers. From 1991 to 1996 she was the project worker with the Shared Rearing Project, developing fostering by Travellers for Traveller children. She is now a senior social worker with Cerebral Palsy Ireland.

Zofia Waleria Stelmaszuk is an Assistant Professor at the University of Warsaw, Faculty of Pedagogics, where she teaches and conducts research in child welfare. She has written extensively and given conference papers on child protection and foster care. She has also been active in international collaboration and is a member of the Executive Committee of the European Scientific Association on Residential and Foster Care for Children and Adolescents.

Julia Waldman worked for many years as a community and youth worker. More recently she has developed her work as an independent researcher, university teacher and business change consultant. For seven years she has been a foster carer for children and young people.

Suzette Waterhouse is a social worker/researcher with experience in Social Services, NSPCC and as a Guardian *ad litem*. Areas of research and publication include communicating with children, particularly in court, and the attitudes of short-term foster carers. She was project worker for the research published by NFCA as *The Organisation of Fostering Services in England*.

Ann Wheal is with the Department of Social Work Studies at the University of Southampton. She previously spent 17 years teaching young people in inner-city multi-racial schools and colleges. She has a wide experience of obtaining the views of young people and families and her publications include *The Foster Carer's Handbook*.

Joan Marcella Williams is a New Yorker of West Indian descent. She has a Masters degree in Counsellor Education and in Social Work. She has worked as a social worker in fostering and with the Child Welfare Administration. For the last seven years she has been Director of a residential group care programme for 115 adolescents in foster care in New York City.

Jill Worrall is a lecturer in Social Work at Massey University, Auckland, New Zealand. She was formerly Manager of Regional Child and Family Services for Barnardo's New Zealand and is National Consultant for the New Zealand Family and Foster Care Federation. Her research interests are in the Care and Protection of children and young persons.

Tables and Figures

Introduction

> Informal care by relatives seems to be an integral part of the cultural framework of a majority of countries, and even in those countries where kinship links are weaker, relatives are increasingly being seen as an under-utilised resource and a way of maintaining the child's links with the biological family. (Colton and Williams 1997: 285)

Most children in most cultures are likely to be supported not just by a nuclear family unit, but by a network of concerned adults. In most cases, this network will largely coincide with the child's extended family. The commitment of this kinship network towards the child is an important source of support, concern and care for the child, and it will often be members of this network who offer a child a temporary home if she needs alternative care. Several of the contributors to this book make the point that the network of support for a child can often be wider than just relatives, including neighbours and friends of the family: most of the ideas in this book will apply equally to the wider 'network'.

It is important to be clear that the focus of this book is not upon *kinship care* in general, but more specifically upon *kinship foster care* of children and young people. We will be focusing on those situations where relatives are caring for a child in partnership with the state, and where social workers therefore play a key role.

Our motivation in producing this book stems from a growing realisation that kinship foster care does in fact play a very significant role in child care in a wide range of countries and communities. Research suggests that fostering by relatives now accounts for 20–30 per cent of all fostering in many countries, and that the proportion is rising. There are specific issues and dilemmas in this area for social work practitioners, managers and policy

1

makers. We hope that the international perspectives offered within this book will prove helpful in escaping the 'taken-for-granted' nature of a particular way of seeing things within a specific national context. Historical patterns of family life, law and social policy may all have helped to shape established social work strategies within particular national contexts, but there may be very different perspectives and lessons to be learned from elsewhere.

Similarly, two of the chapters examine the issues from the perspective of Black and ethnic minorities: fostering by relatives may well prove a very important way of avoiding the removal of children from their own community and culture. It is crucial to good anti-oppressive social work that we incorporate these perspectives into our practice, and ensure that fostering services do not operate as a form of colonialism.

This book aims to combine the contributions of researchers and practitioners so as to offer a set of ideas which will challenge existing practice, but also suggest models of good practice. Case examples are offered and, wherever possible, we have given voice to the families themselves. There are four pieces of new research – on the experiences of kinship foster carers; on how social workers select placements for children and whether they consider kinship care; on how kinship foster carers see their training needs, and on the dynamics which develop within placements between the parents, the carers and the agency.

We will be suggesting that the available research indicates that foster care with relatives is of real value to the child, and should therefore be regarded as a placement of choice, not just as a fall-back when resources are short.

A theme throughout the book will be the need for social workers to think systemically. Too easily, current practice encourages a focus on nuclear family households. We will suggest that a full assessment of the whole network is essential if the worker is to assess the potential of a kinship placement and any risks involved. A systemic perspective will also be crucial if she is to support the carers once the placement is established, and two chapters look specifically at the complex dynamics involved when relatives become foster parents.

A widespread concern is that policy makers have neglected this area of practice. Some seem almost to assume that assessment, training and support are not really needed by these families – an assumption which contributors to this book would want to challenge. Similarly, there seems to be widespread uncertainty about the financial support of kinship fostering; should carers receive full fostering payments, reduced allowances, or no financial support at all?

The main thrust of this book will be to argue that kinship fostering is already a significant element in child placement, and is in many ways an ideal way of minimising disruption to the child and working in genuine partnership with the family. As such, we will be arguing that increased attention needs to be given to developing sound policy and practice, and to giving these placements priority when a child must move.

There are, however, some cautionary notes, and in particular, we draw attention to the difficult and sophisticated assessments which will be needed where social workers are considering a kinship placement following the neglect or abuse of a child. This will be particularly necessary where there has been sexual abuse. Not only the potential placement itself, but also any proposed contact arrangements may need careful scrutiny if further abuse is to be avoided.

Similarly, it is a theme of the book that this pattern of care, like all others, needs viewing in the light of larger developments in social policy. We shall point out that kinship fostering misused has the potential to extend the exploitation of women as carers, and to foist onto families some of the responsibilities that rightly belong with the (Welfare) State.

Finally, as we examine some of the issues in kinship fostering, we also provide a contrast with 'regular' fostering practice and raise questions about the nature of fostering itself. Social workers have tended to view fostering by carers unrelated to the child as the 'norm'. In post-communist Europe, this may draw policy makers into rushing to establish such a fostering service, while largely ignoring the existing pattern of kinship care which continues to thrive within the community.

In addition, the dominant definition of fostering has assumed one or two adults in a nuclear household: this is in fact a very narrow view of how children are supported, and we should, perhaps, consider the value of recruiting a network, not a household. Similarly, ideas about 'permanence' often assume that security for the child is best achieved by a legal transfer of the child into a new family: this orthodoxy is brought into question when we examine kinship foster care. Arguably children can be offered much greater security in kinship placements, living with someone 'who shares [her] own most basic and important memories' and who can 'polish up the fading memory before it is too late' (Kellmer Pringle 1975).

In summary, this book will examine issues and argue for good practice in kinship fostering, but it will also invite a re-examination of some of our common assumptions about what we mean by fostering.

References

Colton, M.J. and Williams, M. (1997), *The World of Fostercare: An International Sourcebook on Foster Family Care Systems*, Aldershot: Arena.
Kellmer Pringle, M. (1975), *The Needs of Children*, London: Hutchinson.

Part I

The Policy Dimension

1 Kinship, Fostering, Obligations and the State

Roger Greeff
Britain

When, over the last fifty years, social workers in western Europe and North America have talked about fostering, they have almost invariably meant placements with foster carers unrelated to the child. In fact, though, some of the placements they have been working with have always been placements with members of the child's extended family. The 1980s have seen a serious recognition of kinship foster care for the first time, and positive developments in its use, in, for example, Sweden, the Netherlands, the United States and Britain.

There are, though, very different patterns in other social and economic contexts. In the developing world – the economic 'South' – the care of a child often still rests with the kinship network and the local community, and the emphasis in fostering services is on developing for the first time a system of non-relative fosterers to deal with those situations where the traditional system of care cannot cope.

In southern Europe, even with a welfare state in place, social workers may struggle to introduce non-relative fostering. Triseliotis (1994) observes that in these societies there are strong extended family systems where 'the boundary line between members of the extended family appears very loose, allowing for support and exchanges, including the care of related children.' 'However,' he continues, 'the boundary line between the extended family system and the outside world is rather rigid, leading to . . . some reluctance to look after non-related children' (1994: 4).

Finally, in central and eastern Europe, until the liberalisation of the 1980s, substitute care for children rested mostly either with the extended family, or with State institutions. Now, social workers in these countries are, like colleagues in the South, seeking to fill the gap by developing non-relative foster care, but should the extensive kinship care which already exists now be regarded as foster care?

Who are kin?

It may be helpful to be clear at this stage what this book will be taking into account as 'kin'. We will be considering any relative, by blood or marriage, apart from the parents of the child in question. But the possibilities are in fact wider than this; it has been pointed out that among African-American families, as many as two-thirds had 'fictive kin' – people who are not related either by blood or marriage, but who are none the less clearly treated as kin. Similar attributions will apply, to a greater or lesser extent, in most cultures. Such people may not carry any moral or legal obligation to the child in the way that actual relatives may, but if we are concerned to identify who matters to a child or young person – and who may be able to offer a supportive home – then surely we must allow our focus to widen on occasion to include 'fictive kin'.

One factor of which we must be aware in a collection of papers such as this is the way that patterns of contact and commitment between kin will vary considerably in different communities and in differing eras. Any discussion – and certainly any sensitive social work practice - must take care to tune into the particular dynamics of the specific community to which this individual child belongs. We must therefore take care not to universalise from any one model or discussion within an international collection such as this. Ideas from Poland or New Zealand may be very relevant to social work in Sweden or Britain, but those paradigms may need significant adjustment to the different social patterns in a different society.

Sociologists have devoted much debate to the question why family forms have varied as society has changed. In pre-capitalist societies, do we note some relics of a 'feudal' family form, or is there even here the emergence of the nuclear family unit? Is there an inevitable movement, if a society adopts more intensely capitalist and individualist patterns, from kinship and community to a more limited network we may call the 'extended family', and from that to an isolated nuclear family unit with rather uncertain levels of support from a very few close kin?

Over against the tendency to regard kinship as a rapidly declining aspect of family life in modern societies, writers such as Greer (1985) have argued that it is in fact the extended family which has endured, albeit making adjustments to changing social circumstances, through generations of change. She sees the tension not as pre-capitalist vs. capitalist, but rather between 'traditional community' forms and 'the doctrine of instant gratification' prevalent in the consumerist West. It is possible to identify communities within capitalist societies which are still genuinely communitarian.

Similarly, Finch (1989: 85) argues that 'Industrialisation and urbanisation did not destroy either domestic relationships or kin relationships but clearly they did . . . transform their character.' She points out that although the particular patterns of support may have changed, extended families in modern Britain still operate to offer a whole range of support – with finances, accommodation, physical/health care, stress and relationship problems, and of course with child care.

She suggests that what alters over time is on the one hand, the particular pattern of *'need'* for support, and on the other hand the *'capacity'* of relatives to offer help. Both 'need' and 'capacity' are affected by the prevailing social, economic and demographic conditions at any particular time:

> In reality the amount and type of support that kin give each other varies with the particular historical circumstances within which family relationships are played out . . . there is variation both in people's need for support and in the capacity of relatives to provide it. (Finch 1989: 81)

One further question is whether the pattern of support within kinship networks is now defined more narrowly in intergenerational patterns, from parent to child to grandchild, with a decline in involvement from 'lateral' relatives such as aunts, uncles and cousins? Lengthening life expectancy means that, for instance, by 1962 in industrialised countries one in four older people with children also had great-grandchildren (Shanas et al. 1968). For a far larger proportion of families than ever before, there are as many as three other generations of family members to relate to. Morgan (1975: 81) suggests that 'generational relationships' are of first importance – the primary relationship and sense of obligation is from parent to child – followed by sibling relationships, and then wider kinship. This analysis represents another example of ideas which need to be tested in differing social contexts; for instance, even in Britain, the link between sisters-in-law may be very important in communities of South Asian background (Wilson 1978).

This last point is helpful in pointing up the contrasts and changes in patterns of marriage and divorce, and their effects upon family networks. Some societies now see something close to 'serial monogamy', with the consequence that children may have step relationships and links with more than one family of 'in-laws'. Some of these relationships may be tenuous and insignificant; others may matter a great deal, and amount to real attachments.

Finally, Finch (1989: 86) offers a reminder that kinship support is 'patterned by the position of individuals in wider social structures – their class position, their gender, their ethnic identity.' In particular, the question must be asked whether in pursuing the cause of kinship care, we may be perpetuating the subordination and exploitation of women? In societies structured by patriarchy, Dalley (1988) may be right in arguing that in the end *any* care arrangement based on a familial model will inevitably perpetuate inequalities between women and men. I would want to argue that any practitioner planning care arrangements for children should be monitoring the effects of their intervention on the position of the women (and men) involved, and attempting to ensure that the responsibilities are shared in anti-sexist ways. For instance, the ecology of an extended family should not be defined in terms of men in authority and women as carers – we should not be scrutinising the network of a child looking for a *woman* with a sense of obligation.

The question of ethnicity is dealt with later in this chapter at a political level, but it must be acknowledged here that most societies are now clearly pluralist, and there is therefore an obvious need to recognise the particular patterns of closeness and distance, freedom and obligation which apply within different communities, and to work with, not against them.

The needs of children

The fundamental justification for kinship foster care is that it is often the best way of meeting the needs of the child, particularly the needs for continuity of experience and for a clear sense of identity and belonging.

When parents are unable to carry on with the immediate care of the child, the kinship network often steps in quite naturally and without any involvement from social workers or the State. A particular example of this phenomenon in recent British history would be the experience of children in the Caribbean who stayed on with grandparents when in the 1950s and 60s their parents came on ahead in the move to living in Britain. In some cases, several years went by before the child was reunited with her parent in Britain. What is interesting about many of the accounts of this process is to note that the child often seems to have adapted relatively easily to the loss of the parent – the child was still in the same place, with the same friends, cared for by a familiar figure, within the same community. What was actually very difficult was the move to Britain, and the readjustment involved in re-forming a relationship with your parent, at the same time as coping with a new country, new school, completely different way of life – and an appalling climate (Riley 1985).

Too often, the experience of children who are admitted to public, State care can be similar to that of the child arriving from the Caribbean. Although foster carers have been carefully selected, the move from home may involve the loss of almost everything that is familiar. You find yourself with new carers in a new home, in a neighbourhood you don't know, with no existing friends, feeling lost (Winter 1977).

White (1983) suggested that some key themes which emerge when theorists and practitioners try to identify the prerequisites for growth, development and fulfilment in a child are a secure base, significance and community. Arguably, if alternative care is needed, then kinship care can provide a new base which is contiguous with the old one, a sense of significance (mattering enough to a relative for them to welcome you) and a sense of community, ideally the opportunity to remain within the same neighbourhood. Hegar (1993) has suggested that the three key factors to be taken into account in planning a child's placement are the child's emotional attachments, her need for 'permanence' and security and her kinship relationships.

We are learning that, in planning alternative care for children and young people, one of the key hazards for the child is the sheer extent of the disruption involved in the move. A child will be carrying a personal sense of security which rests upon the reliability and continuity of a whole range of factors, including, along with parenting, their network of friends, their school, a sense of place which centres upon their family home and the neighbourhood where they play, and a patchwork of familiar people – teachers, neighbours and of course, relatives.

If the damaging effects of a breakdown in parenting are to be minimised, then the greater the number of elements of the child's sense of self and security we can leave in place, the better. It is in this context that social workers and others have come to realise that a placement within the existing family network is often the first choice. Research in Sweden, Israel and the UK suggests that kinship fostering leads to positive identity outcomes for the young people involved.

Recent policy guidelines in England and Wales demonstrate the growing recognition of the child's need for *continuity*:

> A child's need for continuity in life and care should be a consistent factor in choice of placement. In most cases, this suggests a need for placement with a family of the same race, religion and culture in a neighbourhood within reach of [the child's] family, school or day nursery, church, friends and leisure activities. Continuity also requires placement in a . . . home which a child can find familiar and sympathetic and not remote from [her] own experience in social background, attitudes and expectations. (Department of Health 1991: 4.4)

This statement spells out very clearly the reasons why, in the child's best interests, kinship placements should be high in the list of alternative care arrangements for many children.

Trading in children?

We have considered the costs to the child when she is separated from her parents and family, but there is another side to the equation: the loss of the child matters to the community to which she belonged. When parents are unable to continue with the care of their child, there is a danger that the child will be lost – temporarily or permanently – not just to the parents, but also to the community.

Children are important members of any community, and represent very clearly, the potential of the community: to lose its children is to lose its future. This concern has been voiced very forcefully in Britain and the US by the Black communities, who have seen disproportionate numbers of their children entering the care system. Until recently, those children were too often 'transplanted' into white families or institutions; they then grew up without any clear sense of themselves as Black, and they seldom had any significant contacts with the Black community, nor any real sense of belonging to it. 'These Black children have been made white in all but skin colour' (Gill and Jackson 1983: 137). Children are effectively being 'exported' from the Black community to the white community: 'The one-way traffic of Black children into white families begs fundamental questions of power and ideology' (Small 1986: 83).

One example of this phenomenon is the experience of the aboriginal community in Aotearoa/New Zealand. The Maori community has experienced extreme marginalisation and economic and social deprivation: one effect of this has been that a disproportionately large number of Maori children and young people have been placed in care. Many of these children were then placed in foster homes, often with white foster carers. In 1989, the new Children Young Persons and their Families Act in New Zealand placed the primary responsibility for children in crisis with their kinship network; family conferences would be called, and the people within the child's network would be asked to decide upon the best course of action. This resulted in a major reduction in the use of foster care, as the kinship network found less far-reaching solutions – to the disappointment of a large number of (white) foster carers who found themselves without children to take in!

Gypsy communities have faced persecution, ranging from marginalisation to genocide, in many European countries (Powell 1994: Zamfir and Zamfir 1993). One of the most frightening strategies has been the removal of children to boarding schools and children's homes, where they have been systematically 're-made' as if they had no connection with the gypsy community. If followed through, these policies may effectively eliminate that community. This is an extreme example of the social engineering involved when social policy seeks to enforce 'integration' (assimilation) as a response to diversity.

This theme – of children stripped from their communities – has many echoes in child care social work around the globe. There is always the potential that the families who are in a position to offer space to an extra child will be from the more affluent strata in society, while the families who are struggling with the care of their children will be from economically deprived sectors (Frost and Stein 1989). If this is true, then the child welfare system is in danger of acting to remove children from working-class backgrounds and to place them in middle-class families and communities. This may be difficult and inappropriate for the child – it may also be the negation of social justice. For instance, foster carers will usually be given financial help which would not have been available to the birth family (Beresford et al. 1987).

The other 'trade in children' which must concern social workers is the practice of inter-country adoption. Social workers may be playing a part in a process where large numbers of children are being 'rescued' from countries in economic distress and transported to affluent homes in economically powerful states. This process can be viewed as a positive response to children in need (as it often is within the 'receiving' countries) – or as a modified form of colonialism, with children being removed from their homeland in order to meet a shortfall in the supply of babies and young children for childless couples in the richer parts of the world. This process has developed at first with a South–North dimension, with children from the economically marginalised 'shanties' of South America, Asia and Africa being placed with families in the North. This is, by definition, a transfer of Black children to white homes, and we must immediately beware of any underlying assumption that to grow up in a white family in a Western economy is 'better' than to spend a childhood with Black parents in a developing country.

A similar pattern has grown up in the period of liberalisation in eastern Europe in the last ten years. As the West has gained greater access to eastern European communities, one consequence has been the rise in the number of couples and agencies who have sought to 'relieve' children living in poverty, or more particularly in institutions, by removing them down the road to adoption in the West. While some governments have been sanguine about this development, an increasing number of East European countries have found the need to put in place new legislative frameworks to regulate this process, at least ensuring that the parents have given genuine consent. In some states the legislation has gone further, effectively attempting to put a cap on the whole process.

Why should we hold reservations about this process, which in one light appears to be giving a number of children a 'better chance'? The first and most significant objection is that although the numbers of children involved may at times appear to be growing very rapidly, this process can never do more than cream off a tiny proportion of children who are living in extreme poverty or less-than-satisfactory institutional care. The majority of the children about whom Western couples and agencies have apparent concern will remain exactly where they are. The obvious question to ask is whether there are not better ways of attempting to improve the life of more of these children, than to remove a tiny minority for a 'fresh start'? As in many other areas of child welfare practice, we must face the fact that the key factor which is diminishing the life chances of these children is quite simply poverty.

What we are seeing in focusing upon the trade in children for adoption from South to North and East to West is a reflection of the wider issue which pervades child welfare practice: finding alternative family placements for children can often amount to the export of children from economically deprived communities to economically favoured families elsewhere.

The relevance of kinship foster care to this debate is that if those seeking alternative homes for children make real and strenuous efforts to locate and support carers within the child's extended family, the child can be retained within the community to which she belongs. This proposition will be illustrated in Chapters 11 and 12 which examine developments in Ireland with Traveller children and in New Zealand with Maori children. In a real sense, then, the active use of kinship foster care can be seen as a good example of anti-discriminatory practice.

Family obligation and the State

In reviewing patterns of what he termed 'gift relationships' within society, Titmuss acknowledged 'the reciprocal rights and obligations of family and kinship' as one form of these transactions (1970: 212). He felt, however, that such giving could be regarded as 'obligatory': 'within all such gift transactions of a personal face-to-face nature lie embedded some elements of moral enforcement or bond' (p. 210). It may be useful in the context of this book to pause and ask in what sense is kinship care obligatory?

Finch (1989) chooses to use the term 'sense of obligation' in this context.

Is the sense of obligation moral or legal; is it acted out willingly or grudgingly; is it reliable? Morgan (1975) has suggested that sociologists have regarded the giving of support in families as either 'instrumental' or 'expressive'.

'*Instrumental*' support is driven by necessity – the pay-off is mutual survival and some expectation of reciprocity. Gittins (1985) and Ross (1983) show how in nineteenth-century Britain whole communities needed to share child care in order to maximise the number of wage earners in their collective struggle for survival: 'Child care for the poorer sections of the working class was very much an informal arrangement based around the women in the community, rather than being a specific kin-related or mother-specific task (Gittins 1985: 29).

On the other hand, '*expressive*' support is offered as an active expression of the underlying commitment and affection felt towards the other family member. It may still be balanced against the cost of giving, of course. For the social worker, an assessment of the nature of the 'sense of obligation' working in a particular case may be important in concluding whether that sense of obligation carries enough real commitment to the child to provide a genuinely nurturing environment. Some of the accounts of young people's experience of foster placements with relatives in Chapter 10 will illustrate poignantly that placements based on a grudging sense of duty may leave children feeling unwanted, 'second-class' outsiders – the Cinderella phenomenon.

As we said at the start of this chapter, the commitment of the extended family will in many situations be enough to provide a suitable home for the child without any involvement or knowledge of the State. In all but the simplest of societies, however, the State, and social policy, will be exercising some influence. Here the questions become, who knows what is best for this child – the family or the State; and who is responsible for this child – the family or the State?

In societies where the State has little role to play, there may still be disputes within the kinship network about who knows the child's needs best, or who within the extended family group should actually be caring for the child. Here the role of the State is to mediate or adjudicate, perhaps by way of the law courts, but the responsibility for the child remains clearly with the family. This position may be enshrined in public policy and law: until the Poor Law was abolished in Britain in 1948 (with the advent of the welfare state), 'there was a legal expectation that, if the need arose . . . grandparents as well as parents had a responsibility to support children' (Finch and Mason 1993).

Where, however, the State is a major player, we face the tension characterised by Fox-Harding (1991) as that between a *laissez-faire* position, and one which emphasises the need for at least some State intervention in family life. Frost and Stein (1989) make the point that the boundaries between 'family', 'community', and 'State' are not fixed, but under constant renegotiation. This process is well illustrated in Chapter 12, where it can be seen that the greater involvement of the kinship network brought about by the new legal framework in New Zealand is inherently linked to a social policy objective to 'roll back the welfare state'.

It is in this context that the question of finance can become problematic. The State has a well-established interest in pursuing foster care as a cheaper option than residential care. But when kinship foster care is considered, could this be even cheaper? If the placement with family members is accepted as a foster placement, need the carers be paid an allowance, like all other foster carers? At one level, the answer would appear to be a simple 'yes'. The complication is with the notion of 'obligation'; if this is an obligation the relatives are meeting, why should they be subsidised? In a number of countries, there is debate as to whether kinship foster carers should be paid a lower allowance than non-related foster carers. In some legal systems, there may even be a requirement on grandparents or other relatives, as well as parents, to contribute financially if a child is in State care. In these circumstances, they may feel pressurised to offer care themselves, in order to avoid a financial burden.

This issue also brings into sharp focus the distinction we drew at the beginning between kinship care and kinship foster care. If some kinship care becomes recognised as foster care and is then supported financially, it is essential that the criteria to define which placements are to be seen as kinship fostering are clear, well thought-through and widely accepted. This dilemma is at its most problematic when, as in Poland (Chapter 2), there is already widespread kinship care, and social workers have the task of establishing a new foster care service.

Table 1.1 lists a number of possible roles for the State in kinship care.

Table 1.1   Possible roles for the State in kinship care

Laissez-faire	Family has sole responsibility
Last resort	State as reluctant safety net
Support to family	State helps family to do its job
Partnership	State and family work together for child
Regulator	Family accountable for quality of care
Policing the family	State role in protecting child from family
State as parent	State has ultimate responsibility for all children

- The State may play *virtually no role*. The extended family and the community to which it belongs will cope
- The State may act purely as the *last resort*, in providing for children who would otherwise be living on the streets. This was often the case in western Europe prior to the inception of welfare state ideologies
- The State may play a *supportive role* through positive policies to support families and promote child welfare. This model – what Finch (1989) terms 'supporting the family in order to enable it properly to care for its members' – suggests that primary responsibility remains with the family: the family cares for the child; the State supports the family in doing so
- There may be a genuine commitment for families and the State to work together in *partnership* with an assumption that both parties share responsibility for the child's welfare. This model itself may be based either on the principle of empowerment, or alternatively on a consumerist model (Wilson and James 1995)
- The State may take on the role of *regulator*. This is based upon a suspicion that people other than parents and close relatives may not be safe or reliable in offering care to children; their activities should therefore be scrutinised. Interestingly, in Britain today, placements with relatives other than grandparents, aunts, uncles or siblings – cousins, for instance – are seen as needing to be registered and supervised by social workers on the same basis as if the carer was a stranger to the child, even if the family would be happy to carry on alone
- The State is seen as holding a legitimate role in *policing the family*. The right of children to protection is seen as clearly overriding the need to respect the integrity of the family unit. Children may therefore be removed from their parents in order to protect them from harm. Even here, there may be possibilities for partnership between the State and the wider family: Chapter 5 examines the possibilities and challenges involved in working with kinship foster care when implementing a child protection plan
- Finally, there may be a model where some, or all, children are regarded as the *'children of the State'*. This was perhaps the case in eastern Europe under communism: of Russia until liberalisation, Harwin (1995) writes: 'Under socialism the State had always maintained a clear entitlement to define the political obligations of parents in child-rearing . . . it required parents to nurture a love of the Motherland and a respect of socialism in their children.' This political framework may also at times have generated an assumption that if a family could not cope, they need feel no great remorse in passing their children on to State care.

Social work practice

The attitudes of social work practitioners and policy makers towards kinship fostering do show links with all these positions. Perhaps the predominant starting point still seems to be the 'hands off' *laissez-faire* attitude that if families can be left to manage, then that is the best model. In Western economies, this model may be reinforced by the sharp decline in State resourcing for welfare. In other societies, it may be founded on a clear legal expectation that relatives have an obligation to the child. Whatever the value base, it seems that many social workers still assume that they need not engage with kinship care unless some special circumstance applies. This can then lead to the situation where social workers engage with the situation after the event, and can consequently feel disenfranchised and uncertain of their role.

At the opposite end of the spectrum, but with a similar assumption of distance from the family, social workers may define their role as purely to check on the safety and well-being of the child. They view the family (sometimes quite rightly) with suspicion, and look to the family to establish that it is trustworthy.

In the centre of the range are the strategies which aim to support the family in its endeavour, and to establish a genuine partnership. It is the central argument of this book that this is the model which will most fully benefit the child, though much of the evidence suggests that partnership with extended families is still only developing slowly, and at times reluctantly.

References

Beresford, P., Kemmis, J. and Tunstill, J. (1987), *In Care in North Battersea*, London: North Battersea Research Group.

Dalley, G. (1988), *Ideologies of Caring*, London: Macmillan.

Department of Health (1991), *The Children Act 1989 Guidance and Regulations Vol. 3 Family Placements*, London: HMSO.

Finch, J. (1989), *Family Obligations and Social Change*, London: Polity Press.

Finch, J. and Mason, J. (1993), *Negotiating Family Responsibilities*, London: Tavistock/ Routledge.

Fox-Harding, L. (1991), *Perspectives in Child Care Policy*, London: Longman.

Frost, N. and Stein, M. (1989), *The Politics of Child Welfare*, London: Harvester Wheatsheaf.

Gill, O. and Jackson, B. (1983), *Adoption and Race*, London: Batsford.

Gittins, D. (1985), *The Family in Question*, London: Macmillan.

Hartman, A. (1979), *Finding Families*, London: Sage.

Harwin, J. (1995), *Russian Children's Rights*, in Franklin, B. (ed.), *The Handbook of*

Children's Rights, London: Routledge.

Hegar, R.L. (1993), 'Assessing Attachment: Permanence and Kinship in Choosing Permanent Homes', *Child Welfare* 72(4).

Holman, R. (1975), 'Exclusive and Inclusive Concepts of Fostering', *British Journal of Social Work* 5(1).

Morgan, D.H.J. (1975), *Social Theory and the Family*, London: Routledge Kegan Paul.

Powell, C. (1994), 'Time for Another Immoral Panic', *International Journal of the Sociology of Law*, 22(2).

Riley, J. (1985), *The Unbelonging*, London: Women's Press.

Ross, E. (1983), 'Survival Networks: Women's Neighbourhood Sharing in London', *History Workshop Journal*, 15.

Shanas, E. et al. (1968), *Old People in Three Industrial Societies*, London: Routledge Kegan Paul.

Small, J. (1986), 'Transracial Placements: Conflicts and Contradictions', in Ahmed, S., Cheetham, J. and Small, J. (eds), *Social Work with Black Children and their Families*, London: Batsford.

Titmuss, R.M. (1970), *The Gift Relationship*, London: Allen & Unwin.

Triseliotis, J. (1994), 'Setting Up Foster Care Programmes in Romania; A European Perspective', paper delivered to the International Foster Care Organisation European Conference, Berlin.

White, K. (1983), 'Welfare of the Child', *Social Work Today*, 14(38).

Winter, A. (1977), 'Only People Cry', in Association of British Adoption and Fostering Agencies (ed.), *Working with Children Who are Joining New Families*, London: ABAFA.

Wilson, E.O. (1978), *On Human Nature*, Cambridge, MA: Harvard University Press.

Wilson, K. and James, A. (1995), *The Child Protection Handbook*, London: Balliere Tindall.

Zamfir, E. and Zamfir, C. (1993), *The Romany Population*, Bucharest: Bucharest University.

2 The Continuing Role of Kinship Care in a Changing Society

Zofia Waleria Stelmaszuk
Poland

Introduction

This chapter will focus on kinship care in Poland; it will start with the long-established pattern of caring for children within the kinship system when parents are prevented from providing the care their child needs. It will then examine the ways in which changing political regimes and shifts in social policy have affected kinship care, and will show that the commitment of extended families is remarkably resilient, continuing strongly whether supported, ignored or opposed by the State.

The current population of Poland is 38.6 million, of whom 10.4 million are under 18. Over 120,000 children are in out-of-home placement (in various forms of care); of these, 49,000 are in the care of 38,000 foster families, almost all of them relatives of the child (as of 15 December 1996: Glowny Urzad Statystyczny 1997). In recent years, more and more children are being placed in the guardianship or care of relatives rather than in institutions. Among the different factors contributing to this phenomenon, the most significant are the deterioration of the communist Welfare State and growing social problems and pauperisation. There is also increasing criticism of State residential care as well as new policies resulting in regulations recognising kinship care as kinship fostering. The wider context of this shift is democratisation, a growing awareness of children's rights as well as human and individual rights in general, and the development of active citizenship.

Recognition of kinship care as kinship fostering mirrors, in a way, the state's efforts to meet the new challenges of a society in transition, to prevent more severe and widespread problems and to gain social acceptance by respecting traditional and religious patterns and values. On the other hand, it is also an attempt to maintain State control over child welfare in a situation

21

where emerging private and non-governmental sectors are offering alternatives to the rigid, ineffective and expensive services dating from the time of communist State monopoly.

Historical background

The care of children by relatives has always been a significant resource for the child welfare system in Poland. Families and communities were always strong in this part of Europe where traditional family solidarity was strengthened by a strong adherence to Catholicism and a shared rural background. Industrialisation evolved much later than in the West and there continued to be a sharp divide – families were clearly of either noble or peasant stock. The extended family remained, therefore, a powerful institution much longer than in Western countries, taking responsibility for their dependent members including orphans, disabled relatives and even those who remained unmarried. The historical experience of the country, involving a number of tragic wars and years living under imposed rule, made the family exceptionally important as the only reliable and trustworthy institution and the main source of mutual support. Years of hardship and frequent shortages – a constant situation in the State-controlled, centralised economy – made sharing a necessity. Out of necessity, extended family members developed strong links and a commitment to support each other.

In Poland, grandparents are traditionally involved in their grand-children's upbringing and general well-being. Research shows that the most important goal for the majority of grandparents is the education and prospects of their grandchildren. For example, 75 per cent in a sample of 77 rural grandparents interviewed by the author, were more concerned with supporting their grandchildren, than saving for themselves. They seemed to enjoy being a resource for the family and feeling appreciated in this way (Stelmaszuk 1990). It is quite common to support even grown-up grandchildren, if the grandparents have the greater financial means. It is also known for grandparents to move in with their children in order to make their apartment available for their grandchildren. Therefore bringing up or fostering grandchildren could be a natural consequence of being grandparents, except that fostering grandparents faced much more serious challenges.

Before the Second World War, kinship care was the most common way of providing care for orphans and children from large families, although professional foster care programmes had already been introduced by several municipalities in order to meet the needs of children in a more modern way

(Kepski 1991). During the war, kinship and social networks were the most effective means of providing help and saving the lives of thousands of children including war orphans. Also foster care campaigns organised just after the war were very successful and secured care for children orphaned or lost during the war. As a result of these campaigns children from the big cities or parts of the country which had been devastated were sent to the countryside for better care and nutrition. These children remained placed with families and communities until their health and conditions improved. The authorities strongly supported these campaigns and provided financial help for children so placed – governmental reports mention nearly 125,000 children in foster care (Akta Ministerstwa Oswiaty 1946).

The Communist State

After 1945, when Poland became a communist state, many significant changes were made to both child welfare and family systems. These changes, introduced gradually, were aimed at strengthening the dictatorship of a communist party (officially the Polish United Worker's Party) and the organisation of society based on the soviet model. The nationalisation of the country's economy and 'preparation' of a young generation was seen as of special importance in this process. The changes were introduced gradually, as they were in opposition to the traditional values and attitudes held by most of Polish society. For instance, in some schools religious lessons continued even into the 1950s. In the school year 1955/56 religious lessons were still taught in 30 per cent of schools in Poland. After the 1956 riots against the system, religion was reinstated in schools and only in 1961 did the Act of Education definitely take religion out of schools (Misiaszek and Potocki 1995: 56–61).

In 1946 the newly formed Department of Child Welfare in the Ministry of Education took control over child and youth welfare while babies under the age of three were the concern of the Ministry of Health. The whole system of education and child care was entirely centralised. Any kind of private or nongovernmental initiative in the social and humanitarian area, including education and child welfare, was strongly prohibited from then on. In 1947, there were still over 73,000 children placed in foster care and probably a very large number of children in the informal care of relatives (Majewska 1948). However, with the strong political regime of the 1950s calling for collective education and upbringing, education 'by the State and for the State' became a priority of the new system. Young people were strongly encouraged to join the 'young socialists' organisation, and this could be important in gaining entry to university, for instance.

State control also affected private and family life, employment and education. Full employment and fixed flat wages imposed a two-income family model: mothers were expected to work, and comprehensive State education of children included pre-school day care, after-school care and weekday residential nurseries (week creches). All schools and kindergartens and all children's institutions (children's homes, special schools or leisure facilities) were public, with programmes strictly controlled by the state. Pre-school care was subsidised and available for long hours. There was also after-school care organised in schools, so children, especially in the cities, spent the whole day in school while their mothers were at work.

In theory, social policy was the centrepiece of policy but in practice it was always subordinate to economic policy (Millard 1992: 122). Family allowances were part of the wage package but eligibility for such benefits was limited to those in State employment and/or participating in the social insurance system. Until the 1970s, children of farmers, artists and other private or self-employed people (about half of the population) did not receive these allowances. Housing posed a big problem: many families did not have accommodation of their own, while the waiting time on the housing list was over twenty years. Consumer prices for goods and services essential to daily family life (for example, milk, bread, school books, summer camps, holiday resorts, energy, transportation) were subsidised but constant shortages were frustrating. Only some employees (military and police) acquired protected status.

Children from families unable to provide the necessary nurturing conditions were placed in large, State-run children's homes. These were secular institutions with trained personnel and a highly ideologised programme of State upbringing. In the view of the State, foster family care, for all intents and purposes, did not exist. Kinship care was not promoted or even discouraged – it was ignored. If it was seen as existing at all, kinship care was somewhere in the shadows, almost underground, or at least, the 'old-fashioned' approach. As it was rather hard to trust the State, which was perceived by the majority as strange, imposing, fearful and controlling, grandparents or relatives caring for children did not make demands, knowing that they could lose the child forever. They would not even try to compete with the official system which provided their young wards with an apartment and job, along with extra help after moving on from placement. If caring relatives asked for help, it would be through informal channels or through the Catholic Church (although the Church was at that time not allowed to be involved in any social or charitable activities).

At that time, and until recently, placement in an institution was intended to be permanent. Maintaining links (for children in care) with their birth parents or extended family was not encouraged. The intention was to break these links to the 'faulty past' and to connect children with a 'friend family' (an official programme introduced by many institutions) in order to learn about 'proper' family life. It was common that children in residential placement spent their life there until they were able to live independently, with no chance for reunification with their biological family and no contacts or links outside the institution.

'Social orphan' was quite a convenient label, which fulfilled a useful role within communist society. Children 'of the State' were needed to prove the State's caring attitude. For instance, State propaganda encouraged big factories (State industries) to become 'patron' institutions for a children's home. The media portrayed representatives of such factories sponsoring a child from the institution to fund an apartment. Birth parents or relatives providing care were unable to equip their children with anything comparable. Besides, if they were diagnosed as dysfunctional or unable to cope, their motivation was discounted. In my current research I have found the court documentation of a case in which a mother and grandmother fought dramatically for the return of two young children. They received help from the Catholic Church (unofficially), and from relatives and friends; no court or child welfare authorities ever supported their efforts (the mother was diagnosed dysfunctional). The children were systematically prevented from having contact with their mother and grandmother and were never returned home. Meanwhile, attempts were made to give the children up for adoption or to connect them with two different 'friend' families provided by the children's home. When I recently saw them, both children were in their twenties and still in an institution. Their grandmother had died, and their mother had become socially isolated and finally homeless but was still trying to keep in contact with her children. Her daughter, however, remained attached to the 'friend family' and didn't want to see her mother. Fortunately, her son was still eager to see her and was trying to help her to settle down.

Another example involved three young children who were placed in an institution after their mother, who experienced severe beatings from her alcoholic husband, escaped from home. As a result she was deprived of parental rights. Her husband died from alcohol abuse some time later. She stabilised her life, starting seeing her children in placement. Their contacts were successful and the children were very happy to be back in touch with their mother again. She later remarried and had two other children. Supported by her new husband and mother-in-law, she tried to regain custody of her older children but never succeeded. She was not well regarded by the staff in the institution 'as coming too often and disturbing their work'. Staff were also critical because she moved close to the institution and the children were now often absconding to be with their mother and younger siblings. The institution's plan was for the children to remain in placement until they would be able to live independently.

Recognition of kinship care

Within the new political shift of the 'modern' 1970s, kinship care by grandparents became more politically acceptable and, gradually, a more recognised form of care. The new rhetoric of the communist party was promoting a 'socialistic family' rather than a collective. Family policies did not change but standards of living improved. In the great need for foreign technologies, government turned to the West for credits and, at least for some time, the economy seemed to be improving. The loosening of the regime resulted in more freedom and open borders, and exposed the universities to Western social sciences. The Friends of Children Society (TPD), a State-controlled organisation which was the only one allowed to act in the area of child welfare, started to organise adoption centres and promote family-like forms of care. This was connected with the expansion of psychology and social psychiatry, and was greatly stimulated by Western influences. Under new leadership, Poland was trying to be more open to Europe and to present itself outwardly as a democratic country, concerned with the rights of children. In 1978 the Polish government even proposed the idea of a Children's Rights Convention to the UN Human Rights Commission (Lopatka 1991). There were now also new people in the Ministry, allowing for 'experiments' in the child care sector.

In 1971, the Council of Ministers passed the first comprehensive legislation which allowed for the placement of children with foster families, including relatives (Uchwala Rady Ministrow nr 254). Regional Boards of Education were responsible for the organisation, financial support and supervision of foster care (schoolteachers served as supervisors). In the beginning, only unrelated care givers were entitled to a state subsidy for caring for a child. The subsequent regulations, by order of the Minister of Education in 1974, provided all foster carers with an allowance for a foster child, but kinship care providers were only entitled to one-half of the allowance given to unrelated foster care providers (Zarzadzenie Ministra Oswiaty 1974). In 1975, the Family Welfare Code of 1965 was updated with respect to foster care issues and in the same year kinship foster families first appeared in court statistics (Ignatowicz et al. 1990; Zegadlo 1996). The more comprehensive regulations of 1979 by the Council of Ministers and the subsequent order by the Minister of Education that year gave a priority to kinship care (Rozporzadzenie Rady Ministrow 1979; Zarzadzenie Ministra

Oswiaty 1979). These regulations initiated the 'expansion' of kinship fostering. It was at that time, therefore, that kinship care was officially recognised as kinship fostering.

Since then, kinship foster care has become the preferred form of placement by the courts, which are the new Family and Juvenile Courts, set up to deal specifically with all family problems. The court 'curators' (the equivalent to a court social worker) were assigned to provide supervision of foster care. In 1975, courts placed 8,843 children with kinship foster carers, while in 1980 this had risen to 20,402 children (Zegadlo 1996). In comparison, there were at the same time only 461 children in professional foster care, which is modelled on a large family and entirely financed by the State – so-called 'Family Children's Homes' (Ziemska 1981). Very few children were placed with unrelated foster care providers (Jaworska-Maj 1990), usually either placement within a social network of friends/neighbours, or with a prospective adoptive family.

It is important to mention the 'alimony obligation' as an additional factor in the prevailing attitudes regarding kinship placement. In Poland, the law obliges not only parents but also extended family members (grandparents, step-parents or siblings) to provide care or financial support for children in need of care (Ignatowicz et al. 1990: 525–8). This so-called alimony obligation (which is also mandatory for children towards dependent older relatives) is deeply rooted in Polish tradition. For many years, it was used to justify giving a lower State subsidy for children living in kinship foster families; why should the State subsidise people to do something which they are already legally bound to do?

The amount of money given to a foster child was based on the average monthly national wage. The foster care allowance, defined as 'financial help for the child', was set at 40 per cent of that measure, while a kinship foster family would only receive 20 per cent of that amount. Only families fostering babies and children with special needs were eligible for 100 per cent of the national wage. Until 1993, the State subsidy for kinship families remained at 20 per cent, which was insufficient considering the drastically high inflation present in the Polish economy in the 1980s and continuing in the 1990s. No financial support was provided for care given informally by the extended family

None the less, kinship foster families were now recognised and continued to get on with the job quietly, regardless of their serious lack of funds. Forgotten by the State, which was then busy with serious political problems, kinship foster families were not at the centre of attention of either the educational or court bureaucracies. They were, however, noticed by a number of university researchers. Their rather small-scale studies are now the only source of knowledge regarding the development of kinship fostering, as very little data was recorded on the national level. These studies describe kinship foster families as stable and supportive environments for children but showed that unrelated caregivers were able to provide much better living conditions (Rozanska and Tynelski 1981). Children, however, seemed to feel safe and assured in the care of relatives, most often grandparents. Generally, kinship foster care provided a better social climate and better relationships than residential care (Bedkowska 1979). The majority of researchers stressed the strong emotional bonds between children and their caregivers (Kelm 1983; Safjan 1982; Jaworska-Maj 1990). Children brought up within a kinship care environment were more attached to their carers than to their biological parents (Jaworska-Maj 1990). Their health and development seemed to be much better than that of children brought up in an institution (Luczak 1994).

The present situation and current developments

Since 1989, when Poland became independent, accompanied by dramatic and fundamental political changes and the transformation of the communist State into democracy, more and more efforts have been made towards necessary social reforms. The new Social Welfare Act of 1990 guarantees State assistance to people in need. The Ministry of Labour and Social Policy is now responsible for social and family welfare, and social work centres provide assistance at the community level. Also, the emergent non-governmental and private sectors provide different kinds of services for various client populations.

Child protection issues are regulated by the new 1991 Act of Education. The child welfare services (including foster care and adoption) up to this point remained centralised; changes are slow but a green light was once again given to foster care by relatives. First of all, efforts were made to improve the financial situation of kinship foster carers. New foster care regulations, implemented in 1993, stress a preference for kinship fostering when placing children in need of alternative care. Kinship and unrelated foster families are now treated equally and receive equal financial help for a child. There were also subsequent 1993 regulations guaranteeing necessary support from professionals.

In fact, the above move has a very practical basis. In cutting off state subsidies and imposing market prices on citizens, the only way to keep children with their long-term carers – mostly elderly grandparents living on a fixed 'socialist' pension – was to provide them with a more substantial allowance. Forty per cent of the average monthly national wage was set for each healthy child and 100 per cent for a child under two years of age or with special needs; kinship is no different. As before, no payment is provided for family members giving care informally.

Besides, the 'new' State faced unpredictable levels of social demands and economic problems. Practically all sectors require reforms. The situation of children and families is particularly challenging. It was not possible and too costly to implement child welfare reforms but much easier to seek collaboration within the familiar resources. Kinship care providers reacted immediately. As twenty years before, unexpected State 'generosity' resulted in a sudden increase in the number of children in foster families (from 37,591 in 1991 to 43,911 in 1994 and 49,366 in 1996). The circumstances were like those in the 1970s, that is, a more democratic state perceived as more friendly and fair and less intimidating. It seems very likely that the surge in the number of kinship foster families was due to many people formalising their existing status as caregivers to their grandchildren or relatives, which was previously informal and unrecognised.

Kinship foster care remains under the control of the state. Placement decisions are taken, as before, by the Family Court; the Board of Education continues to be responsible for overseeing foster families and there are plans for it to be responsible for pre-placement assessment (now only briefly carried out by court workers). This should be a task of the Adoption and Fostering Centres (some of them are now private or run by non-governmental organisations, but still controlled by the State) employing foster care specialists. In practice, these centres, faced with rapidly growing numbers of foster families, and staff shortages, have to prioritise, and tend to concentrate on adoption work.

Current political developments form a new context. After four years of post-communist domination in the Parliament, the new coalition formed in 1997 by post-Solidarity parties is calling for decentralisation, pro-family policies and community-based social services. It is possible that foster care issues, and child protection in general, will be moved from education to the social policy sector. If the problems of children are to be solved on a community level, kinship fostering will probably once again prove its relevance and flexibility.

Contemporary kinship foster families

The first nationwide foster care survey carried out by the Ministry of Education in 1995 showed that the majority of kinship foster families face continuing difficulties. Kinship fostering occurs mainly within families of lower social and economic status. Among 46,101 children concerned, 15 per cent were orphans while 85 per cent were placed because of problems within the nuclear family, but only 25 per cent of parents were deprived of their parental rights. Ninety-eight per cent of the children were placed by the Family Court. The majority of children in care are aged 7–15. Only 1 per cent of babies under two and only 5 per cent of the remaining children were classified as having special needs (only these children are entitled to the highest level of foster care allowance). The care in 90 per cent of families was assessed as being of a good quality and in 10 per cent as unsatisfactory. Grandparents are most prominent among the care providers. They are older people, mostly in their 50s but some in their 60s or more. Apart from financial problems, they suffer serious health problems. The majority of fostering grandparents cannot rely on their own children for support – this is often why they are fostering the grandchildren (Ministerstwo Edukacji 1996).

Placement of the children is intended to be permanent or long-term (the majority remain in care more than ten years) but, at least in some families, arrangements are quite flexible in practice. For example, a number of children spend some time with their parents, no matter what the formal arrangements are. Sometimes, the placement takes the form of shared care. Research shows, however, that in many families, children are not seeing their parents and siblings at all, and that there are often serious conflicts between the natural parents and care providers (Stelmaszuk 1996). Those families are in immediate need of mediation and support.

Currently, there has been a strong push by child welfare professionals to develop specialised foster care services – to make available trained, salaried foster care providers, ready to take children in at any time. This form of care, widely publicised as a 'contract family', but still not yet included into the system, can sound like the ideal model if not the 'panacea' for child welfare in Poland. A recent child welfare conference which took place in early 1998 also called for more 'Family Children's Homes' where several children could be placed permanently with 'professional' parents. With great media involvement, a campaign is now under way which aims to collect funds for 'Family Children's Homes'.

The existing system, relying on kinship caregivers, has therefore been under attack from the 'professional foster care' lobby. Kinship fostering has been criticised for providing a low quality of care. Accusations have been made that authorities are supporting dysfunctional families while neglecting other poor families who function better, but where the State has no basis for intervening. Kinship foster caregivers are suspected of using the system, even collaborating with the natural parents in order to take advantage of the State subsidy. Help to kinship families is criticised as a waste of public money (Polkowski 1997).

Current research by the Ministry of Justice does not necessarily confirm the accusation, although it calls for better pre-placement assessment and better quality assistance to families providing care. The report shows that in most cases grandparents try their best to cope with their circumstances (Zegadlo 1996). It also makes clear that recognising kinship care as kinship fostering provides an opportunity to assist families in difficulty in the best interests of the child. Kinship foster families remain under the supervision of court workers in order to prevent out-of-home placement in an institution. Their status as foster families entitles caregivers to an allowance for a foster child and other kinds of assistance provided by the educational authorities. The goal of kinship foster care is then 'preservation of family ties and providing help in the environment closest to the child', as was stressed in the new child welfare policies accepted by the Polish Parliament in 1994 (Ministerstwo Edukacji Narodowej 1994).

It is true that contemporary kinship foster families are vulnerable and some of them are hardly able to cope with their responsibilities. Grandparents feel guilty about their children who failed as parents and feel responsible for the family's problems. They are caught in between the official and the family systems. Despite their exceptional efforts, the situation has continued to be difficult while the assistance they needed so much has been insufficient. Grandparents – older people who have experienced a lot of the State control through their life span – do not necessarily trust intruders coming from the court or social services. They are afraid of losing the funding that they are receiving for the child and they, of course, try to cooperate with the authorities while finding their own way of dealing with the situation. In fact, the supervision received from the court and educational authorities often takes the form of control rather than genuine support. Therefore, instead of receiving acceptance and recognition, they may feel threatened or even condemned.

The free market and the development of new life styles present a challenge to extended families and social networks in Poland. However, they also pose a threat to kinship fostering. There is hope that, despite the multitude of ideas, programmes and philosophies so rapidly developing and competing with one another, extended family care will continue to be a recognised and valued form of care. There are still important goals to achieve, including proper assessment, clear guidelines, a framework for support and adequate assistance by professionals, as well as gaining a voice through cooperation and networking with other kinship foster families, groups and associations.

The complex experience of kinship foster care in Poland goes to prove the resilience and the universal value of this form of care over time. It is significant that whenever the State declined in power, individual families took more control over their own family life, with more family-like forms of care developing immediately. More freedom in the social sphere resulted in the development of alternatives to placement in institutions. Generally, these were outside the family. With some encouragement, or even just permission from the State, relatives would be immediately available, ready to take over their traditional responsibilities.

References

Akta Ministerstwa Oswiaty (1946), Archiwum Akt Nowych Warszawa, sygn. 3598. Unpublished.

Bedkowska, V. (1979), 'Sytuacja emocjonalna dzieci w rodzinach zastepczych', *Problemy Rodziny*, 5.

Glowny Urzad Statystyczny (1997), *Oswiata i wychowanie w roku szkolnym 1996/1997*, Warsaw.

Ignatowicz, P. et al. (1990), *Kodeks rodzinny i opiekunczy z komentarzem*, Warsaw: Wydawnictwo Prawnicze.

Jaworska-Maj, H. (1990), *Sytuacja zyciowa bylych wychowankow rodzin zastepczych*, Warsaw: Instytut Badan Pedagogicznych.

Kelm, A. (1983), *Formy opieki nad dzieckiem w Polsce Ludowej*, Warsaw: Wydawnictwa Szkolne i Pedagogiczne.

Kepski, C. (1991), *Dziecko sieroce i opieka nad nim w Polsce w okresie miedzywojennym*, Lublin: Uniwersytet Marii Curie-Sklodowskiej.

Lopatka, A. (1991), *Konwencja o Prawach Dziecka a prawo polskie*, Warszawa: Wydawnictwo Sejmowe.

Luczak, E. (1994), 'Srodowisko wychowawcze rodzin zastepczych', Opieka. Terapia, Wychowanie, 17.

Majewska, A. (ed.) (1948), *Rodziny zastepcze Lodzi*, Lodz: Polski Instytut Sluzby Spolecznej.

Millard, F. (1992), 'Social Policy in Poland', in Deacon, B. (ed.), *The New Eastern Europe: Social Policy Past, Present and Future*, London: Sage Publications Ltd.

Ministerstwo Edukacji Narodowej (1994), *Glowne kierunki doskonalenia systemu edukacji w Polsce. Materialy na debate sejmowa*. Unpublished.

Ministerstwo Edukacji Narodowej (1996), *Informacja dotyczaca przegladu rodzin zastepczych dokonanego w 1995r.* Unpublished.

Misiaszek, K., Potocki, A. (1995), *Katecheta i katecheza w polskiej szkole*. Warszawa: Wydawnictwo Salezjanskie.

Polkowski, T. (1997), 'Czekamy na spelnienie obietnic', Zycie, 11 listopada.

Rozporzadzenie Ministerstwa Edukacji Narodowej z dnia 17 sierpnia 1993r. *w sprawie osrodkow adopcyjno-opiekunczych* (Dz. U. Nr 84, poz. 394).

Rozporzadzenie Rady Ministrow z dnia 26 stycznia 1979r. *w sprawie rodzin zastepczych* (Dz. U. Nr. 48, poz. 256, z pozn. zm.).

Rozporzadzenie Rady Ministrow z dnia 21 pazdziernika 1993r. *w sprawie rodzin zastepczych* (Dz. U. Nr. 103, poz. 470, z pozn. zm.).

Rozanska, E., Tynelski, A. (1981), *Rodzina zastepcza jako forma opieki nad dzieckiem*, Kielce: Wyzsza Szkola Pedagogiczna.

Safjan, M. (1982), *Instytucja rodzin zastepczych. Problemy prawno-organizacyjne*, Warsaw: Wydawnictwo Prawnicze.

Stelmaszuk, Z.W. (1990), 'Wartosci wychowawcze w rodzinach wiejskich', *Ruch Pedagogiczny*, 33 (7).
Stelmaszuk, Z.W. (1996), *Reintegracja rodziny jako cel i efekt opieki zastepczej nad dzieckiem*, Raport z badan wykonanych na zlecenie Komitetu Badan Naukowych. Unpublished.
Uchwala nr 254 Rady Ministrow z dnia 22 listopada 1971 r. *w sprawie pomocy materialnej dla dzieci i mlodziezy w rodzinach zastepczych* (M.P. 7.12.1971, Nr. 56, poz. 364).
Ustawa z dnia 29 listopada 1990 o pomocy spolecznej (Dz. U. Nr 87, poz. 506).
Ustawa z dnia 7 wrzesnia 1991r. o systemie oswiaty (Dz. U. nr 95, poz. 425 z pozn. zm.).
Zarzadzenie Ministra Oswiaty i Wychowania z dnia 13 grudnia 1974 r. *w sprawie doboru rodzin zastepczych i udzielania pomocy materialnej dzieciom pozostajacym pod ich opieka* (Dz. Urz. Min. Osw. i Wych. 20.01.1075, Nr. 1, poz. 2).
Zarzadzenie Ministra Oswiaty i Wychowania z dnia 21 wrzesnia 1979 r. *w sprawie doboru rodzin zastepczych i szczegolowych zasad udzielania pomocy tym rodzinom* (M.P. Nr. 24, poz. 135).
Zegadlo, R. (1996), *Analiza stanu prawnego i praktyki sadowej w zakresie ustanawiania rodzin zastepczych*. Unpublished.
Ziemska, M. (1981), 'Poland: Foster Family Homes', in Payne, C.J. and White, K.J. (eds), *Caring for Deprived Children: International Case Studies of Residential Settings*, London: Croom Helm.

3 Kinship Fostering – Research, Policy and Practice in England

Roger Greeff,
with Suzette Waterhouse and
Edwina Brocklesby
Britain

In Britain, kinship foster care has always been a feature of foster care in the post-war Welfare State, but has seldom been given specific attention. In some ways, social work attitudes have tended to avoid acknowledging its existence – placements with relatives seemed an anomaly when non-relative foster care was being developed as the dominant model. Such placements were often referred to as *'de facto'* fostering, as if the social worker had experienced no option but to accept a situation which was already in existence. There was perhaps an implication that the social worker would work with the situation, but was keen not to be seen as positively endorsing it.

This approach was echoed at a policy level: Rowe et al. (1984) draw attention to a passage in an authoritative policy document from the Department of Health and Social Security, *Foster Care: A Guide to Practice* (DHSS 1976):

> The stresses of fostering by relatives are considerable and are sometimes underestimated both by the family and by the social work agency involved. At its best the child has the love and security of familiar care; at its worst [she] may become a vehicle for bitter jealousies and disputes and the object of a tug of love which neither side can win. In the latter situation the child is exposed to much conflict and thus to the greater possibility of serious emotional damage. (DHSS, in Rowe et al. 1984: 174)

The alternative view is eloquently put by King and Trowell; although they are in fact commenting on a specific case, I believe their sentiment has wider relevance:

> By concentrating narrowly on the nuclear family, the welfare professionals seemed to have overlooked entirely the possibility of retaining the children in the

35

wider family network. Although hostility and lack of contact between the extended family members may initially make it appear that the parents and children exist as an isolated unit, and also make it difficult for the parents to involve their relatives in their problems, the prospect that the children will be damaged or lost often leads to cooperation and solidarity between the family members and to help and support for the children and parents. (King and Trowell 1992: 126)

More recently, there has been a change in attitude, policy and practice. This might be attributed to a combination of two factors: the difficulty of recruiting increasing numbers of 'standard' foster carers, coupled with the 'discovery' of kinship care, and research which points to the strengths of this form of care.

First, it seems to have become apparent that a limit has been reached in the number of non-relative foster carers who can be recruited. Despite continuing recruitment efforts by foster care social workers, a liberalisation of criteria which has allowed, for instance, more single and 'older' people to act as foster carers, and despite significant moves towards regarding foster care as the job it is, and so demanding remuneration rather than just expenses, the number of foster carers in England and Wales has reached a plateau. This experience appears to have been mirrored in other Western societies, such as Sweden and the US. Some of the reasons why this plateau has occurred have been discussed by Parker (1978).

Secondly, research has begun to portray kinship foster care as a much more attractive alternative than has previously been thought. Most importantly, Jane Rowe's study of long-term foster placements (those which had already lasted over three years) 'discovered' a significant sub-group of kinship placements, in fact one in four of her overall sample. The researchers' overall conclusions were that 'children fostered by relatives seemed to be doing better in virtually all respects than those fostered by others' (Rowe et al. 1984: 175).

In common with other studies in the UK and other countries, Rowe and her colleagues found that 70 per cent of related foster carers were grandparents and another 20 per cent were aunts, and that relatives were twice as likely to come from the mother's side of the family. Almost two-thirds of carers were at least forty years older than the child, and over a quarter were widows; several were in ill health (but in turn had the support of other family members in most cases.) They were of lower social class than unrelated foster carers, but household standards were generally no worse. Perhaps surprisingly, the kinship foster carers tended to welcome the involvement of the social worker rather more than did non-related foster carers.

Almost two-thirds of the children had been placed directly by their parent, prior to social work involvement. Most placements were seen as long term, and the children showed a 'basic feeling of security'. Only one in five felt a sense of stigma about their placement, compared with half the children with non-relatives, and two-thirds had contact with their parents, compared with only one in five of children in standard foster homes. Parents generally preferred their child being looked after within the family, though there were some strained relationships, particularly where the carers were on the other parent's side of the family.

The child's behaviour was only a cause for concern at the time of placement in one in ten cases, and the proportion was the same in the present. In non-relative placements, both proportions were three times higher. Six out of seven children placed with relatives were seen by their social workers to be achieving satisfactorily at school.

Incidence

There is some evidence to suggest that the use of network fostering placements is increasing in England and Wales, although there is uncertainty about the true statistics as children can be placed within their wider family by way of a number of mechanisms including:

- Informal arrangements within the family, with or without transfer of finances
- Use of funding under Section 17 of the Children Act 1989 to support the informal placement, but without formalising it within the care system
- Using a residence order either with or without payment of a residence allowance
- Placement under fostering regulations (reg. 3)
- Emergency placement under fostering regulations (reg. 11)
- Adoption.

In 1989, in a large sample of children in the care system, Rowe identified 3 per cent of her study placements as being with relative carers. Waterhouse (1997) found that for the 94 English authorities responding in the fostering services organisation study, an average of 12 per cent of all approved foster carers were relatives or friends of the child. There were striking variations in practice between authorities, a finding echoing that of Berridge and Cleaver (1987). In Waterhouse's study, at one end of the spectrum one authority reported no kinship carers approved under the Foster Placement (Children) Regulations, choosing instead to 'support' such placements through funding under section 17 of the Children Act. At the other end of the spectrum, one authority stated that over 30 per cent of approved carers were kinship carers. Significantly, 12 per cent of the family placement managers completing the questionnaires could not easily access the kinship information for the survey, because often the arrangements were made directly by the field social work teams and were not funded from within a budget for 'looked-after' children. This was particularly true for those authorities with purchaser–provider divisions.

Contact with family

Research in the 1980s pointed out how easily children are 'Lost in Care' (Milham et al. 1986); in particular the Dartington study showed that of children remaining in the care system for two years, half had lost contact with their mothers, while as many as one in three had no contact with their mother *or any other relative*. This has been confirmed by Biehal et al. (1995): a quarter of teenage care leavers had little or no contact with any members of their family. The care system can thus have the effect of separating children not only from their parents, but also from their wider family, community and established friendship networks. When looking generally at contact between children in long-term foster care and their families, Rowe commented on how few had contact with grandparents, but that when it did happen, it was 'almost wholly beneficial' (Rowe et al. 1984: 116).

We have also begun to develop some understanding of the part played by the extended family in a child's experience before their formal admission to the care system. Thoburn reviews the emerging evidence which suggests that the nuclear family units to which these children belong are often very unstable, and concludes that 'in view of this pattern of movement [within the nuclear family unit], families of children looked after by local authorities are often estranged from their extended families' (1994: 6). This impression is confirmed when looking at teenagers entering the care system: half had poor relationships with their wider family (Sinclair et al. 1995). On the other hand, Rowe et al. (1984) found that only 24 per cent of parents of children in long-term foster care had been in the position 'where no family support seemed available at the time of admission'.

Later research by the Dartington team – Bullock et al. (1993) – has suggested that almost 90 per cent of children admitted to the care system are back with their family within five years of admission; an even higher proportion – 95 per cent – will return to their original community, sooner or later. Biehal et al. (1995) found that one in five of their sample of teenagers leaving care regarded members of their extended family as 'there for them', people with whom they belonged in some sense, even if they were unable to live with them. Bullock et al. (1993) concludes: 'Whatever the circumstances, the wider family continues to be a vital resource which can be enhanced by social work support and encouragement.'

Similarly, Hoggett (1993: 114) reviewing the research, comments that whilst the preferred model of fostering is 'inclusive', most long-term placements seem not to achieve it. On the other hand, the 'favourable results of many placements with relatives' may be attributable to their built-in 'inclusiveness', and their success may thus reinforce the argument for inclusive substitute care. Aldgate (1984) has coined the term 'inclusive permanency', and it does seem that kinship foster care has this characteristic – in the long term, return to the parent is not that likely, but on the other hand the chances of continuing contact are good. Colton and Williams (1997: 290) summarise: 'Relatives, whether or not they get on with the natural parents (and often they do not), succeed in maintaining family ties because they are family.'

Stability of kinship care

We are not aware of any British research that has had kinship care as its prime focus, although some specific findings regarding the efficacy of kinship care have emerged from broader research. Rowe et al. (1984) and Milham et al. (1986) found that children enjoyed a high level of stability and satisfaction when fostered with relatives. Rowe noted that the children were older, and the plans tended to be for longer-term placement, with the increasing use of court orders. Berridge and Cleaver (1987) found a remarkable success rate: within their sample of 25 there was an average 9 per cent breakdown within the first year of placement with a relative, and no breakdowns in the subsequent four years, as compared with a rate of 15–40 per cent in non-relative placements.

When Triseliotis (1989) looked at factors associated with successful placements, he confirmed that placements with relatives stood out as more effective. In the overall fostering context, he also found that carers over 40, carers with no children of the same sex and age as the foster child, and foster carers whose attitude was 'inclusive' (Holman 1975), were more successful. It could be argued that many kinship care placements are likely to have these additional characteristics: grandparents will be older, and unlikely to have children in the same age range, and kinship foster care has clear 'inclusive' properties.

There is no recent research on breakdown rates in kinship placements in the UK, although within Waterhouse and Brocklesby's (forthcoming) sample of 50 general foster care placements five of them involved a move from the care of a relative or friend into temporary foster care. Three of the placements (6 per cent) were considered to result directly from a breakdown of those kinship care arrangements. This is of course a comment on informal kinship care rather than relatives as foster carers, but it does caution against regarding kinship care as a panacea. Overall, however, Berridge concludes in his review of foster care research that fostering with relatives is a 'proven success' and that 'In the light of its success it seems curious that such arrangements are not more common' (1997: 78, 26).

We can thus summarise the current evidence about network fostering from research in four key points:

- The number of network placements is substantial – perhaps 10 per cent of all foster placements, and probably rising both in numbers and proportion of all foster placements (Rowe 1984, 1989; Berridge and Cleaver 1987; Waterhouse 1997)
- Network placements are genuinely 'inclusive' – parents prefer them, and continuing contact between parent and child is three times more likely than in standard fostering (Rowe et al. 1984)
- These placements are very likely to last (Berridge and Cleaver 1987; Triseliotis 1989; Berridge 1997)
- Children feel secure when placed with relatives or friends (Rowe 1984; Millham et al. 1986).

New policy

Attention to kinship fostering has been encouraged in Britain by recent developments in the law and policy governing social work with children and their families. The most important change has been the introduction of the new Children Act of 1989, the key legislation on child care in England and Wales. This Act is built round three central principles – partnership, contact and restoration – and each has the effect of encouraging social workers to work actively and positively with a child's wider family and network.

Partnership is implicit within the Act, rather than being spelled out as such. However the guidance on good social work practice issued by the Department of Health states: 'One of the key principles of the Children Act is that *responsible authorities should work in partnership with the parents of a child* who is being looked after' (DoH 1991: para. 2.10). The aim of this partnership is to share the process of making plans, decisions and agreements about what is best for the child. The guidance goes on to suggest that where a child is mature enough, she too should form part of the partnership.

The guidance makes it clear that one key element of partnership is that all the people involved should be consulted and involved whenever important plans or decisions are to be made. At this point, it is recognised that there are others who have important relationships with the child, and therefore a valuable insight into her needs:

> The child's family, parents, grandparents and other relatives involved with the child should be invited to participate actively in planning and to make their views known . . . members of the child's family or others who play a significant part in the child's life should be involved in the making of arrangements for the child. Such sharing of information and participation should be the norm . . . (DoH 1991: 2.49, expanding on s.22(4,5))

It may be argued that there is a distinction between partnership, which includes the parents and the older child, and participation, which involves the wider circle of extended family and friends. Interestingly, in Stein's (1983) taxonomy of levels of participation by the citizen, partnership is characterised as giving power to the citizen, while consultation is categorised as a form of tokenism. The Children Act may still be falling short of involving the wider family in a really significant way.

The second core principle of the Act is *contact*. The tendency of the care system to attenuate the child's contact with her family and community (Milham 1986) should be actively resisted by the social worker. Thus the legislation requires that positive efforts are made to *promote* and maintain contact between the child and her parents – and also with other 'relatives and friends' of the child (Children Act 1989: sch. 2 para 15(1)). There is still some distinction between parents and other relatives, if the child is in compulsory care following child protection action and a court order. In this situation parents have a legal right to 'reasonable contact' with their child, unless a court has been convinced that contact is against the child's best interests (Children Act 1989: s. 34(1)). Other family members are not given this automatic entitlement to reasonable contact, but a lesser right to apply for a court order allowing contact. It is very apparent, however, that the importance of contact with a network wider than just the child's parents is clearly recognised and endorsed in this legislation; this is a major step forward from previous frameworks which made little or no reference to the extended family, and often left the responsibility for maintaining contact with the parent, in circumstances which were often stacked against her (George 1970).

The third core principle of the Children Act is *restoration*, the belief that whenever possible, the child should be returned to her parents or somewhere in her own community at the earliest moment consistent with her welfare – she is best served by an opportunity to live within her own family and community. This is based upon a recognition of the child's need for *continuity*:

> A child's need for continuity in life and care should be a consistent factor in choice of placement. In most cases, this suggests a need for placement with a family of the same race, religion and culture in a neighbourhood within reach of [the child's] family, school or day nursery, church, friends and leisure activities. Continuity also requires placement in a . . . home which a child can find familiar and sympathetic and not remote from [her] own experience in social background, attitudes and expectations. (DoH 1991: 4.4)

This statement makes a clear case (at least indirectly) for kinship placements as placements of first choice! This is in fact spelled out when the official guidance states that 'Possibilities for a child to be cared for within the extended family should have been investigated and considered as an alternative to [care] by the authority.'

Even if admission to the Care system does prove necessary, 'placement with a relative will often provide the best opportunities for promoting and maintaining family links in a familiar setting' (DoH 1991: 3.33).

Finally, the law requires that wherever appropriate, arrangements are made for the return of the child to the care of 'parents, relatives or friends' (Children Act 1989: s.23(6)).

The framework and principles of the 1989 Children Act thus provide social workers with six key stages where the extended family should be involved :

- *Preventing admission*: placement with members of the extended family should be an alternative to admission if possible
- *Incorporating existing placements*: if the child is already placed within the extended family, there may be a case for her to remain there, although she is formally admitted to the care system. The relatives then become foster carers, and will receive financial allowances; the authority will have the right to supervise the placement
- *Preference for kinship placement*: if the child needs to move, the preferred choice of placement should be with the extended family
- *Consultation*: relatives should be invited to participate in all key planning decisions, and should be consulted before decisions are made
- *Contact*: contact with members of the wider family should be actively promoted during the period away from home
- *Leaving care*: the child should be returned from the care system to live with a parent, relative or friend at the earliest appropriate moment.

Social work practice

What conclusions can we then draw for good social work practice, in the light of the research findings and the Children Act framework? If the social worker is to act on the research findings, and put the spirit of the Children Act into play, she will need to use a wide repertoire of skills.

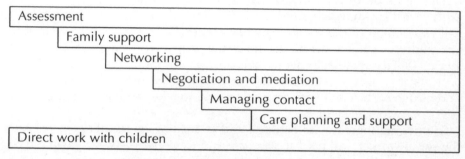

Figure 3.1   Social work roles and skills

First, *assessment* entails the social worker actively seeking care possibilities within the extended family. Assessment should be based on a partnership model, and involve the child, the parents and the wider family: the worker will need to avoid a 'procedural' model of assessment, and try to develop an 'exchange' model, based on user involvement and empowerment (Smale and Tuson 1993). Assessment should avoid taking a nucleated focus, and needs to explore the complete range of strengths and options within the child's full network of relationships. Seed (1990) has pointed out that traditional social work assessments, based on an assumption that families are essentially nuclear, tend to make the extended family invisible, and Darvill and Smale (1990) make the point that 'families', 'networks', and 'communities' are not easily identified, homogeneous entities.

If the worker develops a systemic overview she will be able not only to identify possible carers, but also to anticipate the way that family dynamics may enable – or disable – any potential placements (cf. Hartman 1979). In order to locate alternative placements which are already familiar, and to note which have been tried but have not worked out, it may be important to track any earlier moves and separations the child has made (DHSS 1985: 69).

Secondly, the importance of *family support* strategies should be emphasised, and as well as the need to focus support on the whole family network, not just the children and their parents. Such an approach needs to look for strengths within the family network, and to adopt a genuinely empowering approach without the baggage of stigma and threat (Holman 1988: 100), a balanced approach which avoids a preoccupation with risk without denying that risk exists within some extended families. The research suggests that support may be available even from relatives whose relationship with the parent is far from perfect.

This leads on directly to the use of *networking skills* to engage all those with particular knowledge and understanding of the child and her needs. A full exploration of the child's network and existing links will be central to any understanding of her needs and of the people who matter to her (DHSS 1985: 44). This may well involve the calling of a family group conference, with its emphasis on allowing the members of the network to share their knowledge of the child with each other, and to take the lead in defining the best option for the child.

In bringing together the network and in helping its members to engage, the social worker will need to *negotiate* and to *mediate* between people who may have distinct perspectives on the child's history and needs, and who may have a variety of scripts already established between them. Placements within the extended family network will often perpetuate old tensions within the family, and the adjustment of family members to the new care situation may be hard: the addition of a new member (or members) to the household will inevitably mean a reworking of family dynamics. Mediation skills will be important in helping to sustain the new arrangements which emerge for the child's care: people may need help with communication and with making arrangements work out.

A particular application of these skills will be in *managing contact*. Linking back to assessment, the earlier mapping of the full network of people who are significant to the child – her 'community of attachment' (Willmott 1986) – will prove to be a crucial tool in developing the full range of continuing contact arrangements required by the law and by concerns for the child's continuing sense of self. In the same way that the worker cannot make the benign but naive assumption that extended families are risk-free zones, so she cannot assume that contact arrangements within a family network will be trouble-free. Many of the same issues may arise as with non-relative fostering – for instance, is contact about visiting or about parenting? But in addition, there will be extra twists in terms of different sectors of the family and their history; in particular relatives by marriage will probably feel some loyalty to the 'other' parent. Negotiation by the social worker, with a clear focus on the needs of the child, may be the key to clear, workable arrangements which allow continuing parent–child contact without dispute and distress.

Once a placement is established, the worker will need to exercise *care-planning* and *support* roles. Both of these tasks will test the extent to which she has been able to negotiate entry to the family on terms which allow genuine partnership: has she breached the sense (for her and for the family) that she is an outsider to be fended off? The research suggests that if this relationship can be established, relative foster carers are actually very appreciative of having support available.

Most importantly, there may be a need for continuing *work with the child* herself. The process leading to the placement with relatives may well have been disruptive or traumatic: it may have involved abuse of the child. Sensitive work which helps the child to make sense of this experience, and to move forward with an intact sense of self may be central to meeting the child's needs.

Finally, and inevitably, we arrive at the question of power dynamics. The development of kinship foster care has the potential to express social work's aspiration to be anti-oppressive. As in other areas of anti-oppressive action, it will involve a reworking of traditional or existing power dynamics. If workers are to avoid exploiting women as carers, and the unnecessary removal of children from Black communities and working-class neighbourhoods, then they must be willing to allow the women, Black people and working-class people – and of course the children themselves – to take the lead. Here again the New Zealand family conference model is apposite.

In Chapter 4, Portengen and van der Neut have pointed out that in 'standard' foster care the social worker is in a pivotal position, holding key information about the child, the birth family and the foster family and deciding how widely to share it. In kinship foster care, by contrast, the child, parents and kinship carers already know each other, and know far more about each other than the social worker does.

This can leave the social worker less certain of her role than in 'standard' foster care. The carers may know a great deal more about the child than the worker does; they may be convinced (and may be right!) that they know better than the worker what the child needs; the family may already have, and continue to have, family secrets. At a fundamental level, there is the question whether the worker is essentially an 'insider' or an 'outsider'. This mirrors Holman's (1975) analysis of foster placements as 'inclusive' or 'exclusive': is this carer welcoming a partnership approach, or attempting to construct a family unit free from outside interference? Ironically, O'Brien suggests that if the social worker is welcomed, it may be at the cost of the birth parent's exclusion (see Chapter 8). In these circumstances, the worker needs to develop a genuine partnership approach which combines professional authority with appropriate humility!

References

Aldgate, J. (1984), *Making or Breaking Families*, Oxford: Oxford University Press.

Berridge, D. and Cleaver, H. (1987), *Foster Home Breakdown*, Oxford: Basil Blackwell.

Berridge, D. (1997), *Foster Care: A Research Review*, London: HMSO.

Biehal, N., Clayden, J., Stein, M. and Wade, J. (1995), *Moving On: Young People & Leaving Care Schemes*, London: HMSO.

Bullock, R., Little, M. and Millham, S. (1993), *Going Home: The Return of Children Separated from their Families*, Aldershot: Dartmouth.

Colton, M.J. and Williams, M. (1997), *The World of Fostercare: An International Sourcebook on Foster Family Care Systems*, Aldershot: Arena.

Darvill, G. and Smale, G. (1990), *Partners in Empowerment*, London: NISW.

DHSS (Department of Health and Social Security) (1976), *Foster Care: A Guide to Practice*, London: HMSO.

DHSS (Department of Health and Social Security) (1985), *Social Work Decisions in Child Care*, London: HMSO.

DoH (Department of Health) (1991), *The Children Act 1989 – Guidance and Regulations, Vol. 3, Family Placements*, London: HMSO.

George, V. (1970), *Foster Care*, London: RKP.

Hartman, A. (1979), *Finding Families*, London: Sage.

Hoggett, B. (1993), *Parents & Children* (4th edn), London: Sweet & Maxwell.

Holman, R. (1975), 'Exclusive & Inclusive Concepts of Fostering', *British Journal of Social Work*, 5(1).

Holman, R. (1988), *Putting Families First*, London: Macmillan.

King, M. and Trowell, J. (1992), *Children's Welfare & the Law*, London: Sage.

Milham, S., Bullock, R., Hosie, K. and Haak, M. (1986), *Lost in Care*, Dorset: Blackmore.

Parker, R. (1971), *Planning for Deprived Children*, London: National Children's Homes.

Parker, R. (1978), 'Foster Care in Context', *Adoption and Fostering*, 3: 27–32.

Rowe, J., Cain, H., Hundleby, M. and Keane, A. (1984), *Long-term Foster Care*, London: Batsford.

Rowe, J. (1989), *Child Care Now*, London: British Agencies for Adoption and Fostering.

Seed, P. (1990), *Introducing Network Analysis in Social Work*, London: Jessica Kingsley.

Sinclair, R., Garnett, L. and Berridge, D. (1995), *Social Work & Assessment with Adolescents*, London: National Children's Bureau.

Smale, G. and Tuson, G. (1993), *Empowerment, Assessment & the Skilled Worker*, London: HMSO.

Stein, M. (1983), 'Protest in Care' in Jordan, B. and Parton, N. (eds), *The Political Dimension of Social Work*, Oxford: Basil Blackwell.

Thoburn, J. (1994), *Child Placement: Principles & Practice*, Aldershot: Wildwood House.

Triseliotis, J. (1989), 'Foster Care Outcomes: A Review of Key Research Findings', *Adoption and Fostering* 13(3): 5–17.

Waterhouse, S. (1997), *The Organisation of Fostering Services: A Study of the Arrangements for the Delivery of Fostering Services in England*, London: NFCA.

Waterhouse, S. and Brocklesby, E. (forthcoming), *Placement Choices for Children in Temporary Foster Care*, London: NFCA.

Willmott, P. (1986), *Social Networks Informal Care & Public Policy*, London: Policy Studies Institute.

Part II

The Social Work Role

The Social Work Role

4 Assessing Family Strengths – A Family Systems Approach

Riet Portengen and Bart van der Neut
Netherlands

Working with members of the family and the social network in kinship care means building on the strengths of the system: the parents, the child, the foster parents and other important people in the family and social network. Two key concepts in the assessment and support of kinship families are *empowerment* and *activating* the system. This demands a particular attitude from the social workers. Techniques like working with genograms, ecograms and sociograms, and a consultation with the family or social network are helpful in enabling social workers to work with the strengths and potential of the family and the social network, instead of focusing on the problems. These techniques and related skills enable kinship care to be an interactive process between parents, children, foster parents and foster care organisations, to create tailor-made kinship care. These are the central elements in the method of working and training for social workers which we have developed.

Activating the system

Kinship care must involve working with members of the family and the wider social network who are significant for the parents, the child and the foster carers. Key players are the children who need care, parents who have to trust others with this care, foster-parents who want to take on the responsibility, and children of the foster parents who have to share their parent's attention with the foster child. In kinship care the members of the foster care system already know each other to a greater or lesser extent. This would seem to be a good recipe for working in partnership with a social worker from the foster care organisation, but many social workers experience kinship systems, in comparison to regular foster care, as difficult to assess and to support. One of the most important sources of this difficulty for social workers is that their professional training focuses on individuals and problems. They have learned to focus on the problems of their clients, on the individual who causes or experiences the problem and on finding solutions for them. Empowerment through activating the system requires different attitudes and professional skills, working with and building on the strengths of the members of the family and the social network to solve the problems in partnership with them. In this way members of the kinship care system learn to trust in their own abilities. The social worker supports the process and teaches new skills with the aim that the members of the family or social network can use them by themselves when new situations arise.

Empowerment has been defined as 'the attempt to find ways of working with others that permit them the maximum say in decisions about their own lives' (Ryburn 1993, 1996). He suggests that traditionally the foster care organisation claims the expert knowledge, deciding whether the parents are incompetent, whether the foster parents are capable and whether a child is suitably matched with the foster family. The 'professional as expert' attitude doesn't attempt to involve the parents, children and important members of the family and social network in decisions about foster care. Ryburn (1993) states: 'The risk assessment approach is one that sees families as dangerous. It does not distinguish the actions of some members of some families as dangerous, but rather the whole family network is labelled that way.' The consequence is that the most important source of support, the family and the social network, is not involved in the assessment and the choice of a 'good' placement for the child.

Portengen (1994) indicated four starting points for social work in kinship care.

- Support of a kinship care system demands a family-centred and network-centred approach; the individual family member is part of the system, and problems can be solved in relation to this system. The strengths in this system help the individual to solve their problems
- The foster family is a part of the kinship care system, as are the parents and their child. So foster care organisations are bound to work directly with the parents of the child. Boszormenyi-Nagy and Krasner (1994) emphasise the unbreakable tie between parents and children. Just recognising this unbreakable tie is not enough to make the foster care system function properly. All participants of the foster care system need skills to build bridges among themselves in order to handle and to do justice to this unbreakable tie

- Parents, children and foster parents are quite capable of formulating their own goals, enabling them to change the situation according to their own ideas and wishes
- Parents, children and foster parents don't want the social worker to solve their problems for them: they want her to help them develop skills and knowledge to change the situation themselves.

Empowerment through activating the members of the kinship care system means for the professionals that they respect the opinions of all the members of the family or social network who are important for the parents and the child. They have to trust in the strengths of those people who are really concerned with the future of the child and her parents. In relation to the parents it means working in partnership to investigate the parents' suggestions for possible solutions within the family or the social network. Especially when the foster parents are family, the parents are capable of judging the potential of the foster family. A positive attitude from the parents towards the foster parents enhances the chance of success for the placement. When the parents have the opportunity of participating in the decision where their child is going to live, it contributes to a more positive self-image and feeling of responsibility in a disempowering situation.

Empowerment also means maximising the potential and developing the skills of the parents, in order to reunite the child with her parents. In respect to the foster children and the foster parents' own children, it means listening to them. They have their own opinions, solutions and strengths. It's also important to help them develop the skills to attain their goals. And, last but not least in respect to the foster parents, it means supporting them in deciding what they have to offer, tuning in to the potential of the foster parents for taking care of this specific child in their specific situation, and to offer adequate support and training.

Assessing family strengths must be a continuing process, building on the strengths and potential of the family and the social network in a changing context. The social worker uses specific techniques to assess these strengths and to monitor changes in the family and social network. The foster care organisations of course have their responsibility; they are responsible for the formalisation of the placement and they cannot take the risk of a child being harmed emotionally, physically or psychologically in a kinship family. But the foster care organisations have an obligation to children to look first in their own family or social network for a foster care family. The rights of children confirm these starting points.

Kinship care: an interactive process

Kinship care is an interactive process; at many different points in time there are decisions to take. The process of recruitment, appraisal, selection and support for the kinship system demands skills from the social worker to structure the process of decision making and requires trust in the expertise of the family and the social network who know the child better than anyone does. This is a different role and position to 'traditional' foster care, where the foster parents didn't previously know the child and her parents. Figure 4.1 shows the difference in position.

Traditional foster care

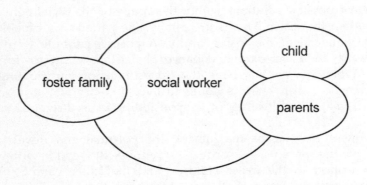

Family and social network foster care

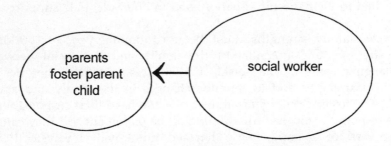

Figure 4.1   The social worker's position in traditional and network foster care

In 'traditional' foster care, the social workers link and filter the information; they decide what information should be told to the parent about the foster parents and what information should be told to the foster parents about the child and her parents. All parties are dependent on that information and this puts the social workers in a powerful position. They are like the spider in the centre of the web: all parties need them for information about and contact with each other. In kinship care, the parents, child and foster parents know each other; they know many things about family life style, the history of the family, the way they raise children, family secrets and so on. They do not need the social worker for information; the social worker needs them to get information. She has to prove that she is worth trusting with this information before they will give it.

In aiming to deliver tailor-made foster care we can consider foster care as a continuum in terms of how much the foster carers know about the child and her family history.

Kinship fostering				'Regular' fostering
A	D	M	W	Z
+-----------------	+ -----------------	+-----------------	+ ----------------- +

Figure 4.2   A continuum of fostering

In Figure 4.2, 'A' is the situation of kinship care in the family; for example a child living with her grandparents or her aunt. In situation 'A' everybody knows each other as described above. 'Z' is the situation of a 'traditional' foster family, in which the child and the parents didn't previously know the family who are offering themselves for foster care. But there is a lot of variation between these two extremes. For example, a child may live far away from her extended family and without contact between her parents and the wider family for many years: actually this child does not know her family-members. The extended family knows a lot about the common history of the family but not about the life of the parents and the child over recent years. So the family needs a lot of information, and so do the parents and the child. This situation is shown as 'M' on the continuum.

Another example is when neighbours have been good friends of the parents for many years and have gone through all the ups and downs with the parents and child. They have shared everything with them and have had a lot of contact with the family. So the right place on the continuum is 'D'.

These different scenarios have important implications for the process of recruitment, appraisal, selection and support, and for the position of the social worker.

There are three different starting points in foster care within the family and the social network:

- The child is already living with the foster parents and they ask for support
- The child and/or the parents have a proposal and ask for permission for a placement to go ahead
- The child needs to be placed in a foster family but the child and/or her parents don't know of any possibility within the family or the social network.

You can say there are three types of foster care families, but you can't say there are only three ways to work with these different families when you want to give tailor-made support to the child, her parents and foster parents. They have their own strengths, context, (family) history, problems, etc. and the foster care organisations need to tune in to these elements in the recruitment, appraisal, selection and support of the foster care system. The process of a foster care placement is an interactive one between the child, parents, foster parents and social worker. The decisions relate to the starting point and should permit the child and the parents the maximum say in decisions about their own lives.

As with regular foster care, the foster care organisation has to come to a conclusion whether they can take the responsibility for the placement of that child in that family. There are some legal demands from government and the organisation must have insight into the development of the child and the context, dynamics and history of the foster care placement and the decisions the family have already made.

Recruitment

An active recruitment takes place when the child and/or her parents didn't know of any placement possibility or when you want to research all the possibilities in the family or social network. With the help of genograms, ecograms or sociograms, the social worker holds consultations with the parents, the children and eventually other important persons, to trace systematically all the possibilities in the family or the social network. In this way parents and children play an active role in finding a foster family. Even if the decision for placement away from home is taken by an institute of Child Welfare or a judge, parents can still actively be involved in the decision over who can take care of their child. The next step is to talk with one or more possible foster families. Dependent on the situation the parents can talk directly with the possible foster parents: this can be facilitated if necessary by the social worker or another important person in the family or the social network (a teacher, religious leader, etc.). A consultation with the family or the social network can be very helpful in this situation. The central issue is to gain a perspective on their capacity to function as a foster family. One important aspect is the situation when the family, the foster family or the social worker decide they are not suitable to be a foster family, but when their motivation is high to help the parents and the child – can we help work out what they need to do to make it possible to become a foster family?

Appraisal

The appraisal is a next step to get more insight into the family and the social network and the decisions which have already been made. Appraisal takes place in all the three starting points mentioned above. Important questions to the potential foster parents are:

- *Whose choice was it to become a foster family?* In many situations, one family member feels more concerned with the child and/or her parents than the others because it is his family or friend, etc. Most of the time family members have different motivations for wanting to take care of the child
- *How were they confronted with the request?* Has the child run away from home and stayed with the foster family or did the parents ask the foster parents to take over the care of the child for a time? Have the foster parents the opportunity to say 'no' or are they obliged to the family to take the child into their family?
- *What changes (roles, tasks, position, attention, space, etc.) will occur for all the family members when the child goes to live in the foster family?* Will the foster carers' own children have to share bedrooms after the foster child arrives? Will the eldest one no longer be the eldest child in the family? And which of the parents will have to handle the extra caring tasks?
- *What will change in the relationship between the parents and the foster parents when the child is living in the foster family?* What will happen when your best friend is not only your best friend, but becomes the care giver to your child?
- *Are the foster parents aware of the problems of the child and her parents?* Do they have a realistic view of the reason why the child isn't able to live with the parent for a while?
- *Have the foster parents the skills to look at the consequences of their own actions towards the child and the parents and can they communicate about that?*

The appraisal should make clear if:

- *the foster family is able to cope with a foster child.* For instance: a single working mother with two children offers a (temporary) home for her sister's daughter. Will she be able to give her niece the time and attention she needs?
- *the foster parents can create the conditions necessary for the foster child that are attuned to her needs.* For instance: a child who needs a lot of structure is placed in a family without a daily routine. Is this family able to handle this child's need for structure?
- *the foster parents have the skills to monitor the consequences of their actions and can communicate about that.* For instance: an aunt has many problems with her own children, who have left home. Can the parenting of her own children be discussed, or is this put aside as not relevant?
- *the foster parents have a realistic image of the problems of the child and her parents (development, communication, behaviour, drugs, etc.).* For instance: a 15-year-old boy has run away from home because of conflicts at home, part of which were caused by his attitude of blaming everyone else for the problems he caused. He didn't take any responsibility for his actions. The foster parents, the parents of a school friend, think the boy is reasonable and reproach the parents for showing too little flexibility
- *the foster parents are able to respect and to handle the child's feelings of loyalty.* For instance: when the foster parents in the previous example encourage the boy to give up his loyalty to his parents by blaming them for all the conflicts. On the one hand the parents will experience the attitude of the foster parents as disqualifying. On the other hand, in the future the boy will find it difficult, due to his dependence on the foster parents, to differentiate his story of the conflicts and the way he experienced them.

In the process of appraisal, possibilities and ideas are central. In selection, the process of taking the decision about working together in support of the foster-parents is the central item.

Selection

In this context selection is to be seen as mapping strengths, protective factors and stress factors, in partnership with the foster family, in order to determine what kind of support is needed for them to fulfil their task. The result of this stage in foster care is the decision of the family, the social network and the foster care organisation to work together in the placement of the child in that specific family and to work together to maximise the success of the placement and to reduce the risk factors. In this decision the members of the family and the social network and the foster care organisation take on their final responsibilities.

When there are contra-indications for the placement of the child with a certain family, the child can't be placed. The decision that the organisation cannot accept a foster family should be described as one where the risk factors outweigh the strengths and the protective factors in the system. These are the cases where the safety of the child, parents or foster parents cannot be guaranteed, when the child would be restricted in her development (emotional, physical or psychological), or when the foster parents don't satisfy the legal conditions. In these cases the foster care organisation can't accept the responsibility for the placement. It may also happen that the family or social network comes to the conclusion that there is no possibility within the family or social network for taking care of the child. Most of the time they then give their permission to place the child in a regular foster family. This permission is very important for the well-being of the child in this family and for partnership with the regular foster parents.

We accept that the primary motivation of the foster parents lays in the relationship they have with the child and its parents. The decision to accept them as foster carers is based on their competence and strengths rather than focusing only upon the risks and problems involved in placement. They are then asked how they can grow into the role of foster carers alongside their role as a relative or friend and what do they need in the way of support from the social worker.

To work with the network the following techniques can be used:

- genograms
- ecograms
- sociograms
- lifelines
- consultation with the family and the social network.

These techniques are all based on social network strategies.

Social network strategies

Everyone needs a social network for affection, connection, means of living and social significance (Baars et al. 1990). In the sphere of foster care work, the social network consists of all the people who have a more or less durable relationship in daily life with the parents, the child or the foster parent.

Within the family or social network we meet a lot of cases in which the social network is already exhausted, that is, the network members did everything they could, but nothing seemed to work. They didn't know they could get support from the foster care organisation. Once the network is exhausted, this can lead to damage to contacts and relationships, often with people who are very important for the child and the parents. Social network strategies will help people to strengthen the social network, to make the care of the child not the responsibility of just one person, but shared among other people who are important to the parents, the child and the foster parents. Social network strategies can be used for foster care placements which are already in place to strengthen the situation and to relieve someone caring for the child. Besides that, social network strategies will help to search for a possible foster family in the case where there are no possibilities in the family, and the parents and the child, at the first glance, don't know of a family in which the child could (temporarily) live.

In social network strategies Baars et al. (1990) distinguish four steps:

1.   investigation of the (quantity) of contact with the social environment.
2.   analysis of the quality of the stucture of the existing network.
3.   making plans to strengthen the social network (strategies).
4.   carrying plans into effect.

Genograms are useful when investigating the family structure. A lifeline will give a view about important events, both stressful and happy, in the life of the child and of the parents. To make a map of the social network of the child and/or the parents, an ecogram is very useful. A sociogram will analyse the quality of the relationships. A consultation with the family or the social network is essential if we are to work with the social network to strengthen the situation.

Genograms in foster care

In foster care it is necessary to investigate methodically, together with the foster parents, which capacities and abilities they have to offer in relation to caring for and educating a foster child. This investigation provides us with a profile of the foster family and tells us what needs to be done, in order to support the foster parents while they are doing their job. In our experience genograms can be very useful in clarifying the possibilities and capacities of the (aspiring) foster parents. Making and working with genograms with the family or a group of family members is a technique in itself. Therefore we will only describe their use in assessing the strength in the family.

Genograms are a way of mapping a few generations of the family. (See Figure 4.3). They can help us to structure the process of gathering information and diagnosing the family system, and in making interventions in working with the family.

The genogram has two important functions in working with families in foster care. The first function is to gather and share information about the system with the members of that system. The collected information can be split into two important sections:

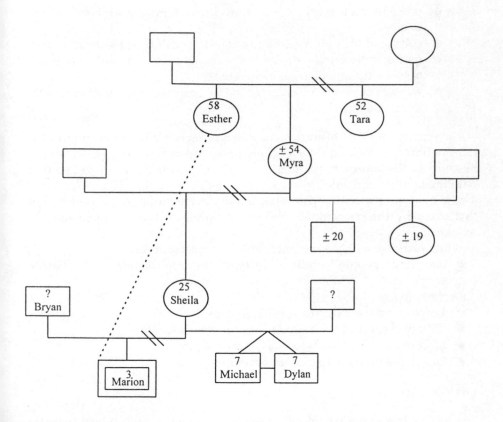

Figure 4.3   Genogram: possible placement of Marion with Esther

1. About family history

    - the constellation of the family over three generations (the child involved, her parents and her grandparents)
    - important dates (birth, death, marriage, divorce, etc.)
    - coincidence of dates (relationship between dates and events)
    - development and stages in the life-cycle of individual family members and the family as a system
    - coincidence of important events and stages in the life-cycle; repetition in patterns and symptoms (in behaviour, life style, profession, partner choice, etc.).

2. About relationships

    - intensity and reciprocity of relationship
    - position and roles of the individual family members in the system
    - culture of the family (eating, rituals for birthdays, mourning, etc.)
    - norms, values and patterns in the family (how to handle emotions, to live with others, friendship, etc.)
    - ways of dealing with changes in the family (a new member, death, marriage, etc.).

The second important function for genograms is giving a meaning to the information and making interventions based upon what we see. Giving a meaning to the information (diagnosing) should explicitly be done together with the family members. This is an intervention in itself. Giving life events a new context or meaning can cause a shift in the emotional experience of that event by the participants and the meaning of that event in today's relationships.

When working with genograms, *during information-gathering*,

- encourage people to talk about both important events and relationships.

During support:

- Empower the good, strong relationships
- Organise support for difficult situations and events
- Mobilise people who were 'out of the picture'
- Give a positive interpretation to relationships.

Lifeline

The lifeline is another technique, along with the genogram, which helps to outline the important life-events – marriage, death, divorce, birth, etc. – of the child and her parents. Figure 4.3 is an example of a lifeline.

Year	Age	Events
1980	0	Rodney born (Aruba)
1982	2	Sister Janice born
1984	4	Parents divorce – living with mother near grandparents; starting school
1987	7	Mother emigrates to Holland, with Janice; Rodney stays with aunt
1992	12	Rodney finishes basic school; emigrates to Holland – reunification with mother and Janice
1994	14	Mother finds new partner, who moves into family home
1995	14	Conflict starts between Rodney and stepfather – Rodney runs away for the first time, returning after three days
1995	15	Rodney runs away second time, to parents of a friend; Rodney says he wants to stay there
1995	15	Mother requests help from social workers

Figure 4.4   Lifeline: an example – Rodney

These events influence Rodney's personal development and can be connected with his problems and the mother's request for help. Repeating patterns and combinations of events are visible at a glance. The genogram shows these events from an intergenerational perspective, the lifeline from an individual perspective. In combination they give an overall view of the individual development of the child, the relationships within the family, and the context, with its strengths and problems, in which the child grew up.

The function of the lifeline is diverse. It offers opportunities for the client to talk about important events in her life. She decides what is written down, thus giving herself a chronological view of the things that happened in her life and the possible connections she sees with the problems. At the same time, the lifeline offers the client an opportunity to talk about the way she overcame problems in earlier times, identifying points of contact, hope and power to work on a solution for the current problems.

Secondly, the lifeline gives an overview for the social workers through the intake and the appraisal. When social workers exchange information with each other, it is often time-consuming and the reproduction of the information is frequently a problem: everyone gives their own interpretation to the information. The lifeline provides the information directly from the client and will not change due to the interpretation or misunderstanding of the social worker.

Ecograms

Ecograms are a very useful tool to investigate the social network of the parents, the child and the family. They create a picture of the client and the contacts she has in her own context. The quality of the contact can be shown by different lines.

The functions of the ecogram are the same as the genogram: a help in obtaining information and pursuing the question of support. The ecogram is a technique to find contacts and help which can support the family or even a foster family for the child in a surrounding which is familiar to the child. The starting point can be solely the contacts of the child (see Figure 4.5.i) or the contacts of the parents and the children together (Figure 4.5.ii).

It must be clear for both the social worker and the client why they are making an ecogram. The ecogram (like the genogram) is not a goal on its own, but is used as a means to reach a particular objective. Social workers and family members make the ecogram together: the family are the experts about their own environment. The social worker sketches out a basic framework incorporating all the main aspects of a social environment. This prevents 'blind spots' in the social network of the client, that is, relationships that are not part of their immediate life or world of experience that could be forgotten. These might be components of the social network which might be built up to support the parents in finding a solution to the problems.

After completing the ecogram the client and the social worker appraise the difference between the actual and the desirable or necessary contacts:

- the need for support for parents, the child and/or foster parents
- the sources of support and in some cases, a possible foster family
- the lack of support which had to be organised.

After this they make an action plan, built on the identified strengths and skills of the family members and the social network. For example, one of the members of the social network who is not able to act as a possible foster parent, could be asked to babysit or arrange a visit to the doctor. The social worker makes an agreement with the parents that if they do that by themselves, the social worker will support them, or, if necessary, she will meet with the helping person. Following an ecogram, a sociogram can be created with the client to look at the quality of the contacts in the network, or a family consultation can be arranged with all the important members of the network. An ecogram is a help in evaluating if goals have been reached and the family's ecogram has taken on the desired appearance.

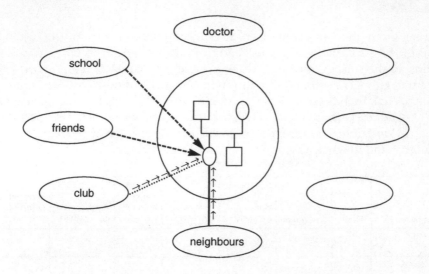

Figure 4.5.i   Ecogram for the child

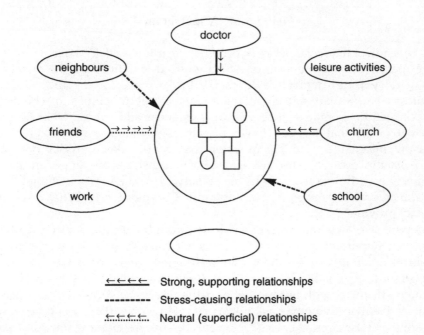

←←←←	Strong, supporting relationships
----------	Stress-causing relationships
←.←.←.←.	Neutral (superficial) relationships

Figure 4.5.ii   Ecogram for the family

Sociogram

A sociogram gives an inventory of the structure and quality of the contacts within the social network. The genogram and ecogram can be guides in filling in the sociogram. It schedules the existing contacts (see Figure 4.6). The sociogram is separated into different categories: family (parents, family-in-law, etc.), friends (schoolfriends, neighbours, etc.) and institutions (social services, doctor, church, etc.) The structure of the social network becomes clear in describing how many contacts there are (intensity), frequency of contacts, and in what way (telephone, writing letters, visits).

Contacts	Who?	Description	How many contacts? How frequent?	What form of contact?	What do you get from the contact?	What do you do together?	How much control do you have?
FAMILY							
FRIENDS							
INSTITUTIONS							

Figure 4.6   A sociogram

The function of the social network becomes clear if we ask to what extent the other person is fulfilling a need. Affective need is defined by the question 'What do you get out of the contact?', for example having fun, finding comfort when you are sad, trusting someone to tell difficulties to. The need for connection refers to sharing the same interests and values: what do you do together? What do you have in common? Material needs refers to housing, information, etc. The question that can be asked is 'What can you get from this contact?'. The need for social security is the question about connection with organisations in the society to arrange certain things (like assurance, social services, labour contract). The question is 'What does the contact provide?'.

Step by step the social worker works it through with the family member. It is very important to explain the different categories as the professional jargon is unfamiliar to the client. When the client gives an answer it is very important to give value-free reactions. If someone tells you that she has a very good contact with her mother and then says she speaks to her once a year by telephone, you may ask in surprise 'How on earth is a good contact possible in those circumstances?'. You can be sure the client will not tell you everything when you ask the next question. The social worker needs to tune into the experience of the client: changes in the structure and the quality of the social network are always connected with the request for help and the need of the client.

Working with the sociogram gives an analysis of the quality of the structure of the existing network. Making plans to strengthen the social network (strategies) gives aims and direction in carrying plans into effect. The sociogram is a working-out of the contacts with the persons in the genogram and the ecogram. In this way we can be confident that all the important people for the parents, the child and the foster parents are identified and could be invited for a consultation with the family and the social network.

Consultation with the family and/or the social network

As empowerment is one of the central principles in kinship care, consultation with the family and/or the social network is an essential part of the working method. The power of this consultation is that the members of the family and/or social network discuss together their responsibility regarding a good outcome for the child who needs care, the consensus about the placement of the child and the support they can offer the kinship-parents.

In our experience many people are involved in helping the family system when a child is at risk. In particular, members of the extended family (grandparents or brothers and sisters of the parents) have often invested a great deal in supporting the family before social workers or therapists come in. For that they deserve our respect and recognition. One of the aims of a family consultation is to amplify the commitment and skill present within the family and social network. The consultation offers an opportunity to develop the problem-solving skills of the family and the social network. It contributes to empowerment for the future and makes them less dependent on the professional.

Family consultations have four different goals in foster care:

1. *Getting to know the family history and family constellation and the social network*. To understand the implications of placement we need to know the family history and its meaning for today's relationships.
2. *Activating and mobilising support and resources*. The process of placing a child away from home is often very complex and many family members besides the actual foster family have something to offer to support each other.
3. *Obtaining approval and support*. Approval of all family members is

important because in our experience those who do not approve can have a powerful position during the rest of the placement. They may also be correct in their objections, a possibility which should be considered. Support for the actual foster family is very important. In many cases it is important to reach explicit agreement about what kind of support people will give.

4.   *Constructing a framework for agency support.* A family consultation will tell us a lot about what should be done by the foster care institute to support the family as a whole to help it fulfil the task of raising the foster child and bringing the placement to a successful end.

Over the past few years we have experienced four different major applications for conducting a family consultation:

1.   To hear from important family members about their ideas about what should happen when a crisis occurs and what they can contribute. This application is not just important in foster care; in all sorts of complex situations it can be useful to mobilise the family and social network.
2.   To examine possibilities for foster care within the social network or family if a placement away from home is inevitable.
3.   If the child is already living with a family within the network, to examine the possibility of foster care.
4.   To obtain consent from the family for initiating other solutions like placing the child in a traditional foster home.

The consultation demands the specific skills of the social worker. Like working with genograms, conducting a family consultation relies upon knowledge of systems theories and the ability to communicate methodically with a large group of family members. We will not discuss these skills and theories here but will limit ourselves to the ten important steps we have developed in working with family consultations:

1.   *Decide who should participate:* together with the parents and the child we determine who is to take part in a consultation. Reasons for who is and isn't to take part must be made clear.
2.   *Invite the participants:* decide how should the participants be invited (by telephone or letter) and by whom (the parents, the foster care institute or the guardian).
3.   *Be aware of the need for an individual preparatory conversation:* sometimes it is necessary to speak to individual participants in advance of the consultation because of their resistance to participating. However, be

careful of too many sessions with individual participants because of the risk of hearing too many family secrets or being drawn in to one side of the system.

4. *Welcome and respect everyone who is coming:* this may sound obvious but we tend to forget the efforts people make to attend a session, often during working hours at a child welfare or foster care institute. With this effort they show their involvement and willingness to invest in the situation.

5. *Know the motivation of participants for coming to the consultation:* each individual may have an individual reason for taking part in the consultation. It is important to make an inventory of these goals. They tell a lot about the relationships and what should be achieved to come to a widely accepted solution to the problems involved. At the end of the session we check whether all participants are satisfied with the final conclusions.

6. *Have a common goal: a positive formulation in terms of the interests of the child:* it is possible that the participants think differently about what is in the best interests of the child. However the interest of the child must be a common goal regardless of differences as to how this can be achieved.

7. *Empowerment: emphasise the strengths of the members of the family and the social network:* even in the most troublesome situations people show strength in the way they deal with it. It is important to mention these skills and behaviours.

8. *Mention the support they can offer each other:* each participant can offer something. Let them organise the support they can give each other.

9. *Set up the next consultation, both its timing and purpose:* sometimes one session is not enough to handle all items. Make an appointment for a next session and determine together with the participants the subjects for discussion.

10. *Confirm the results of the consultation:* show respect and thanks for coming. All participants have made a great investment in meeting; through their attendance they show involvement with the child.

Conclusion

In the recent past, kinship care (in the family and the social network) has developed very quickly. From being a kind of 'second choice' foster care it is becoming more and more a 'first choice'. It is increasingly becoming the policy of foster care organisations that social workers should look first into the family and the social network. The method described above is in further development. It puts kinship foster care in a broader perspective, one in which the parents and the child dare to believe in a future where the situation will have moved on in a direction they have chosen for themselves.

References

Baars, H.M.J., Uffing, J.T.F. and Dekkers, G.F.H.M. (1990), *Sociale Netwerkstrategieen in de Sociale Psychiatrie*, Houten/Antwerpen: Bohn Stafleu van loghum bv.

Boszormenyi-Nagy, I. and Krasner, B.R. (1994), *Tussen geven en nemen, over contextuele therapie*, Haarlem: De Toorts (translation of *Between Give and Take – A Clinical Guide to Contextual Therapy* (1986), New York: Brunner/Mazel Inc.).

Portengen, M.C. (1995), 'Foster Care in Times of Socio Economic Change: Expectations and Perspectives', keynote speech at the IFCO Conference, Berlin in *Foster Children in a Changing World: Documentation of the IFCO Conference*, Berlin: VOTUM Verlag.

Ryburn, M. (1993), 'A new model for decision making in child care and protection', *Early Child Development and Care*, 86: 1–10.

Ryburn, M. (1996), 'Besluitvorming binnen de familie: een model van empowerment', keynote speech at conference 'Familie – en sociale netwerkplaatsingen', Amersfoort, the Netherlands.

5 Kinship Fostering and Child Protection

Janet Foulds
Britain

Introduction

Research and received wisdom about good child care practice highlights the crucial importance of family and kinship groups in providing the best possible nurturing experience for children.

In non-abusive families there are many situations where children are fostered very successfully within their kinship network. Where grandparents or other relatives offer support, care and continuity for a child, there is often an excellent outcome with few of the long-term harmful effects that separation can bring (Rowe et al. 1984)

In families where abuse is not a factor, relatives are frequently highly motivated to offer substitute care. Their own love for and attachment to the child ensure the child is cared for as one of the family. Responsibilities are shared and motivation to sustain regular and enjoyable contact between child and birth parents is usually high. For parents who are suffering from temporary illness or incapacity, extended family members can provide a lifeline. Inexperienced parents or those who have learning difficulties may benefit from the guidance, wisdom and support of relatives in learning the practical tasks of good parenting.

In our efforts to support children and keep families together, there is a danger that children's rights and safety can be overlooked or the significance of risk factors diminished. It is the power of the bond between children and their families that is so enriching for children. It is also the very same power that can trap children and condemn them to very damaging experiences.

Children themselves, on the whole, are in no doubt about where they wish to be cared for. Experience teaches us that even children who have suffered severe deprivation or abuse will cling loyally to those who have harmed

69

them. They are often unable to envisage leaving their families and will strive to maintain themselves at home:

> Children fear disruption of family life, even if that has been traumatic and problematic for them. For children, especially, fear of the unknown and fear of separation usually outweigh their negative responses to a known situation (Sgroi 1982: 23).

Children deserve our respect for the determination and tenacity they show in attempting to remain with their families, often despite overwhelming adversity. We must be mindful that despite our best efforts, ascertaining children's true wishes and feelings is far from easy, especially when they are powerless and dependent. Children and young people will not always be able or willing, because of their age, experiences and loyalties, to let us know what is happening to them.

This chapter examines some of the benefits, complexities and implications of kinship fostering for children who have experienced abuse, particularly sexual abuse within their families. It seeks to identify the challenges for social workers when assisting families to make safe decisions for their children and to highlight the particular issues relating to sexual abuse which would make placements within extended families risky or positively dangerous. It argues that over-optimism and positive assumptions about the advantages of kinship fostering for children may lead, in some cases, to dangerous practice and have long-term costs for the children concerned.

Physical abuse

As well as a commitment to partnership, careful planning and rigorous assessment, professionals need to equip themselves with knowledge about the nature of abuse, its impact on victims and the influence of abuse on relationships and communication, if they are to avoid placing children in harmful situations. Whilst it is accepted that children are best cared for by their families, we also know, for example, that the majority of abuse against children occurs within the context of family and kinship groups.

The following case provides a positive example of fostering within the extended family:

> A young baby, Kirsty, was born with a physical illness which placed heavy demands on her parents, particularly with feeding and nursing care. At the time of her birth, her parents were under considerable stress emotionally and financially. The couple had two older children to care

for. Kirsty's father was unemployed and her mother was being treated for depression.

Child protection services were alerted when Kirsty received physical injuries which could not have been caused accidentally. Immediate legal steps were taken to protect the child as there was no clear explanation for the injuries, and a full child protection investigation was undertaken. Kirsty's grandparents offered to foster their granddaughter to provide some respite to her parents and in the hope that she could, in time, be rehabilitated to them. This placement allowed a full assessment to be undertaken and a planned piece of work involving social workers, health workers and family support services were commenced.

Kirsty quickly recovered from her injuries and thrived in the care of her grandparents. Her parents took a very active part in her care, gradually regaining the confidence as parents which had been very evident with their older children. Having received appropriate counselling and practical help to reduce the stresses, Kirsty's parents were able (within a relatively short period of time) gradually to resume full-time care of their daughter. Kirsty was able to go home where her progress was carefully monitored.

There were particular factors in this family which I believe led to a very positive outcome:

- *Motivation* – on the part of the parents to resume the care of their child. There was a strong attachment between parents and child, and the goal of rehabilitation was shared by the wider family who committed themselves to ensuring the plan worked
- *Good existing relationships* – Relationships within the wider family were close, affectionate and mutually supportive
- *Open communication* – It was possible to engage all family members in discussion of difficult and sensitive issues. There was apparent a high degree of trust between the parties which allowed confidences to be shared and problems identified and resolved
- *Willingness to work together* – The family as a whole demonstrated a willingness to work cooperatively with the helping agencies. The expectations of everyone involved were made very explicit and there was open acknowledgement of the potential for conflict
- *Contribution to the assessment process* – A child with injuries where there is no satisfactory explanation gives rise to very serious concern. In Kirsty's case the concern was lessened by the detailed contribution made by the grandparents to the assessment process. This was tremendously helpful in permitting the injuries and the crisis to be

viewed in a much wider context
- *Willingness of grandparents to assume a monitoring role* – The demands made by this role can be extremely problematic and can test family loyalties to the extreme. Any denial or minimising of the risk to the child, for whatever reason, can jeopardise the child's safety and make working in partnership extremely difficult to achieve. In Kirsty's case the family members were able successfully to manage the inherent tensions.

In any such arrangement the dynamics within the family group will inevitably be affected and great sensitivity is needed to avoid de-skilling and disempowering the child's parents. It is essential, where a child is deemed to be at risk, for the substitute family carers to demonstrate an accurate and realistic understanding of the risks to the child and to make a commitment to remain vigilant even where there is conflict or disagreement with social workers.

It is wise to remember that such an arrangement has costs for all concerned. The child may benefit from remaining within a loving family but the changed roles may evoke very strong feelings of distress, anger and loss and revive old conflicts for family members. Attention must be paid to these issues if a successful rehabilitation process is to be achieved, and feelings of jealousy and powerlessness should not be underestimated. It can never be easy for relatives to accept that a beloved child has been injured or neglected by someone within the family. This reflects on every family member. Denial is common and is an understandable human response but it can be dangerous in child protection work.

In this case example, Kirsty was fortunate to have a loving family with sufficient maturity and strengths to cope with a most distressing and potentially damaging episode. The partnership was successful and Kirsty was able to settle back with her parents and grow into a healthy little girl.

Another case example illustrates a less positive outcome:

Emma, aged six, was fostered by her grandparents following physical abuse by her father. As in Kirsty's case, rehabilitation was considered possible after appropriate work, and the family was fully involved in planning the necessary assessment and programme of therapeutic work.

During the assessment process, serious concerns were raised about the parents' capacity to care for their child. Information received from various sources indicated a worrying degree of violence within the marital relationship and it became clear that the child was being blamed for her parents' difficulties.

During individual work with Emma, she expressed fears to her social worker about returning home. She could not tell her grandparents how she felt because she knew that they wanted her to be reunited with her mum and dad. The adults were in agreement but Emma was unhappy. Her grandparents were devoted to her but were unable to 'hear' or accept that their son was capable of such violent behaviour. Emma could not tell them how she really felt.

Not surprisingly, relationships between the family and social services became antagonistic and difficult. Emma, aware of the 'battle' and feeling somewhat responsible for the problem, worked hard to placate everyone. She told her family that she wanted to go home. She told her social worker that she didn't. For the family there was only one possible outcome and it became increasingly difficult to work cooperatively with the family. Although her grandparents provided excellent care for Emma, their level of denial and their own needs would have left Emma at risk. The loyalty towards their son had prevented them listening to their granddaughter's fears.

In situations like these there is a danger that family members collude in constructing a false 'reality'. The child can easily become a hostage to the family 'script' and close families can sometimes become *closed* families with unhappy consequences for the children.

In a review of child abuse tragedies, Reder, Duncan and Gray refer to the 'closure' of families to the outside world and more specifically towards professionals. This was identified as a very significant factor in over half of the families where children were fatally injured. Closure was seen as attempts by families to regain control over their lives: 'We understood closure to be primarily an issue about control, with parents feeling that they were in precarious control of their lives and that outsiders were unwelcome intruders who would further undermine them' (Reder et al. 1993: 99). Clearly, if the involvement of professionals poses a threat to the family system, effective partnership cannot be achieved and the ability to make a thorough assessment can be severely compromised.

Child sexual abuse

NB: For the purpose of this discussion the child is referred to as female and the offender as male. It must be emphasised though that victims and offenders can be of either gender.

The dynamics at work in families where child sexual abuse has occurred are more complex still, and it is essential for workers to have an understanding of these dynamics when considering foster placements within extended families. Many of the positive features which enabled effective partnership to work in Kirsty's case will not be available to workers or will be unreliable in families where sexual abuse is a factor.

Reflecting on our knowledge of sexual abuse, we might expect working relationships with families to be less straightforward. Instead of openness and honesty, we are likely to be faced with secrecy and denial. Building trust can be problematic. Sex offenders attempt to 'groom' not only children and other family members, but also professionals. We can expect, because of the secrecy and minimalisation involved, that we will rarely be given the whole picture when making assessments. Making decisions about safe placements in such families, therefore, is challenging in the extreme.

Sexual abuse of children is primarily the abuse of power relationships between adults and children. We know that sexual abuse is widespread, occurs mainly in families, and that most offences are committed by people known to the children: 'The fact that the perpetrator is often in a trusted and apparently loving position only increases the imbalance of power and underscores the helplessness of the child' (Summit 1983: 177–93). Children are threatened, bribed or coerced into silence, making disclosure and discovery very difficult. Hence, very few offenders are prosecuted for their crimes.

Undiscovered abuse

The nature of sexual offending and the secrecy and denial that contributes to the silencing of children means that social workers must not assume that the full extent of sexual abuse has necessarily been disclosed. In a survey of prevalence, Kelly et al. (1991) found that a substantial amount of sexual abuse, as much as 95 per cent, goes unreported to child protection agencies. In one study, Finkelhor (1984) found there was differential reporting of abuse by parents depending on the relationship of the offender to the child. When the offender was a stranger, 73 per cent reported the abuse. When the offender was an acquaintance, only 23 per cent did so. However, when the offender was a relative, none reported the abuse.

Despite recent changes in law and practice, most notably the partly implemented Pigot Report (1989) which opened the door to child witnesses being allowed to give evidence on video in criminal proceedings, the criminal justice system cannot be relied upon to convict offenders or to protect children. We may reasonably conclude therefore, with the level of under-reporting and low conviction rates, that many sexual offenders remain firmly rooted within families, living with children and continuing to create opportunities for further offending. Children cannot rely on being protected from abuse even if they are able to tell. All too often the abuse continues with long-term damage to the child's emotional health.

The process of abuse and the child sexual abuse accommodation syndrome

To understand how children and families may be affected by sexual abuse, it is important to know how offenders work. We must acknowledge that the majority of sexual abuse takes place within a child's own family: 'Who is the perpetrator likely to be? Almost always it is someone in the child's own family who has access and opportunity by residing in the house or family circle' (Sgroi 1982: 13).

We know that sexual offenders fantasise about abusing children, plan their abusive acts and 'groom' children and their environment to provide opportunities to abuse. Having offended against a child, the abuse becomes self-reinforcing and a pattern of repeated offences follows, usually with progressively more serious behaviours (see Wolf's cycle of offending – Wolf 1984). Finkelhor and Browne (1986) identified four preconditions necessary for sexual abuse to occur:

- Motivation to abuse
- Overcoming internal inhibitors
- Overcoming external inhibitors
- Overcoming the child's resistance.

In order to overcome their own internal inhibitors abusers develop what Finkelhor and Browne call 'cognitive distortions'.

The cognitive distortions, or 'thinking errors', used to justify the abuse are absorbed by the victims. Children who have been groomed into compliance by the offender often believe themselves to be equally guilty and responsible for the abuse, and feel intense shame and self-disgust about their own victimisation. Because of this many children (and adults) see themselves as unworthy of help and protection. This results in increased vulnerability to further assault.

Summit concludes that the only option for the children in such situations is to learn to accept the situation and survive: 'The only acceptable alternative for the child is to believe that she has provoked the painful encounters and to hope that by learning to be good she can earn love and acceptance' (Summit 1983).

The child sexual abuse accommodation syndrome is extremely helpful in making sense of children's reactions to abuse and explains how children's attempts to cope with trauma often lead, sadly, to their continuing abuse.

Where children have become accommodated to their abuse, there is a danger that professionals may misread the lack of obvious emotional distress and the apparent strong attachment to family members as indicators of safety.

With little power to influence events, greater dependence on adults and a distorted view of their own complicity, children remain trapped. If the abuser is a parent or close relative, the child is easily targeted for repeated abuse: 'The intrafamily perpetrator will, of course, be able to control the child far more effectively because of the likelihood of ongoing access to the child' (Sgroi 1982: 22). The abuser may, through family contacts or baby-sitting arrangements, be well placed to get sufficiently close to the child for abuse to continue.

The potentially devastating effects of childhood sexual abuse are well documented in research and first-person accounts. Finkelhor and Browne's four 'traumagenic dynamics' describe the main sources of trauma in child sexual abuse:

- Traumatic sexualisation
- Stigmatisation
- Betrayal
- Powerlessness (Finkelhor and Browne 1986).

Children who are sexually traumatised within abusing families or networks, betrayed by those who should be protecting them and who are powerless to change their circumstances, must find ways to survive, or risk being psychologically overwhelmed. Knowledge about these survival strategies helps to inform judgements about the advisability or otherwise of foster placements with relatives.

Denial and dissociation

To survive in hostile environments, children may deny or mentally block out what is happening to them. Hall and Lloyd provide an explanation for this: 'By denying this reality, she learns to dissociate herself from the accompanying psychological and physical pain, trauma and confusion' (1989: 89).

Abused children learn to suppress emotion, refuse to cry when hurt and may invent another self (or selves) whose role it is to take the abuse. Some children describe being 'outside' their bodies looking on when the assaults are taking place. Others take refuge by focusing their thoughts on a nearby toy or object. Some escape into a fantasy world as a means of dealing with unbearable events. Sometimes children cope by mentally constructing an alternative reality and, despite their victimisation, will idealise those who are responsible for hurting them (Summit 1983). These coping mechanisms have a protective function and help the child victim avoid being over-whelmed, but they may also result in the child being unable to disclose the abuse.

Children's feelings about abusers – appeasement, ambivalence and attachment

In a vain attempt to stay safe, a child may seek to appease her abuser just as a hostage might make friends with a captor. The grooming process may have led children to believe that they are being abused either because they are special or because they deserve punishment for behaving badly: 'The grooming of the victim may involve developing a friendship with the child, using bribes of affection and gifts, threats or physical violence' (Morrison et al. 1994: 245. There are numerous variations on this theme but the messages conveyed by perpetrators are extremely powerful and damaging to the child.

When they are able to talk about abuse, children need us to hear also about the love and positive feelings they may have for their families and even for their abusers. Disclosure of abuse and separation from parents are significant experiences of loss for children and it is important for workers to acknowledge the range of feelings children may have. We cannot assume that children will see all of their experiences as harmful, even if in fact they are. Feelings of ambivalence are common. A young girl talking about her abuser:

> I would have liked him to have gone away, and I would have liked for him to have had his beating that he really deserves, one, for my sake and two, for my mum. But it's funny though because I still don't hate him, not when it comes to it, you can't, because no matter what, he was still there for me. (Female, aged 16 – NCH Action for Children 1989: 24)

Many children say that they do not want to lose their families, they just wanted the abuse to stop. However, groomed children with poor self-esteem cannot be expected accurately to understand or express the risks to themselves. It is more likely that a child will minimise or deny the harm and seek to play the role ascribed to her by adults around her. Roles may become blurred, with the child assuming the role of parent or adult. The need for love and approval is strong and children try to meet those needs by attempting to keep the family together.

The distorted attachment bond between offender and victim is described by Anna Salter who warns workers not to make the mistake of assuming that because a bond is there and the child is attached to the perpetrator that the relationship is good for the child (Salter 1992):

> Jonathon (10) only came to social workers' attention when disclosures of sexual abuse within his family were made by his cousins. They alleged that the children had all been sexually and physically abused for many years by various members of the extended family, including Jonathon's parents.
>
> During the ensuing investigation there was considerable evidence gathered to substantiate the children's claims. Jonathon denied that he had suffered abuse and his teachers were shocked to hear of the allegations. They spoke of the close and loving relationship between the child and his father and were horrified to hear that Jonathon was to be removed from home for his own safety.
>
> It was only when Jonathon was moved to a foster home and felt safe that he was able to confirm the allegations made by his cousins. He had been seriously abused by his father for as long as he could remember.

Impact on mothers and other family members

Partnership approaches would suggest that we seek guidance from non-abusing parents as to where their child will be safe, but we need to be aware of the profound ways that the sexual abuse may have affected the parent herself. A child's disclosure is likely to have far-reaching effects on other members of the family, and especially on mothers. Summit (1983) describes how the recognition of her child's victimisation tends to be 'assaultive' to the mother. If a woman has her own history of sexual abuse, the discovery that her child has also been abused may lead to a simultaneous disclosure and provoke a personal crisis for her. Distressing memories may be triggered. If she has received no help with her own abuse the memories may lead to a temporary breakdown in her ability to cope with day-to-day life, and an inability to act appropriately for her child (Curtois and Sprei 1988).

Because of her own pain, she may respond initially by denying what she has been told. Divided loyalties can leave women with extremely difficult choices to be made: 'Choices around divided loyalty will be very intense and the parents may choose to support each other and ignore the child's needs rather than make the significant changes in their own behaviour that would be required' (Sgroi 1982: 249).

If the mother's abuse was perpetrated within her own birth family, she may, even as an adult, still be at risk of ongoing sexual abuse or physical violence. The internalisation of thinking errors from her own abuser can prevent her from recognising the risks to her own and other children. In a number of cases, children are entrusted by parents, victims themselves, to the care of extended family members who have been abusive to the parent in the past. The parent may believe, erroneously, that they were the only one to be abused and may have caused it to happen. Thinking errors have been absorbed. This is illustrated in the following case example:

> Andrew's mother, Jenny, had been brought up in a family where sexual abuse and neglect of children were established patterns of behaviour. As an adult, Jenny had a series of relationships where she was exploited by men who were violent and sexually abusive towards her. It seems she was targeted because she was the mother of young children.
> In time, Jenny's children disclosed sexual abuse by one of her partners. The children were removed from her care when she attempted to conceal the abuser's presence from social workers. The children were placed with foster parents.
> Only when they were away from her did the children talk of extensive sexual abuse by a number of people, including Jenny's family and friends.
> In this case it is of significance that Jenny took action to protect three of her children, but had placed a fourth child, Andrew, with his grand-parents, the very people who had sexually abused her over many years.

The main risk in situations like these is that the parent may have an impaired capacity to judge what is safe or dangerous for their own child. If the mother's abuser is a relative, then the abuser–victim dynamic can remain powerful and, in some cases, regression may occur, leaving the mother feeling childlike herself. Even if she sees the risk and wishes to protect, the mother may become totally powerless in the presence of the offender. In very extreme cases, she may be used to procure children for her own abuser to abuse. It is important to acknowledge that women are often wrongly blamed for their apparent failure to protect children when the situation is far more complex. Everyone in the family group is likely to be affected by the abuse of the child in some way, and therefore careful assessment of family dynamics is clearly of crucial importance.

Contact

The complex dynamics of sexual abuse must also be taken into account when contact arrangements are made. We have seen how children may have less than positive reasons for agreeing to contact with abusing parents. Anna Salter (1992) urges us to consider the dynamics when contact takes place. She argues that if treatment of both child and offender has not taken place, the abuse will continue because the offender–victim dynamic is unchanged: 'When the touching stops, the abuse does not stop.'

Unfortunately, all too often contact arrangements are made with the assumption that safety will be ensured if contact between a child and an offender is supervised. This is not necessarily the case:

> It is submitted, however, that in permitting such contact the courts are taking a narrow view of the concept of risk, in that while supervised contact may prevent physical harm, it fails to acknowledge the further psychological harm that continued contact with the abuser may cause. (Foulds, et al. 1997)

The responsibility for supervision of contact is frequently given to non-abusing carers or members of the extended family. If treatment has not taken place, the dynamics are unchanged and the offender retains control. If a significant shift of power has not been possible, then perpetrators will continue to dictate what happens within the family:

> The perpetrator often dominates all family decision making and is the sole authority on where the family lives, how much is spent for clothing, food and household needs, vacation planning, part-time jobs for family members, contributions to charity, participation of the children in school activities, and so forth. (Sgroi 1982: 27)

Knowing about the grooming behaviour of the abusers, it does not seem reasonable to expect relatives to be able to effectively control the offender's behaviour. In any case, it is virtually impossible to prevent the emotional cueing of children even if physical contact does not take place.

Meeting the challenge

Perhaps the most important safety factor for children is the willingness by professionals to believe the extent to which abuse occurs. Accounts of abuse are painful to hear. We must guard against our own protective denial and be aware that in their attempts to cope professionals may take on thinking errors present in the family and minimise the seriousness of the risks to children.

Myths still abound about sexual abuse and they can lead to dangerous practice. Of particular relevance is the myth that offences perpetrated in the past have diminishing contribution to risk in the present. Offenders do continue to abuse even when they are old or have disabilities. Adults continue to be sexually abused.

We must avoid the over-reliance on the importance of the blood tie and be open-minded to the possibility that children can be harmed by those they love. Sometimes a wide range of family members are involved and several children are abused both singly and together.

Professionals should inform themselves about sexual abuse and the impact it can have on victims. This knowledge can then be used productively to plan and implement appropriate assessments. Assessment should include all aspects of family functioning: An assessor needs to consider the possible contribution of cultural beliefs, patterns in the family's history, parents' unresolved conflicts, current interactional patterns, the child's personal history and the child's characteristics (Reder and Lucey 1995: 45).

Reder and Duncan (1995) stress the importance of understanding the psychological meaning of children to their parents or carers as part of all assessments. In cases of abuse, a child can assume particular significance to her parents which results in the child being at greater risk of harm. For parents with histories of abuse, the child can act as a reflection of themselves, representing their own vulnerability. The parent may be reminded of the abuser by the child and feelings of anger may be directed towards the infant. In certain cases the children are perceived as persecutors by their parents. Sometimes the child comes to represent the part of themselves they despise – the weak and vulnerable part. These dynamics, unchecked, leave children very much at risk.

Assessment of attachments is crucial and, with children in particular, it is important to test out assumptions about their relationships within the family. Children do believe that they have a personal responsibility for keeping their families together, and it is helpful to explore fully the reasons why they might wish to be placed within the family. For example:

Jo (8) told workers that she wanted to be with her father to see if he had 'stopped doing those things' (sexually abusing her).
Kevin (10) said that he wanted to live at home so he could stop his stepfather's drinking. Kevin had been sexually abused by his stepfather.

Knowing about the efforts that children make to put things right should alert workers to the need for careful planning and supervision of contact arrangements.

It is essential that priority is given by social workers to direct work with children and to providing children with a sufficiently safe environment in which to express their wishes and feelings. Children who have been abused take time to trust and need to feel safe before they are able to share feelings. Communication with outsiders is risky for them. However, children regard social workers as important and need them to take seriously what they have to say (BASW 1997). Anna Salter (1982) recommends that key workers should act as 'radical advocates' for children who may be psychologically unable to make decisions for themselves because of their victimisation. We need to listen, support and make brave decisions on their behalf.

Once assessment with a family has commenced, plans for work can be agreed with all members of the family, if they are willing. If safety for children is to be achieved, the work must address the needs of the individual family members and aim to facilitate the adjustments necessary for the family to meet the needs of its children. Positive support networks for mothers are particularly helpful in assisting them to protect their children and reduce further risk. Some families will never be safe for children. Sgroi recommends that as a minimum acceptable goal, the treatment should aim to build in at least one functioning adult ally for the child in the home (1982: 249). If this cannot be achieved then the child cannot safely be left in the family. In the report *Messages from Children* (NCH Action for Children 1989), children describe a mix of painful emotions at having to leave home but agreed in retrospect that it was the right thing to do to escape abuse.

Conclusion

Children have the right to be with their families, and families should, wherever possible, be supported to care for their children. However, when child abuse is discovered and children need alternative care, fostering placements within the extended family may not be as safe as we would wish.

Whilst respecting children's rights, we must avoid collusion with people who abuse them. Children in abusive families are often silenced. Social workers have a duty to listen to children and act as advocates for them when their voices are difficult to hear. To listen effectively, professionals need to acquire knowledge about the nature of child abuse and sexual offending and the implications for family relationships and child protection.

Although fostering placements within the child's kinship group should always be considered, I would argue that they should only be made when it can be demonstrated that the placement is a safe and positive choice. An over-reliance on the importance of the blood tie can leave children at risk of long-term significant harm or abuse. Naivety in child protection work is costly and it is the children who will ultimately pay the price.

References

BASW (British Association of Social Workers) (1997), *Evidence to the House of Commons Health Committee Inquiry into Children Looked After by Local Authorities*, Birmingham: BASW.

Curtois, C. and Sprei, J. (1988), 'Retrospective Incest Therapy for Women', in Walker, E. (ed.), *Handbook on Sexual Abuse of Children*, New York: Springer.

Department of Health (1995), *Child Protection – Messages from Research*, London: HMSO.

Finkelhor, D. (1984), *Child Sexual Abuse: New Theory and Research*, New York: Free Press.

Finkelhor, D. and Browne, A. (1986), 'Initial and long term effects: a conceptual framework', in Finkelhor, D. (ed.) (1986) *A Source Book on Child Sexual Abuse*, London: Sage.

Foulds, J., Hall, G. and Lockton, D. (1996), 'Contact Issues in Cases of Child Sexual Abuse', *Contemporary Issues in Law*, II(3): 19–32.

Hall, L. and Lloyd, S. (1989), *Surviving Child Sexual Abuse*, New York: Falmer Press.

Kelly, L. (1998), 'Domestic Violence and Child Protection', presentation Derby Area Child Protection Committee.

Kelly, L., Reagan, L. and Burton, S. (1991), *An Explanatory Study of Sexual Abuse*, London: Child Abuse Studies Unit.

Morrison, T., Erooga, M. and Beckett, R. (1994), *Sexual Offending Against Children. Assessment and Treatment of Male Abusers*, London: Routledge.

NCH Action for Children (1989), *Messages from Children*, London: NCH.

Pigot, Judge T. (1989), *Report of the Advisory Group on Video Evidence*, London: HMSO.

Reder, P. and Duncan, S. (1995), 'The Meaning of the Child', in Reder and Lucey (1995).

Reder, P., Duncan, S. and Gray, M. (1993), *Beyond Blame – Child Abuse Tragedies Revisited*, London: Routledge.

Reder, P. and Lucey, C. (1995), *Assessment of Parenting Psychiatric and Psychological Contributions*, London: Routledge.

Thoburn, J. (1994), *Child Placement: Principles and Practice*, Aldershot: Arena.

Rowe, J. et al. (1984), *Long-term Foster Care*, London: Batsford.

Salter, A. (1992), *Current Issues in Treatment*, MOSAC (Tayside) Presentation.

Sgroi, S. (1982), *Handbook of Clinical Intervention in Child Sexual Abuse*, Lexington, MA: Lexington Books.

Summit, R. (1983), 'The Child Sexual Abuse Accommodation Syndrome', *Child Abuse and Neglect*, 7: 77–93.

Utting, Sir William (1998), *Review of the Safeguards for Children Living Away From Home*, London and Cardiff: The Department of Health and The Welsh Office.

Wolf, S. (1984), 'A Multifactor Model of Deviant Sexuality', paper presented to the Third International Conference on Victimology, Lisbon.

6 Placement Choices for Children - Giving More Priority to Kinship Placements?

Suzette Waterhouse and Edwina Brocklesby
Britain

This chapter will draw on research from the US to examine whether kinship fostering should be regarded as the first option of placement choice for children needing to be 'looked after'. It will then go on to examine findings from a research project in the UK to see how placement choices are actually made, and how significantly are kinship placements considered.

The growth of kinship care

In the US kinship care is the fastest growing service provided by the child welfare system (Gleeson and Craig 1994), but it is acknowledged that research in this area has not kept up with child placement practice. Such care is particularly used for African American children, where kinship care has proved a successful way of providing culturally appropriate placements, often with maternal grandparents. In the US, Everett (1995) and Meyer and Link (1990) found the growth in the use of kinship carers went from 3 per cent in 1986 to 45.8 per cent in 1990, whilst Scannapieco and Hegar (1994) observed that the estimated numbers of children placed with relatives was expected to rise to half a million. The reason for this dramatic change in the US is uncertain, but is thought to have arisen for two reasons: the increased numbers of children requiring placement (many of whom are drug-affected), and the loss of existing foster carers.

Research from the US has also found that kinship placements last longer but that reunification rates are lower than in traditional foster placements (Scannapieco et al. 1997; Berrick et al.; Meyer and Link 1990; Dubowitz et al. 1990). Placements with relatives do appear to be very stable (Berrick et al. 1994; Inglehart 1994; Dubowitz et al. 1990). However, they tend to be less effectively monitored and supported than is the case with traditional foster care (Scannapieco et al. 1997; Everett 1995). The latter research study emphasised a need for additional supports and professional interventions for relative carers who may be struggling with a wider range of problems than non-relative carers. This would include difficulties with the birth parent/s, divided family loyalties, boundary definitions and the changed role from relative to primary carer. Everett considered that respite might be essential and contingency planning a necessity.

In seeking to explain the lower rehabilitation rate associated with kinship care, Scannapieco et al. (1997) observed that:

> This pattern of fewer services successfully delivered to parents, together with the marked longer stay in kinship homes compared with traditional foster homes, suggests that efforts to work with parents toward the goal of returning children to parental custody may be less successful when children are in kinship care. It may be that many parents are comparatively content to have children raised in the homes of relatives and decline to engage with agencies in working for the children's return. It may be that agencies put less effort into permanency planning efforts when children are in kinship care, or it may be that they select cases for kinship placement when prognosis for return of the children is poor. (Scannapieco et al. 1997: 487)

Wulczyn, in 1990, had found that after two years, that 88 per cent of the kinship foster sample remained in care, compared with 40 per cent of the control foster sample; another study by Thornton (1987, cited in Link, 1996) found that relatives are often unwilling to move on to adopt their kin. Meyer and Link (1990) studied 536 children and found the kinship foster carers were markedly less prepared to follow through to adoption. They hypothesised that within a family placement there is less incentive for a parent to change their life style.

The National Foster Care Association study of the organisation of fostering services

Turning to the UK, in 1997, the National Foster Care Association published the first part of a two-part study commissioned by the Department of Health. It examined how local authorities were organising and delivering their fostering services (Waterhouse 1997). One of the important themes to emerge from this research related to concern about the lack of choice of carers for children, reflecting an overall shortage of carers. There appeared to be a need to explore the mismatch between supply and demand and consider the perspective not only of the family placement teams but also of the other 'users' of the fostering service, specifically the social workers and the foster carers. It seemed that supply of foster carers was going to become even more acute in the light of changing social and demographic trends. Some authorities in the first survey considered that they had already exhausted their supply of carers and they were very despondent about whether they could expand their pool of carers. It therefore appeared that kinship care could offer some potential expansion of the 'pool' of foster carers as had occurred in the US.

In England and Wales, Section 23 (2) of the Children Act 1989 prioritised care by relatives, and the Guidance (DoH 1991: 3.33) emphasised the advantages for children being placed within their wider family:

> Possibilities for a child to be cared for within the extended family should have been investigated and considered as an alternative to the provision of accommodation by the responsible authority. However even when it has become necessary for the responsible authority to arrange provision of accommodation, placement with a relative will often provide the best opportunities for promoting and maintaining family links in a familiar setting. (DoH 1991: 3.3)

Advantages are also thought to lie in easing contact arrangements with parents, achieving a goal of early reunification and ensuring a placement in familiar surroundings. Clearly the use of kinship placements enhances the breadth of choice available for a child, although it has been recognised that there were likely to be some – as yet unmeasured – disadvantages for children. These may include the differing and complex family relationships that can be set up, possible inhibitors to parental reunification or contact, and contentious issues surrounding how to financially support such placements.

Waterhouse had found that a higher use of kinship carers approved under the Foster Placement Regulations was associated with lack of placement choice across the age groups. This was quite pronounced and she suggested that the approval of kinship foster carers might have been forced by expediency as much as by a positive policy and practice.

Placement choices for children in temporary foster care

The second part of the NFCA study (Waterhouse and Brocklesby forthcoming) set out therefore to examine policy and practice relating to placement choice and matching for children requiring temporary foster care, and the way in which organisational arrangements might affect these issues. A prime objective was to examine the factors influencing placement choice for children requiring temporary foster placement in five authorities. Information was gathered from senior managers about their policies and procedures relating to placement choice, and 50 referrals for family placement, ten from each authority, were analysed. Some of the placements were sibling groups so that in total there were 71 children in the placements. A 'triad' of interviewees provided the data for each placement: the family placement worker supporting the foster carers, the fieldworker for the children and the foster carers who accepted the placement.

The questionnaire examined with the respondents the *process* by which the children entered the placements, and specifically enquired about how – if at all – the option of a kinship placement was addressed, and the extent to which kinship placements featured in placement choice for individual children. In each of the five authorities, 'kinship placements' were viewed as a significant and contentious area of policy and practice, with no clear procedures available to staff.

None of the 50 placements in the study were in fact kinship placements, although our sampling procedure could have allowed for their inclusion. That there were no kinship placements reflected in part the diverse ways in which 'looked-after' children are placed in these placements, and the separate organisational arrangements which could exist in terms of how kinship placements formally entered the system. These included:

- informal arrangements with or without transfer of finances
- use of funding under Section 17 of the Children Act 1989
- placement under fostering regulations (Reg. 3)
- emergency placement under fostering regulations (Reg. 11)
- being the subject of a residence order either with or without payment of a residence allowance
- adoption, with or without adoption allowance.

Overview of policy issues within study authorities

In each authority, there appeared to be an absence of written policies and procedures relating to the assessment, approval, support and training of kinship placements. In particular, the fostering allowance structure for kinship placements was usually inferior to that used for non-related carers.

There was robust and ongoing debate within all five authorities about where responsibility for the assessment and support of such placements lay;

it was acknowledged that organisational issues could affect the choice for a child in respect of kinship care. Responsibility for assessing, preparing and supporting kinship carers varied between authorities. Often it was the responsibility of the area social worker to identify and assess a potential kinship placement, a responsibility that they accepted with reluctance. Although the knowledge of the child and their family lay with the area fieldwork teams, social workers there felt that they had not got the skills or the time to undertake a substitute care assessment of this nature. It was pointed out that a full kinship assessment could take in excess of 60 hours' work or 12 weeks to complete.

The family placement team was recognised as having the assessment skills, greater objectivity and access to resources in respect of substitute care. However, they considered that they often had insufficient knowledge of the needs of the individual child located within their wider family system or of any risks or child protection issues involved. In one authority the family placement workers had acted as consultants to the fieldworker, but the increasing pressure on their time to recruit and prepare other carers meant that this work was now taking a lower priority and they were reduced to only sending out information packs.

Family placement workers rarely carried out the emergency 'Regulation 11' assessments of a kinship carer – this task was left to the area social work team. Regulation 11(3) of the Foster Placement (Children) Regulations 1991 is an emergency provision applying to a relative or friend of the child which states that:

> Where a local authority are satisfied that the immediate placement of a child is necessary they may for a period not exceeding six weeks place the child with a person who has not been [fully assessed and approved, with certain safeguards].

However, all the authorities referred to their backlog of families awaiting full assessments. In many cases, the Regulation 11 assessment had been undertaken, the child was in placement and allowances were being paid but the full assessment had not been taken forward within the required time frame. In one authority in the placement choices study, the majority of these cases awaiting a full assessment remained unallocated to either a family placement worker or an area social worker, and had been in that state for up to a year. There were obvious implications for the child of this lack of supervision and support of the carer in what were often complex cases. Additionally the process of preliminary Regulation 11 assessments had set up false expectations for the carer that they would be allocated to a link family placement worker, with the benefits of carer training and support.

The fostering managers who were interviewed spoke of various processes in operation to approve such kinship placements, ranging from approval by the fostering panels to individual workers able to place a child under Regulation 11 without even line manager discussion. In one authority, the team manager could approve in 'an emergency' and the case would subsequently have to be taken back to the panel. This reflects the finding in the US that the screening of kinship families is less stringent than that of non-relative foster carer families (Dubowitz 1994). Certainly we found no coherent or standardised procedures to formalise such carer assessments.

Kinship care as a choice of placement within the study authorities

In summary, Waterhouse and Brocklesby (forthcoming) had found that social workers had little real choice in placements for children who were coming into the care system. However the decision as to whether or not a kinship placement was selected for a child was a choice over which the social worker did appear to have very real discretion. It was clear that the decision whether or not to use a kinship placement was usually made by the social worker prior to the family placement team being approached about the possibility of placement in a non-related foster home:

> 'Before considering fostering we look at a family/relative placement – we are using these as carers more and more now' – social worker
> 'I see the fostering team having the monopoly of the placements unless it is a relative or friend of the child, then we have more control of it' – social worker.

It was surprising in view of this control that when the respondent social workers were asked what options they considered when deciding generally on a placement, only 9 per cent of social workers made specific reference to kinship as an option. It was suggested that social workers were more likely to have considered this option either prior to entry to care as a part of family support, or in the light of changing events once a child was in the 'looked-after' system. There were also instances where it was unclear whether the kinship option had been explored, or whether there was an assumption that this had been done with a previous care episode.

The unplanned and emergency nature of placements in the study appeared to militate against the choice of a kinship carer by the social worker at the point of placement. It was alarming in this context that 66 per cent of the 50 placements in the study were unplanned, with this figure rising to 75 per cent where the child was under five years old, or where the study placement represented an admission to the public care system. The long-term consequences for children of such traumatic moves to strange situations without any preparation cannot be underestimated and, at least as a short-term measure, it is arguable that a kinship placement could minimise the trauma.

However, several social workers observed that a foster placement with 'stranger' carers arranged through the family placement team was a less time-consuming option for the area-based social worker acting in a crisis situation than a kinship placement, because of the additional work involved for the social worker if the latter option was chosen.

Some family placement workers said that they would only support a child being placed with a family member if the social worker had done an assessment; otherwise they favoured a placement in normal foster care whilst the potential carers were assessed:

'If the area is under pressure it is quite possible that they don't pursue the wider family. It is easier to demand a foster placement' – family placement worker.

Even more pragmatically:

'We ask the referring social worker what they've done (about kinship) and if they say 'no' we ask them to explore. If they say "yes" then I'd want to know more. Social workers resent us pressing. Our level of pressing will depend on whether we have a vacancy or no' – family placement worker.

Kinship care and the individual study placements

Looking briefly at the profile of the children placed, 38 per cent of the placements were viewed primarily as risk assessments. Seventy-six per cent were accommodated by agreement with the parents and 24 per cent were the subject of a court order. Eighteen per cent were black Caribbean, 10 per cent black African and 8 per cent mixed parentage.

Overall, 63 per cent of social workers stated that they had considered the option of kinship care. However, a distinct pattern to emerge was that the actual placement decisions could often be made by duty social workers, even though the family was already known to the department, and may have an allocated social worker. Often a series of duty workers were handling the need for a placement as it evolved over several days. When we interviewed the social worker allocated to the child, some were unclear exactly what investigations regarding kinship care had been made. Given the number of duty social workers involved in the placements, and their likely lack of knowledge of the child concerned and of his/her network, it seems probable that kinship placements were an option which was not really explored for some children:

> *'I assumed this had been assessed on a previous care admission'* – social worker
> *'As far as I know there isn't anyone. The case is awaiting a new social worker, I'm not sure how kinship care has been investigated'* – social worker.

Despite the organisational blocks to kinship placements, there were also other clearly stated and valid reasons given by social workers for not considering extended family placements in respect of individual children. These included:

- Belief by social workers that no family member was available or interested
- Too much conflict within the family and it was therefore unhelpful to place the child there
- Child protection concerns precluding such a placement.

The last two reasons appeared to be real barriers to some social workers pursuing the kinship option. Further, the speed with which the study placements were being made, which directly reflected the very high level of unplanned placements, meant that there was no time to resolve such potential difficulties in order to facilitate a kinship placement.

In some cases, part of the ongoing assessment whilst the child was in the temporary foster placement was to explore potential kinship placements. This could involve considerable time demands on the social worker. In one instance a social worker had been ordered by the court to undertake separate assessments of four separate components of the wider family network as possible carers for a child. Other workers commented on the tensions within family networks that complicated the assessment and in some cases meant that wider family placements were not considered as long as the care arrangement was voluntary and the mother was the sole person with parental responsibility:

> *'The paternal grandparents had a poor relationship with the mother, they wanted the baby but were angry and hostile. I felt this was unhealthy for the child and moved him on from them, the mother supported this move'* – social worker. In another case, *'The mother rejected a family placement, she did not want her family to be involved and we accepted this'* – social worker.

Child protection

Despite the positive indicators for kinship placement, it is important to emphasise that our study sample confirms a picture of children currently coming into temporary care with a significant range of problems and unhappy early life experiences, sometimes involving sexual abuse. For 30 per cent of the children, child protection was the primary reason for the child entering the study placement. This is relevant in assessing the merits of a kinship placement where family dynamics are already complex:

> 'Grandmother and mother are not speaking and there is lots of conflict – it is not fair to involve grandma' – social worker
> 'Mother is fearful that if S went to her mother she'd never get her back. Mother is in care herself therefore we need to check it out first' – social worker
> 'Yes we go and see the [wider] family and ask, but if there is a child protection issue then it is complex and very work intensive' – social worker
> 'We didn't really know of anyone else, we excluded the father, although he thought highly of S, because there were child protection concerns, some of which involved him. The father wasn't consulted but we did write to him regarding S's admission to care' – social worker.

Race and cultural issues

The matching of race, ethnicity and culture has clearly come across as a high placement priority to the professionals placing children. Indeed our respondent social workers indicated that it was a dominant feature in determining placement choices. The authorities studied were making strenuous attempts to match refugee and asylum-seeking children with families from similar cultural backgrounds, sometimes by means of a kinship placement. Aside from the case of refugee children, our respondents tended not to emphasise the advantage of kinship placements as a way of ensuring that a placement for a child was culturally appropriate. Six children (8.45 per cent) within the study were of mixed parentage.

The demands of contact

In 78 per cent of the placements in the study, contact was either weekly or more frequent, often in the carer's home or with the carer taking some supervision responsibility. In some cases, the contact arrangements appeared to dominate the child's foster care experience, with the potential to cause considerable disruption to the child's and the carers' lifestyles. This high level of contact, borne out in other recent research, appears to be a trend, which has developed since the implementation of the Children Act 1989.

Department of Health guidance (DoH 1991: 3.33) views placement with a relative as often providing the best opportunities for promoting and maintaining family links in a familiar setting. Often however, there are issues of child protection or neglect arising from alcohol or substance misuse. Crumbleby (1996) has highlighted the complexity of contact within kinship placements and has questioned whether one should assume that such placements do in fact enable more informal contact. Just over half of Meyer and Link's (1990) sample were single children being placed with maternal grandparents – complex dynamics arose when the attentions of grandparents had been diverted from daughter to grandchild and parental roles were changed within the family. Crumbleby emphasised the need to be alert to the longer-term issues and cautioned that the need for professional and mediatory support for contact arrangements could be as great, if not greater than in any other foster situation.

Financial considerations

The issue of payment for 'kinship' carers appeared a contentious area, with fostering managers and family placement workers interviewed in the study often raising issues about what levels of allowances were 'right' for such carers. If a child would otherwise have to be cared for within the 'looked-after' system, there is a strong argument for the same rates of payment and conditions of support services for kinship carers. This rate of 'fostering' remuneration is likely to be significantly more than income support, or even residence allowances (although two of the authorities studied rarely paid residence allowances). The Grandparents Federation (1986) conducted an inquiry into the payment of allowances to support residence orders. This survey highlighted the discretionary nature of residence allowances and recognised the disparity between authorities, the difficulties when the child and the grandparents lived in different authorities and a lack of policy statements about the payment of allowances.

Meyer and Link (1990) identified the potential for family conflict or abuse of the system and calculated that in the US a 'relative' foster carer could be paid twice the amount that would be payable to a birth parent, or even a relative carer on income support. In Illinois kinship placements have a waiver from federal regulations and the authorities are providing a category of 'Kinship Guardianship' which pays less than foster care but more than welfare, with less supervision than foster care. Welfare reform within the US may also mean that families who had accepted a formalised custody arrangement could have their supports cut off after five years. Within the UK local authorities also have the discretion to alter future payments of existing residence allowances.

In the placement choice study, often a lesser rate of fostering allowance was paid to kinship carers:

> *'Kinship is the first choice, there is more pressure to place within the family on a cost basis'* – social worker
> *'We need to have a good argument for management if not using a kinship placement – but the area social worker has to do the assessment and I am too close (to be objective)'* – social worker.

In the US too a range of solutions are being explored, including short-term limited financial support, a lower rate than other forms of foster care, and the promotion of adoption. Link (1996) highlights the very real dilemmas associated with financial issues, and the links with permanency planning for children in kinship care:

> Kinship foster care creates a conundrum: can we, in good conscience create a system that pays more to a stranger to care for children than we are willing to pay a relative for the same care. At the same time can we create a system that pays grandmother more to raise her grandchild than we are willing to pay in welfare to support her daughter and allow the children to remain at home? Determining the answer to these questions will not be simple, especially since children who are in formal kinship care have been removed from their biological families via a family court action, the vast majority as a result of neglect. (Link 1996: 520)

From our own study we have no answers to these questions, nor is there the empirical research on which to base policies and practice. What we do know is that a variety of financial packages is being superimposed on already complex family dynamics, often with less professional support than is normal in foster care. Some longitudinal studies and detailed analyses of outcome measures, particularly in cases where child protection issues have featured, are essential. In the meantime it is small wonder that each one of the five authorities reflected an ongoing and vigorous debate on the merits of kinship placements and a lack of coherent policy and practice.

Summary

Kinship placements were actively considered as an option for only a small minority of children in our sample at the time the study placement was chosen. The importance of wider family and friends in offering substitute care for a child needs to be recognised more consistently but the crisis-led nature of placement-making does not appear conducive to this.

The use of and approval of kinship carers for a child necessitates a partnership or 'bridge' relationship between the skills and knowledge of the social worker and family placement worker. Deciding that a kinship placement is best for a child demands not only an assessment of family members' capacity to care for the child, but also not inconsiderable knowledge of the child, the parents and the wider family setting. It is unrealistic to expect that such assessments will result from family placement and duty social workers working together when neither has a history of contact with the family. It is equally probable under the current system that no one worker has the expertise, knowledge about the case, and objectivity to complete such an assessment.

Developing kinship care appears an important way forward in improving placement choices for children and achieving matches for them that best reflects their cultural origins. The successful making of such placements requires new and creative structures within which social workers and family placement workers can respond together more speedily to assess the opportunities for placing the child in the wider context of their family network on either a short or longer-term basis. If such new structures are not viable within an authority, then consideration could be given to referring assessments for longer-term placements to a specialised agency, capable of extending their skill base and able to offer ongoing specialised group support for kinship placements. Such a project could be piloted on an 'action research basis'. There is a long-term need for professional support in such placements and it cannot be assumed that kinship care is a 'cheap option', or a 'quick fix' for caring for children who come into the care system.

Kinship care provides an important potential alternate placement choice for children and there is much to learn from the rapidly increasing body of knowledge within the US about the recruitment, assessment, preparation and support of kinship carers. We are already aware from the Organisation of Fostering Services Study (Waterhouse 1997) that the extent to which kinship carers are being recruited and approved as foster carers under the Foster Placement Regulations varies enormously between authorities. There is no reason to suppose that such kinship carers have any less need than other carers of skilled training and support but there is no consistency in policy or practice, or indeed body of knowledge or guidance upon which to base practice. There is clearly considerable scope to review the best way forward for the future, so that research and practice in respect of kinship care keep abreast of each other.

References

Berrick, J.D., Barth, R.P and Needell, B. (1993), 'A comparison of kinship foster homes and foster family homes', *Children & Youth Services Review*, 16(1–2): 33–64.

Crumbleby, J. and Little, R. (1997), *Relatives Raising Children: An Overview of Kinship Care*, Washington, DC: CWLA Press.

DoH (Department of Health) (1991), *The Children Act 1989 – Guidance and Regulations, Vol. 3, Family Placements*, London: HMSO.

Dubowitz, H. (1994), 'Kinship Care: Suggestions for Further Research', *Child Welfare*, LXXIII 5: 561.

Dubowitz, H., Feigelman, S., Tepper, V., Sawyer, R. and Davidson, N. (1990), *The Physical and Mental Health and Educational Status of Children Placed with Relatives*, Baltimore: University of Maryland at Baltimore.

Everett, J. (1995), 'Relative Foster Care', *Smith College Studies in Social Work*, June: 235.

Gleeson, J. and Craig, L. (1994), 'Kinship care in Child Welfare: an analysis of states' policies', *Children & Youth Services Review*, 16(2): 7–31.

The Grandparents Federation (1996), Residence Order Allowance Survey, Harlow: Moot House, Stow, Harlow, Essex tel 01279 444964.

Inglehart, A. (1994), 'Kinship Foster Care; Placement, Service and Outcome Issues', *Children and Youth Services Review*, 16 (1–2): 107–22.

Link, M. (1996), 'Permanency Outcomes in Kinship Care. A study of children placed in kinship care in Erie county, New York', *Child Welfare*, LXXV: 529.

Meyer, B. and Link, M. (1990), 'Kinship Foster Care, the Double Edged Dilemma', Rochester, NY: Task force on permanency planning for foster children.

Scannapieco, M. and Hegar, R. (1994), 'Kinship care: Two case management models', *Child & Adolescent Social Work Journal*, 11(4).

Scannapieco, M., Hegar R. and McAlpine, C. (1997), 'Kinship Care and Foster Care: A Comparison of Characteristics and Outcome', *Families in Society: the Journal of Contemporary Human Services*, September: 480–88.

Thornton, J. (1987), 'An Investigation into the Nature of Kinship Foster Homes', unpublished doctoral dissertation, Yeshiva University, New York.

Waterhouse, S. (1997), *The Organisation of Fostering Services: A Study of the Arrangements for the Delivery of Fostering Services in England*, London: NFCA.

Waterhouse, S. and Brocklesby, E. (forthcoming), *Placement Choices for Children in Temporary Foster Care*, London: NFCA.

Wulczyn, F. (1990), 'The Changing Face of Foster Care in New York City', Albany NY: New York State Dept of Social Service.

7 Working with Family Complexity – Supporting the Network

Hermien Marchand and Wilfried Meulenbergs
Belgium

In many families and neighbourhoods, children are brought up by members of their extended family (grandparents, aunts and uncles) or with neighbours or close friends. In more traditional cultures it is taken for granted that the eldest brother (or perhaps his wife) will look after the children of a sister or brother who has died or is away. In some cases a godfather or godmother may still be expected to take up the care of a godchild if necessary.

This clear evidence seems to be in sharp contrast with the evolution of our society from *Gemeinschaft* to *Gesellschaft* (Durkheim). Cocooning within the nuclear family seems very much in fashion, and the ties of the extended family network loosen increasingly as people move in search of work elsewhere and live further away from one another.

Does this mean that caring for children of one's extended family or acquaintances is now outdated because it is no longer relevant in our society? In fact we find that in the most vulnerable section of our society this mobility is not really very great, and bonds and spontaneous solidarity are still very high. It is particularly in this segment of society that we find the larger part of the 'clientele' of youth care in general and foster care in particular.

An estimate by foster care organisations from West-Vlaanderen (the province of West Flanders) suggested that one in three of foster children end up in a family that know them already, either within their wider family or social network.

Defining network placements

In general terms we talk about 'network placements' when talking about

99

care provided for children (and adults too) within an existing network. The foster parents and parents have known each other before fostering and that is why we talk about 'foster care for acquaintances'.

In *family network placements* children are fostered by family. Very often grandparents lend a hand in crisis situations; uncles and aunts also frequently foster. Once in a while children find shelter with a married brother or sister or with a more distant relative.

Fostering in *social networks* is also a frequent occurrence. In these cases children are fostered by confidantes of the parents. These situations usually develop very naturally and gradually: coming in regularly for meals, staying over for one night at a time, then coming for a holiday, and slowly settling in with the friends or neighbours.

Because in most cases these network placements happened spontaneously, assistance is very often called in rather incidentally, or when someone in the neighbourhood expresses concern. Frequently a support team is only brought in after a child has already been living in a foster family for a considerable time (sometimes years). Even the term 'placement' is not wholly appropriate in these circumstances.

New interest in the phenomenon

Why is it that Flemish social workers and foster care organisations have been showing renewed interest in network placements? Caseworkers are increasingly incorporating network carers within the foster care system.

First of all, the idea of network placements coincides closely with the stress on working within the family in an *emancipatory* way. Families that are given the opportunity and support to solve their own problems become stronger and less dependant on organised assistance.

Secondly, a network placement is the logical conclusion of a second important principle in modern juvenile assistance, which is the principle of *subsidiarity*. A crisis situation is best solved by using the least drastic measure that this specific problem calls for. If a child cannot stay home, a network placement is at any rate much less radical than placement in an unknown foster home. Very often those concerned do not consider a network placement as a placement at all, but see it as a natural fact. The trauma of separation and disruption which can be profound and protracted in other situations does not play such a significant part here. Obviously this kind of placement also prevents stigmatisation: it is much easier for a child to say 'I'm staying with my granny for a while.'

Thirdly, network placements fit comfortably with the increasingly popular theories of Dr I. Boszormenyi-Nagy about *contextual thinking*.

'Contextual therapy' was developed by the Hungarian-American psychiatrist and family therapist Ivan Boszormenyi-Nagy, influenced by individual therapy, transactional therapy and systems thinking. The word 'context' refers to the dynamic interaction (connection, alliance) of a person with all their meaningful relationships through the generations, in the past and the future. Each human being is part of a family network with specific relationships. The helper keeps the intergenerational network in mind, even if she is working with one individual. Issues of absent people and future generations can be important.

'Loyalty' is the key word in contextual thinking about human relationships. The alliance between parents and children can never stop: you can never stop being a mother, a father, a son or a daughter ('vertical loyalty'). Loyalty is not a feeling, it has nothing to do with love: it is a fact, derived from giving birth and being born. Loyalty conflicts are inherent in life itself. In the course of life horizontal loyalty (for instance the connection between foster child and foster parents) cuts the vertical, existential loyalty. To break, avoid or deny the vertical loyalty will cause serious pain in new relationships with a partner or children. This can cause a lot of conflicts in ordinary foster care situations. On the other hand, in network care this bonding seems to be an advantage. The gap between foster parents and the home environment is absent, and reintegration with the birth parents can develop naturally with no rupture for the children.

Less cultural distance, more tolerance

When a child is placed in a routine foster family, she will have to deal with greater or lesser cultural differences between the foster family and her own family. These can lead to conflicts of loyalty in the child. In a natural network, these cultural gaps are less acute. The lifestyle of the foster family connects closely with that of the parents. This makes placement less traumatic, both for the child and for the parents. The child's experience will be less like living in two worlds and she will feel less removed from her natural environment. The parents have a lower threshold to cross in getting in contact with their child, and feel less that their child has been 'placed'.

The reverse of this is that some problematic situations may be acceptable to the network foster family but not to society at large. Playing truant may present no more of a problem for the foster parents than it did for the parents themselves, but it does for society at large and thus for the caseworker who is in a way representing society. Furthermore it is the duty of the caseworker to check whether the child is being given adequate opportunity for development. To give an extreme example: a child shall not be taken away from an incestuous family only to be placed with a foster family where the risk of child abuse is high.

However, it seems that a spontaneous selection takes place within the network. The network usually selects a family that has been playing a supportive role in previous crisis situations and has shown itself capable of handling problems.

The specific forces of a network – networks as social systems

Systems thinking has taught us that networks, which are obviously systems themselves, can be very strong. The whole is more than the sum of the parts. The network has its own dynamics which must be taken into account by the caseworker. This can be a very positive factor: family networks can appeal much more forcefully to an unwilling father than any caseworker could.

However, the effect can also be negative: a daughter can be cast off by her family, losing contact with her child who is now living with the mother's parents. While an unrelated foster family can be asked to offer the parents a fresh chance, the grandparents may well respond that they have already done this many times to no avail.

Whatever forces are at play in the network, the fact is that it is not a fragile artificial system as can be the case with a routine foster care placement. In that sense too, the system is 'stronger'. In families, blood ties are still taken seriously regardless of the circumstances: 'They're still my father/son/ daughter, aren't they ?' In social networks there is often more social control which prevents alienation.

Family scripts and balance sheets

The most important feature of network placements may well be that there is always a specific past which people already share when caseworkers join the system. In families this is quite obvious: if a child is staying with its grandparents, the grandparents have a history in common with at least one of the parents, their own child. A typical example is the grandmother talking about how difficult her own daughter was as a child, how she found the wrong husband and how she never cared for her own children as she should, which is why the grandmother has taken over the task.

In a social network placement there is also a shared past, but more restricted and less intense than in a family network. The principle remains the same however: as with every human being, the past impacts on the present. The relationship between the foster parents and the child is not a blank sheet as in a routine foster care placement. There are innumerable variations but there is always a defined relationship between the people involved. Of course, everyone will have their own version of what that relationship is. All this plays a part in how these people will relate to one another during the placement. However, these relationship patterns will not change because all of a sudden a caseworker intervenes and asks questions about them.

Some of the processes and interactions that have a central place in Nagy's contextual thinking have considerable influence on what happens within a family network. Legacies are passed from generation to generation; accounts are balanced or disrupted.

The classic example is grandparents with children who are submerged in problems, leaving the grandparents with a chronic and often unspoken feeling of guilt for having failed in the upbringing of their child. These grandparents want to straighten this out through caring for their grandchild. In this way they want to show society that they can do a good job and that they are setting things right. This mechanism requires that the 'in-between generation' be condemned to a problem-filled life. Without this the grandparents cannot pay off their debt by bringing up their grandchild; otherwise the feeling that it was all their child's fault doesn't hold good. When this grandchild shows behavioural problems in adolescence, comparison with the parents will quickly be made.

Another example of settling accounts is when an uncle takes in the children of his elder sister because she took care of him when their parents had too many problems to cope with.

From these examples it may become clear that in kinship care the motivation to become a foster family must be seen in an intergenerational context and more particularly in the relational-ethical dimension of this context. It is striking how fast you come across this dimension in kinship care and how decisive it can be in the daily functioning of the placement:

Rudy is a two-year-old boy who was born with physical disabilities. His mother and father have mild levels of learning disability. His mother was abused as a child, while his father is an only child who is still spoiled by his parents. Rudy was their first child and the parents had a hard time coming to terms with their little boy's disability. At first Rudy used to visit his paternal grandparents and stay overnight during the weekends, but as time went on these 'weekends' became longer and longer. When Rudy was six months old, he had a cerebal haemorrhage while at home with his mother. Happily he survived, but his mother was then very anxious and when the doctor suggested to her that she leave Rudy with his grandparents on a full-time basis, it seemed a good idea.

When the situation was referred to our office, we found a range of difficulties.

Rudy's father has his evening meal with his parents every day, so Rudy readily recognises him as 'daddy'. They have a good relationship, and it feels comfortable and natural to be together.

On the other hand, although Rudy's mother visits him from time to time, it doesn't feel the same for her. Though she likes this family, she also wants to be loyal to her own parents and they have a major feud with the foster parents. Although her husband spends so much time with his parents, he won't visit hers, so she's torn between his family and her own.

Her parents are asking for the right to have visits from Rudy at their home. The caregivers oppose this strongly: 'They could visit Rudy while he's staying with his parents, every second Sunday, but they don't want to', 'While he was in the hospital, they didn't show much concern for him', 'They mistreated their own daughter', etc.

The mother is asking to be allowed to bring up Rudy herself, but this isn't really her own choice: her parents are pressuring her to take Rudy to prove she is a good mother.

All in all, Rudy's father and mother have very different points of view about what is best for him.

In this example, we see that there's far more at stake than the issue of the little boy's health and development. The caregivers are doing fine work looking after him. During my visits, though, part of the conversation is always about 'how bad the other family is'. They are very scared of losing Rudy, because he's filling their lives.

It's difficult to maintain a good relationship with the mother and with her parents and with the caregivers at the same time. For instance, on one occasion the mother told me that she had often been beaten as a child by her mother. I asked her if there was any danger for her little daughter (a second, healthy child who is treated just fine) and afterwards the maternal grandmother phoned me, awfully mad that I had accused her of beating little children. In this kind of work you have to be extremely careful what you say and do!

So far, we have managed to deal with these problems and there is hope for Rudy.

A network placement support system

It is one thing to acquire a better understanding of the features of network placement, quite another to apply this in developing an effective support system. We now want to outline such a support system and to describe the key principles that follow from this profile of network placements. They are based upon symposia of the West Flemish Foster Care Consultation (Overleg Pleegzorg West-Vlaanderen).

From this perspective the time-honoured network placement seems more modern than ever. However studies show that many social workers feel unable to fulfil their normal tasks (preparation of the foster family, research into the child's background, bringing about a sound attachment between child and foster parents) in network placements. They thus find it much harder to work out their own place in the system that emerges in a network placement, that is, in the triangle of parents – foster parents – child. Hence the demand for a more specific approach focused on network placements, recognising them for what they are and understanding the need for more made-to-measure approaches.

Our key questions are: What is the particular approach needed in a network placement and how does it differ from a routine placement? And how should social workers behave in this specific situation?

A starting point: a new positioning for the caseworker

A foster placement is described in classical manuals as the result of a flow of decisions: each answer leading to a new, more specific, question. For instance, is this a child in need of placement? If so, is she best placed in foster care? If so, which kind of foster care? Or for the foster family: is this family eligible as a foster family? If so, for which kind of children?

This tells us a lot about the position of the caseworker in a routine foster care placement: it is a central and powerful position. At the beginning of a placement the caseworker is the only link between the birth family and the foster family. The caseworker holds all the information from both sides and determines which information will be fed into the system.

In kinship fostering the caseworker's position is totally different. Here the network holds the information and the network has already taken some important decisions. The caseworker is called in when a number of crucial stages are over. This is clearly captured in the expression *'fait accompli'* or *'de facto'* placement. This phrase gives expression to the caseworker's feeling that everything has already been decided and worked out by the time she joins the system, and in addition it reflects a fatalistic and negative starting point. Is a network placement a placement in which you can only do half a job?

From what we have said so far it seems quite clear to us that there are many areas in which a caseworker can do a useful job. Network placements are not 'spontaneously' good and are not 'spontaneously' capable of taking everything into account just because they have emerged 'spontaneously'. On the contrary, the fact that they started spontaneously often implies that clear agreements have not been made between those concerned from the beginning. Everyone just assumes from the start that everything is fine and precisely this assumption contains an extra risk because it can very quickly become clear that each party has their own different expectations.

A point that needs making here is that kinship foster care doesn't necessarily have to follow this *fait accompli* scenario. All major decisions do not necessarily have to have been taken by the time discussions about support start. Another process is conceivable and preferable: at a particular moment a problem situation arises and there is a demand for placement. At this very moment the caseworker could direct herself towards the whole family (and not just towards the members in crisis) and decide together with the family whether a family placement is possible, with whom, on what conditions, within what time limit, with what practical arrangements, etc.

Furthermore family dynamics play an important part: people can be stigmatised for life in their own system, people can be rejected, negative processes can be repeated from generation to generation. The advantages of a network placement should not allow us to forget the risks involved. Consequently, there are more than enough reasons to argue for the necessity of a support system. But the team must realise that it is working from a starting point very different from that in a routine foster care placement where it plays a central role. The team has to accept this position and has to try to play a suitable role in the whole system: 'You have had a whole history together, I must start getting to know the family as an outsider. I shall need your help here.'

Three young brothers were removed from their father, after their mother had left the family. They had been extremely neglected for a long time. The court asked whether the grandparents (the mother's mother who's married to the father's father) could take care of the children, because there was no foster family available where all three children could be together. The parents had the right to visit their children on separate weeks.

Each week there were more difficulties: for instance, the father made a visit at the wrong time (to his own father's house!) and then called the police because he was prevented from seeing his children.

The grandmother wanted to help her daughter because she still believed her daughter was capable of living without drugs and prostitution. After further deception and disappointment, there were big fights between them. The children's mother even thought of buying a gun.

Neither the mother or the father had been brought up by these parents. Mother had lived with her father, and father had lived with his mother. It's understandable that there are many accusations flying around now. For a long period the grandparents asked me not to get in touch with their children because they were afraid that I would interfere. A number of crises later (I will shoot you and the children!) it was time to meet in court.

There was no further opportunity to come to an agreement and the caregivers were exhausted. Grandfather is ill (asthmatic), grandmother is depressed and the relationship between them is strained.

The grandmother feels guilty because she didn't succeed; on the other hand she feels she has to side with her husband, who is certain that they cannot continue. It's very difficult to fail, even though they never asked to have these children.

As a worker I also feel the pain of not having been able to solve these problems. What is going to happen to these children?

What were the issues?

The caregivers do not have the same level of motivation: in this situation the grandfather wants to quit, the grandmother would like to go on.

They feel they have to pay the bill for what's gone wrong in their own life: these children (the parents) were brought up by their 'bad' ex-husband and ex-wife. Life has played a trick on them. They had planned to have a good time together and finally get some rest.

Grandmother wants to explain why she didn't raise her children, that she is not responsible for the behaviour of her daughter. She's very sensitive about this.

The intergenerational script is still being written – often, I heard the remark that one of the children is 'just like his mother/his father', which doesn't suggest there is much chance for the child to develop as an individual in their own right.

In the end, it's a pity that the children cannot stay with their grandparents, just at the very moment when they are getting attached to them. There's only a very small chance that one of their parents will be able to have them back.

> The advantage of a 'neutral' solution (a small institution), will probably be that there's a greater possibility of doing some intensive work with the parents. It will actually be much less complicated trying to work towards rehabilitation with the parents without the grandparents' involvement.

The best way of getting to know the family is to discuss the genogram of the family, with everyone involved. This is the first expression of the multiple partiality of the caseworker.

In our personal experience most people are very open to this concept and it prevents the social worker from coming to the wrong conclusions and choosing wrong approaches. By using the genogram you can also evaluate arrangements that are self-evident in a routine placement, but which do not take into account the relationship patterns in the network. This can save the caseworker a lot of frustration pursuing impractical arrangements or unrealisable objectives.

This method of a general consultation with the family is not just an interesting idea. Several Dutch foster care organisations do apply this method when a child has been referred for fostering. They only resort to unrelated fostering if a solution within the family appears to be impossible. In our view this fits logically and correctly within notions of family-oriented and emancipatory work and subsidiarity.

The actual support

A first principle in supporting network placements is to set realistic targets. You can only formulate what you hope to achieve when the family and their interactions have become familiar to you. You are unlikely to effect quick changes in patterns that have existed and have been repeated for twenty years or more.

It is also quite easy to drop people because they are non-cooperative and not open to guidance. Network families are much more vulnerable in this situation than routine foster families who, so to speak, get the label 'infallible'. It is always important to consider whether apparent contra-indications can be turned into application points for offering support. This is a far more dynamic starting point and opens up new perspectives and possibilities.

Relationship aspects in foster care

All the relationships between those involved have to be taken into account:

who trusts whom, who is called on in emergencies, what alliances exist, what unsettled accounts still play a part in family life (who owes what to whom) and so on. All these questions have a great impact, for instance, on visiting arrangements. The caseworker will need to draw up a chart showing the family relationships. This relational chart becomes the blueprint for setting up arrangements that are going to work.

As an outsider the social worker has a good view of the unspoken interactions and mechanisms in a network. In a way she is an 'unbiased onlooker'. She is the person without a history. This is a situation she can put to good use. She has the authority, more than anyone else, to uncover and to question the existing mechanisms and interactions. For all those in the network these interactions are likely to seem self evident and even inevitable.

A grandmother may think it self-evident that her son will never be able to look after his children 'because he was never able to do so in the past'. It is up to the social worker at least not to agree with her completely. Although she may understand the grandmother's attitude, she will at least want her to give the son the opportunity to prove the opposite.

A daughter may state that she 'has never really been helped by her parents' whereas they maintain: 'If you knew all we have done for her.' The caseworker will have to put these two versions of the same past into perspective, rather than tie herself to one interpretation, thus trying to create openness.

Pedagogical aspects of fostering

Apart from all this the social worker must remain attentive to the pedagogical aspects of foster care. The main focus must remain to provide the best possible environment for the foster child. A standard foster family will have started getting into the habit of discussing this with the social worker even before the actual placement started: it is one element in selecting families that they will talk through the best ways of providing for the child.

In a network placement this theme very often remains elusive. The social worker must not be put off by this. She must find the right approach to talk the subject through. The customary way in to these themes is through discussing the child's development and character.

In this instance too the social worker will best start from a 'one-down' position: 'You know your grandchild better than I do. Tell me what kind of girl she is. How would you describe her?'. An important subject for discussion is not only her personality but also the evolution of the child.

What steps in the child's development have the relative foster parents noticed? The social worker can thus judge whether the foster parents have an insight into child development in general and into their own foster child in particular. Alongside this she will assess the foster parents' aspirations for the child.

From there it is only a small step to evaluate how they treat the child, how they react, what they think important, what behaviour they do not tolerate. If the social worker deals with their questions in a respectful way she will gradually achieve an appropriate role and a mandate to talk these themes over with them.

If this is accomplished, exactly the same pedagogical themes will be touched on in a network placement: health, school, study methods, work attitude, emotional and psychosocial development, linguistic development, social behaviour, ability to cope, conduct and limits within the foster family and how they deal with punishments and rewards.

None the less, in network placements differences in lifestyle may still exist between the parents and foster parents. This may cause minor or major conflicts and the child may also get caught here in a conflict of loyalty between two worlds. Social workers will inevitably have to deal with this.

John is a 13-year-old boy, raised by his father as the lone carer. His mother is an alcoholic; she went through several affairs before leaving home. Mother has three other children: Suzy (12) who's still living with her father, Patrick (6) who's living with his maternal grandmother and Timmy (10 months) who's staying in another foster family.

His father has many debts and he's out working most of the time to pay them off. John was often left alone at home and at one point he broke into a fairground caravan with some friends.

The juvenile court decided that John needed to go and live in a foster home. There was no foster family available for a boy of his age and his aunt (his mother's sister) offered him a chance. He turns out to be a very difficult boy but with the support of his father and maternal grandmother, the situation is tolerable. His aunt and her mother (the grandmother) have a very close relationship.

The difficulties here, are:

● The caregiver wants John to follow the rules of the house but he's taking advantage of the large number of adults involved: if he wants some money, for instance, he asks his aunt, her husband (and his mother), his grandmother (and her husband), his father – and everyone, except his aunt, is spoiling him

- His mother visits her mother from time to time but John doesn't want to see her
- It's very difficult to intervene in the family relationships: we no sooner negotiate a set of arrangements than they are changed. It's difficult to discuss the influence of the past: grandmother's ex-husband (the mother's father) was also an alcoholic but the grandmother can only put the blame for her daughter's drinking on John's father.

We want to support the aunt without interfering too much in her relationships with her husband, her mother, and her sister. Another concern is John's mental health. How can we help him to see clearly in this confusion?

Conclusion

We have argued that the social worker will need to tune in to a wide range of aspects of family history in working with kinship fostering. The family's shared history is an important strength in offering continuity for the child. On the other hand, that same history may mean that the 'offer' to look after the child is far from straightforward, and guilt and indebtedness to other family members may play a part in the decision. There may be very negative views about the child's parents within the family, and this may make it difficult for the parent to visit her child, and may leave the child with a real conflict of loyalties rather than a sense of security. Relationships between different 'sides' of the family may already be complex and strained, and may become more complicated when the placement starts. All this makes real demands on the social worker, who will need all her normal skills and a particular systemic awareness.

Note:
In Autumn 1996 the West Flemish Foster Care Organisation (Overleg Pleegzorg West-Vlaanderen) started research in collaboration with Professor Robbroeckx into this kind of foster care within the foster care organisations in West Flanders: Oikonde (Brugge), Open Thuis (Roeselare), Opvang (Brugge), Westvlaamse dienst voor sociale Integratie (Roeselare), West-Vlaamse pleeggezinnendienst (Roeselare). In preparation two internal symposia were organised on the theme 'network placements' for all staff members of the organisations involved. This chapter is a representation of these two symposia.

Reference

Boszormenyi-Nagy I. and Krasner, B.R. (1994), *Tussen geven en nemen, over contextuele therapie*, Haarlem: De Toorts (translation of *Between Give and Take – A Clinical Guide to Contextual Therapy* (1986) New York: Brunner/Mazel Inc.).

8 Evolving Networks in Relative Care – Alliance and Exclusion

Valerie O'Brien
Ireland

Introduction

This chapter is drawn from a study (O'Brien 1996, 1997) which was undertaken in a child care agency in the Eastern Health Board area of Ireland in 1995. The study, which used a combined qualitative and quantitative methodology, examined the evolution of relative care networks following an emergency placement of a child in a relative's home. It also provided baseline data on a population of 92 children. The study traced the processes involved through the decision making, assessment and post-assessment stages. It examined the ways in which current case management practices, derived primarily from an application of a traditional foster care approach, impact on the evolution of the networks. The multiple perspectives on issues offered by the birth parents, children, relatives and social workers involved was an important feature of the study. A post-Milan systemic framework, drawing principally on the 'fifth province model', was the main theoretical frame used to orientate the study.

In this chapter, the place of relative care in the Irish child welfare system is presented in the first section. The central tenets of the 'fifth province model', which underpins the study are then briefly explained. A typology of relative care networks is presented in the final section. The implications of the different categories in terms of case management are discussed briefly.

Relative Care in an Irish Context

A specific provision enabling relative care was included in the Irish Child Care Act 1991. While the inclusion of relatives was seen 'as an enlightened approach' (Dail Reports 1990: 655), attempts to prioritise placement with relatives over other care options failed to get adequate support in the parliament to be accepted, although this was not pushed forcibly at the time (Dail Reports 1990: 663). The new Child Care Act was followed by the making of the Placement of Children with Relatives Regulations (DoH 1995), which now govern policy and practice in the area. Evidence of growth in the number of relative care placements suggests that it is set to become an increasingly important part of Irish child care services. In 1996, a quarter of all new placements in the agency in which this study was conducted were relative care placements. The actual extent of use of this placement option is however difficult to establish, as national statistics were unavailable at the time of the study. This is a feature of many child welfare systems internationally (Link 1996; Gleeson 1996; Colton and Williams 1997). Child care agencies are now required to compile separate registers for foster and relative care placements, which will undoubtedly assist in the identification of trends in the future.

The broad shifts to which the emergence of relative care is attributed internationally are also evident in Irish child welfare. The underlying philosophy of partnership in the Child Care Act 1991 (Ferguson and Kenny 1995), the shift from residential care to foster care (O'Higgins 1996; DoH 1992a and 1992b, O'Higgins and Boyle 1988), changing demographic patterns affecting the availability of foster homes (Gilligan 1990) and an increased focus on culturally appropriate placements for children in the care system (Pemberton 1996) are relevant.

The Fifth Province Model/Approach

A brief account of the fifth province model, developed by McCarthy, Byrne and Kearney, (Kearney et al. 1989; Colgon 1991; Byrne and McCarthy 1988, 1994; Byrne 1995; McCarthy 1994) within a systemic framework, is presented to illustrate the structural features of the evolving networks presented in this chapter. A systemic framework refers to a mode of practice in which context, relationship and interaction are central conceptual issues. Systemic practice is informed by the definition of system as 'a group of elements in interaction with one another over time such that their recursive patterns of interaction form a stable context for individual and mutual functioning' (Jones 1993: 2).

The fifth province model has been developed since the early 1980s from clinical work in the area of sexual abuse. It has been elaborated as an approach for working with complex systems involving family and state agencies, with particular reference to poverty, inequality, gender and marginalisation. It is defined as 'a linguistic model which figuratively constitutes in diamond form an ensemble of political actors and the discourses in which they are embedded' (Byrne and McCarthy 1994: 51). The model is not in the 'tradition of a grand theory of social action or therapy, rather it is in the developing tradition of post-modernist philosophy which values ambivalence, ambiguity, pluralism, mutual acceptance and respect of other non-dominant value systems' (McCarthy 1991: 238).

The reasons for using a systemic framework, with a particular focus on the fifth province approach, for the study were fourfold. The fifth province provided a conceptual framework:

- to examine family/state relationships
- to conduct field work interviews
- to explore/analyse the network of relationships and
- to work towards co-operative relationships in the relative care networks.

The Diamonds of the Fifth Province: Bateson's Influence

Bateson's description of symmetrical and complementary interactions in systems underpins the diamond structures, which are the hallmark of the fifth province approach (Fig. 8.1). *Symmetrical* movements or escalation refer to those interpersonal patterns where the behaviour of A triggers a similarity of behaviour in B (Bateson 1980: 41). An example of a symmetrical relationship 'is the arms race, which if carried to extremes can lead to the destruction and/or breakdown of the system' (McCarthy 1991: 111). Relationships based on *complementarity* are those which increase differences between the participants, for example, a relationship based on domination and submission. Again if they are taken to their extreme position a gross imbalance is created between the position of domination and submission. The fifth province model developed an application of these two typologies of relationships. They advocate that this analysis can guide the practitioner and offers the potential for enhancing cooperation in the face of competition, conflict and scapegoating (McCarthy 1991; Byrne and McCarthy 1994).

Mythology

The fifth province team invoked the metaphor of the fifth province from Irish mythology, as additional to Ireland's four traditional provinces. 'This province, this place, this centre', was according to Hederman and Kearney 'not a political or geographical position; it is more like a dis-position' (1977: 11). Thus the fifth province was both apart from and a part of the other provinces. For Hederman and Kearney, it was the province of imagination. They envisaged this province as a 'place where all oppositions were resolved ... where unrelated things coincide' (1977: 10). Since the fifth province had no current temporal or spatial existence, it was a transportable guide and defied concrete descriptions of positioning. For the fifth province team it suggested a 'dis-position' towards and beyond all positions constituting the social field in which they operated. They used the fifth province metaphor to create a space within which to examine their own position, and those of other participants, while simultaneously constructing the diamond shapes to map the relationships and discourses emerging in the conversations. By utilising this metaphor the team hoped that 'within this imaginatively created space perhaps different, less competitive, less fragmented and divisive relationships with one another might be possible' (McCarthy 1991: 125).

Diamond structures and the expanded social field

The key instruments and underlying principle of the framework are spatial diagrams, referred to as the diamonds (McCarthy 1991; Byrne and McCarthy 1994). They are used to articulate the structure of 'the expanded social field', to illustrate 'the disparate groups, professionals and families with diverse agencies and mandates' involved in conversations (McCarthy 1991: 219). The 'diamonds structure' applied to the 'expanded social field' provides a frame to represent oppositions, alliances and exclusions of participants in the network of relationships and discourses. Applied to clinical situations 'it provides an analytical moment which points to the lines of conjunction and disjunction in personal narratives anchored in wider and public discourses' (Byrne 1995: 256). Following Bateson's description of complementary and symmetrical interaction in systems, and symbols influenced by the work of Minuchin (McCarthy 1991: 242), two diamond structures were developed within which relationships, themes and discourses could be mapped. These are symmetrical competitive systems and complementary cooperative systems, as illustrated in Figures 8.1.i and 8.1.ii.

A *symmetrical competitive system* is a description for a social field which has an ambivalent structure of opposition and contradiction. This is manifest in the polarity of discourses and the mutually opposed position of participants. The diamond shape used to denote a symmetrical competitive system is in the form of A:B :: C:D (Fig. 8.1.i).

Complementary co-operative systems refer to systems which have an ambivalent structure of contrast and exclusion. According to Byrne in the complementary system 'a combinatory rule operates that establishes a tripartite field of affiliation with the fourth pole excluded' (1995: 256), as illustrated in Figure 8.1.ii. The issue of the exclusion based on difference or inequality has implications for intervention, particularly if by the intervention the voice that is already silenced continues to be silenced or marginalised. Likewise if the intervener aligns with the silenced voice to the exclusion of the other participants, the intervention may be disqualified, leading to either a removal of the intervener from the system, or the system may change to a symmetrical competitive system.

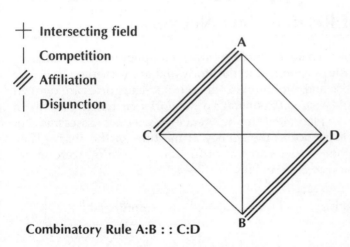

Combinatory Rule A:B : : C:D

Figure 8.1.i   Symmetrical competitive system

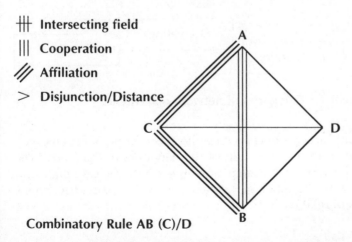

Combinatory Rule AB (C)/D

Figure 8.1.ii   Complementary cooperative system

Source: Byrne (1995: 257)

The diamond structure provides a framework to examine complex relationships, particularly where marginalisation and domination may occur, and can assist theoreticians and practitioners alike. The techniques developed from this approach provide practitioners with an orientation for working with multiple perspectives and processes. Through the exploration of ambivalence, practitioners are provided with a concept that may help to defuse difficulties.

A Typology of Relative Care Networks

Two broad categories, characterised by either co-operative or conflictual networks of relationships, emerged in the study and are presented in Figure 8.2. The characteristics and evolution of the four sub-categories are defined and discussed in this section. Cooperative networks currently describe a minority of the relative placements in the agency, based on an assessment of the 25 networks in existence in the agency at the time of the study. They constitute six of the 25 networks. Conflictual networks were more predominant by a ratio of three to one.

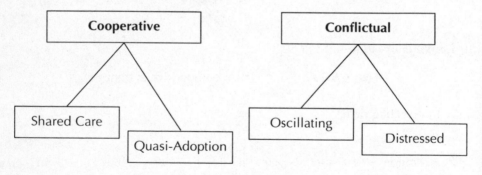

Figure 8.2   Categories of network placements

The positioning of the birth parents *vis-à-vis* the other participants emerged as a major determinant in the evolution of the networks in the study. The extent to which the birth parents were in agreement with the care plan, and were able to work with the other participants, or were enabled to do so, shaped the network of relationships.

Cooperative networks

A cooperative network is described as one in which relationships between the significant participants contain a high level of consensus. These placements are characterised by partnership, collaboration, multi-laterality, mutuality and coordination. Mutual agreement of the care plan by the birth parents and the other participants is required for a cooperative network of relationships to evolve. Agreement is reached, with a broad consensus for the care plan in terms of 'the best interests of the child'. Disagreements or differences may arise on occasion, but the level of distance or difference of opinion is not sufficient to threaten the stability of the overall plan. However in this study, there are two variations in how cooperative networks evolve; these are referred to as 'Shared Care' and 'Quasi-Adoption' sub-categories.

Shared care networks: exclusion of the agency

The relationships in the sub-category called 'shared care: exclusion of the agency' are characterised by a significant and stable cooperative relationship between birth parents and relatives as illustrated in Figure 8.3. The origins of shared care networks are traced to the initial decision-making stage, when a crisis occurs which results in the agency and the family coming together. The care arrangement is described as shared care or joint care, as there are high levels of agreement between relatives and birth parents. Based on a risk assessment, the agency is satisfied to accept a peripheral position, once the formalisation of the placement is completed. However the dominant cooperation of birth parents and relatives excludes the agency from any significant role. From the agency's point of view, the ideal arrangement for the child may be in place, but masks a significant exclusion of themselves.

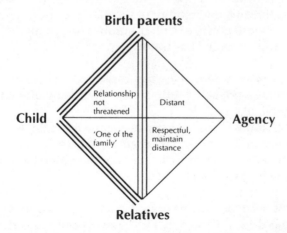

Figure 8.3   Shared care networks: exclusion of agency

The following interconnected factors are associated with shared-care networks of relationships:

- The children tend to be older: they are seen as having a greater capacity to protect themselves
- A voluntary care status (equivalent to accommodation under the UK Children Act 1989 s20)
- A history of informal care within the family network, and general agreement with the care plan
- The agency is satisfied that the protection needs of the child are adequately safeguarded within the family
- Access is problem free and organised informally within the family.

The perceived advantage of the 'shared care' sub-category includes the absence of conflict between the family members, which contributes to a more positive experience for the children, in terms of their psychological and emotional needs. The relatives in the shared care networks generally felt supported by the agency when the assessment process was completed. Like all other relatives in the study they found the assessment process intrusive. The minimum work involved in negotiating contact arrangements and limited financial support were seen as distinct advantages by the social workers. However, despite the stability of the arrangements, issues of disagreement were evident between the relatives and birth parents in the shared care network, for example, the choice of birth parent's partner, financial reimbursements for caring for the child, or a long-standing strained relationship between birth mother and brother-in-law. These differences however did not threaten the stability of the placement. Despite the obvious benefits of this network arrangement, a number of potential constraints for the participants were identified as follows:

- The low priority accorded to the case in the agency may result in family members not being fully aware of or being offered the range of services available
- It is difficult for the social worker to engage the child, which may leave requirements under legislation largely unfilled
- Traditional assessment process may not be understood or considered appropriate by participants.

These constraints need to be incorporated in a case management system, and emphasise the need to consider whether networks of this nature should be diverted out of the current system at an appropriate time, while ensuring that the family have access to adequate financial help and services. It is suggested that network meetings, to include professionals and family members, based on the principles of a 'family group conference' could be used to form a central feature of a case management method, discussing the progress of the placement and current needs and the services to be provided.

Quasi-adoption network: exclusion of birth parents

The sub-category called 'Quasi-Adoption' is also characterised by both cooperative and excluded relationships, and is presented in Figure 8.4. The relationships of cooperation are premised on the care of the child and exclusion of birth parents. In this sub-category, a cooperative network of relationships evolves based on mutual agreement of relatives and agency for the care plan. The difference in this network is that the birth parents are absent. The exclusion or absence of the birth parents results in the network having many characteristics of a 'quasi-adoption' placement. The relationship between the child and relatives is characterised by closeness. The agency's position derives from a risk assessment which indicates that the protection needs of the child are adequately met by the relatives. The absence of birth parents for a prolonged period results in the agency generally respecting the quasi-adoptive nature of the placement. Limited contact between professionals and relatives does not pose a threat to the stability of the plan as a dominant cooperation is in place in 'the best interests of the child'. Unlike the shared care networks, quasi-adoption is characterised by the distance and exclusion of the birth parent from the other participants. The principal relationship is between the relatives and the agency, where responsibility for care of the child is mutually agreed.

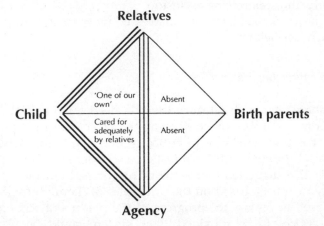

Figure 8.4   Quasi-adoption networks: exclusion of the birth parents

The factors identified as giving rise to a quasi-adoption network are as follows:

- There is a history of care-taking of the child by relatives
- Events surrounding the statutory intervention lead to closure in the relationship between the birth parents and other participants in the network
- The agency is satisfied that the protection needs of the child are safeguarded in the relative's home
- The decision to enter the formal foster care system is made primarily to meet the financial needs of the relatives.

Potential Constraints of Quasi-Adoption Networks

While harmonious, close and respectful relationships existed between the agency, relatives and child, the complaints of the different participants are principally connected to confusion over statutory regulations, as exemplified by the relatives' resistance to the assessment process, and to contact from the agency. In this instance they accepted however that assessment 'was the price they had to pay' for obtaining financial help. The potential constraints arising from quasi-adoption placements are as follows:

- Due to distance of the agency, the child's voice may not be heard adequately
- The story of incompetent birth parents may go unchallenged in the family, thus reinforcing exclusion
- The network may become a distressed network if birth parents try to return (see below).

Case Management Implications

Like the shared care sub-category there is need for financial support and access to a range of services to support the placement in a quasi-adoption network. It is also necessary to critically examine if the network should continue as part of the traditional foster care system when the placement is stable. It is also suggested that network meetings, to include professionals and family members, based on the principles of 'family group conference' could be used to discuss the progress of the placement and current needs and the services to be provided. This system could be used either at the stage when the relatives are moving into the formal care system, or to divert them from the traditional foster care system when the placement is stable.

Discussion of cooperative networks

Many of the features of the quasi-adoption network are similar to the shared care network, which explains the placing of both networks in the broader cooperative category. The difference, which accounts for the separate though connected sub-categories, relates principally to the closure in the relationship between the birth parents and family, child and agency. In the birth parents' absence, the relatives become the principal parental figures for the child. This fundamentally alters the way in which the relationship was experienced and viewed by the different participants. When the assessment procedure is completed, the agency respects the 'special relationship' and is prepared to accept a formal and respectful relationship with the relatives and child.

The primary advantage for the children in cooperative networks is that they are claimed by the family, thus preventing a placement outside their network. Children have membership in their kin, and they appreciate the security this offers. There were no indicators of insecurity from the children in the cooperative networks, or signals that the placements would not work out. Relatives are supported by the agency through payment of allowances, and the relatives in both shared care and quasi-adoption cooperative placements were generally satisfied with the level of support, and felt they could contact the social workers if required, though they had limited experience of doing this in their day to day lives. Financial needs propelled relatives to stay as part of the foster care system: they could not afford to look after the child from their own resources.

It could be argued that the cooperative networks did not evolve as a direct result of an explicit plan being made by the participants. Instead, they are networks that evolved as a response to a particular set of circumstances, such as the agency being satisfied that the child's protection needs were met, low priority of these cases given the demands of other more pressing cases, and the lack of conflictual familial relationships which meant that the child was not involved in torn loyalties. These factors account for the cases being seen as ones that require minimum attention in the overall context of the agency's work. Cooperative networks are therefore propelled through being viewed by the agency as ones that can maintain themselves with minimum help or interference from the agency.

The Conflictual Category: Oscillating and Distressed Networks

Introduction to Conflictual Networks

Conflictual networks are described in the study as placements that are characterised by high levels of tension and conflict among the participants. Two sub-categories, called 'oscillating' and 'distressed' are identified within the conflictual category, as illustrated in Figure 8.2. In the *oscillating* sub-category, the network is dominated by an oscillation in the relationship between the family members, which inadvertently shapes the family–agency relationship. In the *distressed* sub-category, the birth parents are distanced and marginalised. Conflictual networks occur where there are high levels of conflict between a number of participants in the network, either of fixed oppositions or oscillations.

Oscillating Networks: Oscillating/Competition

In this sub-category, presented in Figures 8.5.i and 8.5.ii, the relationship between birth parents and relatives is characterised by intense ambivalence. This arises from the combined/dual roles of being a family member and relative foster parent. This is the central relationship in the network, and in turn shapes other relationships. The family's desire to protect themselves from outside interference (agency) is central to the ambivalence. The agency remains apprehensive about the extent to which the children are protected within the family. The voluntary nature of the care arrangement (or accommodation) results in the agency occupying a more peripheral position, despite their level of apprehension about some of the developments. The oscillation in the relatives' and birth parents' relationship in turn shapes the agency's relationship with both, with each typically on occasion calling on the agency to support their position.

In the scenario outlined in Figure 8.5.i, the relatives and birth parents are affiliated, and the agency is increasingly anxious about the protection of the children. The familial risk emerges from the intense ambivalence which fluctuates between the birth parents and the relatives and is here masked by an alliance which is unstable. The risk to both birth parent and relatives emerges from this potential instability, and may be punctuated by the agency's application for a court order. Here the question of risk is paramount for the agency. Conflict arises in the birth parents' relationship with the relatives, provoked by excessive demands of the latter, or increased questioning of the relatives' capacity to work with the agency. This brings

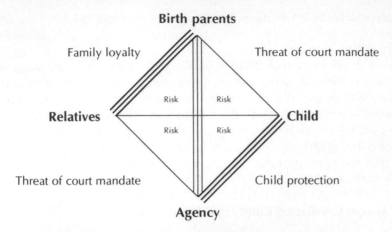

Figure 8.5.i   Family loyalty and child protection

forth a rupture of affiliation between the birth parent and relatives, and raises the birth parent's wish to take the children home despite the lack of adequate parental resources, as presented in Figure 8.5.ii.

In an escalating crisis, the relatives switch their alliance from the birth parents to the agency to secure their role as relative carers and significant complaints about the birth parents emerge. The birth parents situate themselves in a competitive relationship with the agency with the aim of reunification, and the children's desire to protect and support the birth

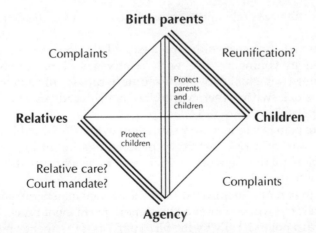

Figure 8.5.ii   The breakdown of family loyalty: relative care vs. reunification

parents emerges more strongly. As the agency attempts to secure the role for relative care through a court mandate, the original alliance based on family loyalty returns (Figure 8.5.i).

The study showed that difficulties are played out at every stage of the relative care process in oscillating placements. The junctures of decision making, assessment, and the actions involved in access, support, planning and reunification, all provide flash points in which the difficulties in the network of relationships can emerge. Each of these events provides a context in which the underlying difficulties in the relationship are played out, and also contribute in part to the continuation of difficulties. Each event positions the participants.

Evolution of Oscillating Conflictual Networks

The main processes identified in the evolution of this type of ambivalent network were:

- Unclear plan due to legal constraints, and failure to explicate the different participants' agenda at the outset
- Mistrust of the agency by both relatives and birth families
- Peripheral position of the agency
- The agency's sense of unease about the impact of the acrimonious relationship on the children, especially if the birth parents' level of distrust of the agency acted as a barrier between the agency and the children.

The central features of ambivalent networks can therefore be described as:

- Care is usually on a voluntary basis. (This does not mean that all children in voluntary care with relatives will be involved in an oscillating conflictual network. Voluntary care is only a determinant if it coincides with other variables considered in the following paragraphs)
- The care plan is vague, with insufficient evidence available to secure a court order, or a risk that court proceedings might produce further disruption in the network, which would jeopardise the children's home with the relatives
- The birth parents are mistrustful of the agency in general, and fear that their children will be removed on a more permanent basis. The family is seen as a potential ally by the birth parents if the agency becomes too intrusive. As the placement progresses, the relatives are seen by the birth parents as being less trustworthy, as their actions are interpreted

as aligning them with the agency, more so than with the birth parents. The theme of family loyalty is invoked which impacts on the relative–agency alliance

- The drama is propelled by the attempts made by the birth parents to claim the children and protect their parenthood. The children in turn do not trust the agency, which they see as having the potential to take them forever from their parents
- The children's attachment and loyalty to their parents, combined with the voluntary nature of the care arrangement, prompts the children to continue to see care with the relatives as temporary
- Relatives are unsure of their position, and themes of loyalty, obligation and mutual protection are core values within which they manage the turbulent family–agency relationships
- Ambivalent networks, although they can absorb a huge amount of agency resources, cannot be sustained indefinitely. They usually lead to the children returning home, either through breakdown or reunification, or evolve into a distressed network, particularly if a care order is used to provide stability for the childrens' care and protection
- In many ways this network can be characterised as a paranoid, mistrustful system.

Potential Constraints of Oscillating Conflictual Networks

The following were seen as the potential constraints of this type of network:

- Impact on the children of loyalty conflicts between adults
- The agency's vulnerability in being involved in a network in which they have such a peripheral position 'if anything goes wrong'
- The agency questions if children's protection needs are safeguarded though they have minimum scope to intervene
- Role ambiguity intensifies for relatives who are torn between being family members and contracted by the agency to do a job
- Separate social workers for different family members further compounds alliances and relationship complexities in the network.

Case Management Implications

It is suggested that this type of network cannot be sustained indefinitely. Three routes are open, which may lead to potentially different and sometimes connected outcomes:

- Planned reunification home as part of family preservation model
- Escalation of conflicts leads relatives to withdraw, necessitating a placement in traditional foster care. The crisis is used to put placement on firmer footing, or reunification home
- Escalation of conflicts leads agency to apply for court order which in turn involves a different contract with relatives, who may or may not be able to continue to work in this new structure.

This analysis suggests that a more proactive stance is needed from the agency at the commencement. This might take the form of network-type meetings with skilled practitioners working as part of a team or conjointly with the objectives of making the care plan explicit, assessing needs and service provision. As the placement develops, different needs may develop. Services can be organised accordingly, but two workers should work conjointly with the network.

Distressed Networks: Court-Mandated Relative Care

The final sub-category of network identified through the study is the distressed network. A network is described as 'distressed' when the relationship between the birth parents and the other participants is characterised by high levels of disagreement. Over time, the birth parents' relationship with the other participants becomes more marginalised. This sub-category is broadly defined as a network where there is an alliance between relatives and the agency around the care and protection of the children, and the birth parents are excluded. The networks in this sub-category share common characteristics. The birth parents are excluded (which occurs over time), children's placements are court-mandated, reunification does not form part of the current care plan, access is problematic, relatives are struggling to hold the care together, sometimes against a background of great personal sacrifice. Pain, disappointment and despair coexist in these families, with a hope that the birth parents will eventually be less resentful of the care plan.

Evolution of Distressed Networks

It is very important to note that, in tracing the development of distressed networks through the different junctures used in the study, they did not enter the care system bearing the hallmarks of the 'distress'. Placement with relatives would not be sanctioned by the agency at the decision-making stage if levels of conflict were such that they would put the child at risk.

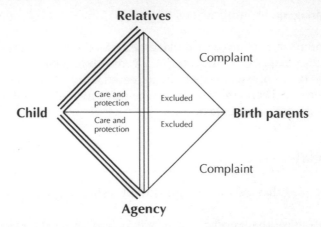

Figure 8.6 Distressed networks: court mandated relative care

Instead the evolution of the distressed networks was traced to the unfolding events over the duration of the placement. The reason for the conflict between the birth parents and the other participants was not ascribed to a single issue. Rather the conflicts were traced to differing interpretations of initial care plans, shattering of hopes that problems would be resolved and children returned, and differing expectations of family relationships and of the agency. The conflicts were played out within the different processes connected with assessment, support and access, and centred on the twin questions of 'who owns this child?' and 'who is in control?'. Of particular note in the study was the high number of networks placed in this category by the social workers at the sampling stage. The seriousness of this finding is compounded by the realisation that, once the networks evolve to this stage, it is very difficult to redress the difficulties, with painful knock-on effects for all concerned.

Potential Constraints

The potential constraints of this type of network were:

- While the children saw the benefit of placement in that they saw it as their home, they were mindful of disruption and stress for relatives
- Exclusion of birth parents and corresponding pain involved for all participants
- If the agency strives to include birth parents, this may be viewed unsympathetically by relatives and distrusted by birth parents.

Case Management Implications

A high number of relative care placements in the agency were described as within this category. The impact of multiple sibling placements and resources requirements needs to be assessed fully prior to a crisis arising in the placement. There are few proactive steps available to the agency when the network gets to this stage.

Proposal

It is suggested that the following principles should guide practice:

- Recognise that conflicts over access and support reflect the issues of 'who owns the child' and 'who is in control'
- Network meetings are needed at the outset where birth parents are encouraged to have their own advocate present
- Coordination and collaboration with multidisciplinary services, particularly addiction and mental health service. (These two areas were prominent in the profile of birth parents which emerged in the study)
- Training is needed for relatives, aimed at enhancing their understanding of the problems of birth parents. This may help to defuse the difficulties as the network develops.

Positioning of the Birth Parents

The positioning of the birth parents in the networks is a major issue which has to be considered in an examination of case management practices. Undoubtedly individual circumstances arise which prevent birth parents from being able to cope despite their best intentions, and their children are removed with all the resulting difficulties. However, a compelling feature of distressed networks is the extent of the marginalisation, as manifested in their anger, resentment and hopelessness, experienced by the birth parents. While the stories of birth parents have tragic contents, when juxtaposed with the stories of the other participants involved in the network, the contradictory emotions of hope and despair, love and hate, and competing claims are better understood. In many of the distressed networks in the study the birth parents said it was too late to build bridges with the relatives, and they were accepting but embittered in concluding that reunification was hardly a possibility.

The accounts of the birth parents were far removed from the principles of partnership, respect and empowerment, which are seen as important foundation stones of good child care practice. Yet amidst the anger and the sense of betrayal, the birth parents' love of and longing for their children was a core feature of their conversations. Unfortunately, for some the hatred was so deep, and the sense of hope so diminished, that they saw little prospect of resolution with agency or relatives. This impacted directly on access to their children. The downward spiral, and exclusion of the birth parents was thus a defining feature of distressed networks, pointing to the importance of striving to manage the networks in a way which avoids this escalation.

Concluding Comments: Tracing Evolving Networks of Relative Care

The study showed that four sub-categories of networks can develop over time. A description of each, the factors that gave rise to its development, the potential constraints of each arrangement and specific proposals to enhance case management practices were presented and discussed above. By examining the evolution of the various networks over time, this study showed that placements commence in a cooperative state, but that increased marginalisation and exclusion of the birth parents leads to the distressed state and confusion that were the hallmarks of both the oscillating and distressed sub-categories. The conflicts which underlie the disputes were traced to confusion and disagreement about the care plan, and these were played out through access arrangements. This led to an intensification of the conflict, in which participants felt confused, misunderstood, and disrespected. The study emphasises the fluidity of the network relationships, and the importance of being vigilant to the changing configuration of relationships as the participants strive to manage sometimes very difficult, turbulent situations.

Based on the emergent findings, which point to the importance of developing a case management model based on the principles of partnership, and where the child is protected, the fifth province model is identified as providing an important conceptual and practice framework to the area of relative care. Through the use of diamond-shaped structural maps, emerging themes can be mapped through a representation of alignments and non-alignments. This enhances an understanding of the place of contradictions and oppositions in the developing networks. It also offers a useful method for facilitating inclusive collaborative conversations among the participants in the relative care network, and may be used to support a new approach aimed at working in a spirit of respect, partnership and collaboration. Relative care has emerged as an important care option for children. However it is embedded in complex relationships at a family–State, and intra-family level, and a conceptual framework is needed to work with the constraints identified and maximise the benefits that this placement option offers.

References

Berridge, D. (1997), *Foster Care: A Research Review*, London: HMSO.

Byrne, N. O'R. and McCarthy, I.C. (1988), 'Moving Statues: Requesting Ambivalence Through Ambiguous Discourse', *Irish Journal of Psychology*, 9: 173–82.

Byrne, N. O'R. and McCarthy, I.C. (1994), 'Abuse, Risk and Protection: A View From the Fifth Province', in Burck, C. and Speed, B. (eds), *Gender Power and Relationships*, London: Routledge.

Byrne N. O'R. (1995), 'Diamond Absolutes: A Daughter's Response to her Mother's Abortion', *Journal of Systemic Consultation and Management*, 6: 255–77.

Byrne, N. O'R. and McCarthy, I.C. (forthcoming), 'Marginal Illuminations: A Fifth Province Approach to Intra-Cultural Issues in an Irish Context', in McGoldrick, M. (ed.), *Revisioning Family Therapy from a Multi-Cultural Perspective*, New York: Guilford.

Bateson G. (1980), *Mind and Nature*, Glasgow: Fontana.

Child Care Act (1991), Dublin: The Stationery Office.

Colgon, F.I. (1991), 'The Fifth Province Model: Father Daughter Incest and System Consultation', Ph.D. Dissertation, University College Dublin.

Colton, M.J. and Williams, M. (1997), *The World of Fostercare: An International Sourcebook on Foster Family Care Systems*, Aldershot: Arena.

Dail Reports (1990), Special Committee Child Care Bill 1988, Parliamentary Debates, Official Report, (Unrevised) Special Committee on Child Care Bill 1988, D 30, No. 12, 4th of April, pp 651–70.

DoH (Department of Health) (1992a), *Survey of Children in the Care of the Health Boards in 1992*: Volume One, Dublin: The Stationery Office.

DoH (Department of Health) (1992b), *Survey of Children in the Care of the Health Boards in 1992*: Volume Two, Dublin: The Stationery Office.

DoH (Department of Health) (1995), *Child Care Regulations. (Placement of Children with Relatives)* S.I. No. 130 of 1995, Dublin: The Stationery Office.

Ferguson, H. and Kenny, P. (eds) (1995), *On Behalf of The Child: Professional Perspectives on The Child Care Act 1991*, Dublin: A & A Farmar.

Gilligan, R. (1990), 'Foster Care For Children in Ireland: Issues and Challenges For The Nineties', Dept of Social Studies, University of Dublin, Occasional Paper 2.

Gleeson, J.P. (1996), 'Kinship Care as a Child Welfare Service: The Policy Debate in an Era of Welfare Reform', *Child Welfare*, 75: 419–49.

Hederman, M.P. and Kearney, R. (1977), 'Editorial', in Hederman, M.P. and Kearney, R. (eds), *The Crane Bag: Book of Irish Studies*, Dublin: Blackwater.

Jones, E. (1993), *Family Systems Therapy. Developments in the Milan Systemic Therapies*, New York: Wiley & Son.

Kearney, P., Byrne, N. and McCarthy, I. (1989), 'Just Metaphors: Marginal Illuminations in a Colonial Retreat', *Family Therapy Case Studies*, 4: 17–31.

Link, M.K. (1996), 'Permanancy Outcomes in Kinship Care: A Study of Children Placed in Kinship Care in Erie County, New York', *Child Welfare*, 75: 509–29.

McCarthy, I.C. (1991), 'Colonial Sentences and Just Subversions: The Potential For Abuse and Love in Therapeutic Encounters', *Feedback: The Magazine of The Family Therapy Network of Ireland*, 3: 3–7.

McCarthy I. (1994), 'Poverty: An Invitation to Colonial Practice. Feedback', *The Magazine of The Family Therapy Network of Ireland*, 5: 17–21.

O'Brien, V. (1996), 'Relative Foster Care: An Untapped Placement Alternative for Children in the Care System? A Discussion of the Central Issues', *Journal of Child Centred Practice*, 3: 7–21.

O'Brien, V. (1997), 'Fostering the Family: A New Systemic Approach to Evolving Networks of Relative Care', Ph.D. Dissertation, University College Dublin.

O'Higgins, K. and Boyle, M. (1988), *State Care – Some Children's Alternatives: An Analysis of the Data From the Returns to the Dept. of Health*, Child Care Division, Dublin: Economic and Social Research Institute.

O'Higgins, K. (1993), *Family Problems and Substitute Care*, 28, Broadsheet Series, Dublin: Economic and Social Research Institute.

O'Higgins, K. (1996), *Disruption, Displacement, Discontinuity: Children in Care and their Families in Ireland*, Aldershot: Avebury.

Pemberton, D. (1996), 'Shared Rearing: Co-Operative Innovation in Foster Care', *Irish Social Worker*, 14: 10–11.

9 Training Needs of Friends and Families Who Are Foster Carers

Julia Waldman and Ann Wheal
on behalf of the National Foster Care Association
Britain

In this chapter we intend to explore issues relating to the training of foster carers who are relatives or friends of the child they are looking after. The discussion of the issues within a United Kingdom (UK) context is based on a research project carried out by the authors on behalf of the National Foster Care Association (NFCA) UK and completed towards the end of 1997.

The research endorses the argument for specialist training provision for this particular group of carers, and for additional training for the social work staff involved in this form of care. A number of key themes emerged from the research which we see as having an important link to training:

- the diversity amongst relative/friend carers
- the concept of transition, and the contexts in which relatives or friends manage the change from a private and personal relationship with a child and their primary carer(s) to one which has a public, legal status
- care management within the public care system.

Background

NFCA has a national role as a voice of foster care in the UK. It recognised that social work departments in the UK have shown, to date, varied practices in the use of relatives and friends as foster carers, and that the needs of this group have not been adequately addressed within the public child care system. Consequently, NFCA applied to the Department of Health for funding to identify and address the training needs of relative and friend foster carers and associated social work staff. Funding was provided for a two-stage project. The first stage was for research work to identify the training needs of the two groups and to make recommendations to support the development of training materials in the second stage. At the time of writing, work has commenced on producing the training materials. It appears that this is one of very few UK studies to focus on training with this particular group of carers.

At this point it may be useful to note that the use of the separate terms 'friends' and 'family' is deliberate. 'Kinship care' is part of professional usage in the international arena but not used commonly in the UK. There is a need for an umbrella term to be relevant to the broad range of carers who are known to the child. Kinship implies at least a notional biological link, yet there are many examples of situations in which somebody close to a child and their immediate family may be suitable to take on a caring role, but falls into neither the category of 'family' nor 'kin' nor 'stranger'. 'Network care' is a term which is more inclusive and is able to encompass the range of social networks in which children may be supported and nurtured. Distinctions are important as they may impact significantly on the training needs of the different groups. We believe the common feature is that the substitute carers have an existing personal relationship with the child and/or the child's primary carer(s).

As part of the project, a small number of other organisations involved in foster care were contacted and their views obtained on training needs and issues which may affect training provision for relative/friend carers. An overview of the interviews suggests that this form of care has been subject to patchy and limited policy attention. There is a picture of a growth rate which has not been paralleled by the policy development which would assist in promoting best practice in the use of relative and friend carers. The following points reflect the prominent themes to emerge.

First, 'foster care' is a problematic term for carers – the term is designed to suit social services not carers. The term 'foster carer' may be used by practitioners to mean approved carers only – many carers looking after children of friends and family may not be part of this group due to *in situ* arrangements and temporary arrangements. There is a concern that the carers who have contact with local authorities represent only the tip of the iceberg of informal and private care networks. Carers undertaking similar caring tasks will be assigned different roles and status according to court decisions and local authorities' practices.

There is a difficult balance to be found in managing potentially competing issues in making decisions about a relative/friend placement. For example, the merits of providing immediate stability and familiarity for a child by placing them with grandparents, versus the reality that the same grandparents' poor parenting skills may be a contributor to their grandchildren needing substitute care. This issue links to care plans for children: what may be best for them in the short term or at a certain life stage may change as the needs of carers and children alter.

Clear information linked to choices and responsibilities should be given early on in the care planning process to potential carers. In particular, Residence Orders are often used inappropriately for relative carers. One of the criticisms raised of Residence Orders was their potential use as a cheaper alternative to fostering arrangements. Caring with Residence Orders also means the family often lies outside access to supportive resources. There is a need for more information to be given to carers about the meaning of different court orders, coupled with time for them to think through the decisions to be made.

When care is crisis-driven it makes it difficult for social workers to raise the question of training early on and, when a care situation is already established, requests to attend training carry little weight. Training may be perceived as another form of authority and interference to those who feel they are doing a job that is bound within a context of duty and long standing experience. Support groups may be more relevant as a training concept.

The research – aims and methodology

During the research, data was collected from relative and friend carers, fostering social workers, children's social workers, resource managers and policy makers. These were consulted in person and by telephone and came from three local authority areas in England. The three authorities reflected demographic and geographical diversity. The authorities were also chosen for their different levels of use of relative and friend carers. The data to support the choice of authorities was obtained from an NFCA report published in 1997 on the arrangements for delivery of fostering services in England (Waterhouse 1997). In two of the local authorities, not all the areas participated.

One aim of the research was to guarantee a representative sample from ethnically diverse groups. As the participants' names were randomly selected this proved difficult, but the sample did include foster carers who were Asian, of Black Caribbean origin and White. The age range was diverse but in terms of socio-economic groups most carers appeared to be in the lower income strata.

The three authorities sent letters on behalf of NFCA to foster carers who they knew to be either friends or relatives of the children they were looking after. The original plan to reach carers via written invitations to group meetings produced a poor response and telephone interviews were used as an additional way of reaching people directly. This flexibility enabled a picture of needs to be built from qualitative data in which the experiences of carers and social work staff were presented in their own words.

The aspects of relative/friend foster care explored in this chapter arise primarily from the views and experiences of carers and social workers. The emphasis is on conveying the individual experience of carers, thus giving voice to the needs of a somewhat invisible group, and offering some general conclusions about training responses. It is acknowledged that these carers chose to speak to the researchers and generally had, therefore, a number of points they wished to make. Some showed a desire to talk through many aspects of their experience which do not relate directly to the research objectives. For these carers this seemed to reflect the isolation they experienced in their role. Indeed one of the challenges of this piece of research was how to reach carers, many of whom it was anticipated would not necessarily see themselves as linked to social services. In the event this proved to be a valid assumption.

The diversity amongst relative/friend carers

One of the aims of the research was to make recommendations for the development of generic training materials for use with all carers falling into the categories of friends or relatives. A challenge to this work was presented by the disparity of the care situations we encountered, all embraced by the term 'relative/friend care'. Circumstances and contexts were infinitely variable, along with the attitudes and expectation of carers. The relationships which existed between child and carer before they took on their new role varied greatly and included:

1. grandmothers, many of whom were lone carers and were the largest group. The reasons for caring for their grandchildren were varied but included parental death, long-term mental illness and drug addiction.
2. aunts and uncles by marriage (in one case, of two girls who had previously been with another elderly relative after their parent's death).
3. older sister.
4. stepfather.
5. male friend of the family.
6. friend of mother.
7. teacher of a child.
8. parents of a friend of the (teenage) child.
9. neighbour who befriended the young child.

It is important to note that women continue to take on the role as main carer, with the vast majority of interviewees being women. All but three of the people interviewed were women, but many referred to their husbands as joint decision maker:

> *'My husband had to take a lot of time off work to go to all the meetings'*
> *'My husband blames me for taking on x but he's very patient and understanding'*
> *'I discuss everything with my partner.'*

Transition: The Start of the Placement

In the majority of situations, the children were already staying with a relative or friend as a result of a crisis, and were *in situ* before social workers became involved. One carer described the process of how she made the decision to look after another child, and how Social Services became involved. Her comment was echoed by many other carers:

> 'I just thought I don't want to see her in a home, that was the initial thing. It wasn't until about two weeks later when we got a visit from social services and we had to read all this stuff, all these forms and then we had to sign it and then had a meeting and so I had to take a lot of time off work.'

Yet the transitional period during which carers and their families made the adjustments to living with a new member was clearly a difficult one for many. As a carer who was looking after a teenage friend of her daughters explained:

> ... it was very disruptive for the other children and it upset them ... because they knew the family they were knowing what was happening and I had to explain an awful lot more than I would have done normally, stuff that you don't really want an 8 or 9-year-old knowing about.

Another grandparent explained the complications and stresses created by not only looking after a young grandchild, but also managing the changeable behaviours of the child's mother, who was suffering from mental ill health. She sought out her own support mechanism by joining a group for families of mentally ill people but she felt very unsupported by health and social services.

She also expressed the fears of other grandparent carers – that of seeing a repeat of the parenting problems they had experienced with their own children. They seemed aware of the complex irony in the fact that due to their own children's failed parenting they were looking after their grandchildren and some were prepared to look hard at how they had brought up their own children. When pressures of duty were applied, sometimes by social workers, they felt that they did not want to fail their children again. As the grandmother in the situation above said, *'They say it's best for x to be with grandparents but it made me feel guilty. They touched a weak spot because I was brought up with grandparents.'*

The involvement of Social Services

The differences in attitudes and expectations amongst carers, especially towards Social Services, was particularly notable. Social workers interviewed were very aware of the effects of these differences on how they were able to work with carers. For example one felt:

> ... as far as doing any work or any sort of assessment I didn't do very well there at all. The children were always well cared for and happy when I saw them but there was this big barrier 'why are you here, why are you asking questions like this?'

A carer described the shock of the assessment: *'The process was gruelling, very personal ... is it necessary for all the intimate questions? – it goes a bit too deep.'*

Not all carers rejected the involvement of social services. One family, for example, told how their concern for their grandchild's safety was finally resolved with the help of a supportive social worker:

> The formal part was all pretty straightforward and the social worker that we had at the time was very good, he gave us a lot of help, because before that we were banging our heads against a brick wall ... we were more or less told that we were interfering at the beginning which, I think if we hadn't persisted, that x might not be [alive].

Mixed emotions were also conveyed regarding the blurring of the grandparent role with that of a local authority foster carer, a tension also experienced by carers with other relationships with the child. For many of them, such a formalisation of the caring role was the only route to financial stability. Without the financial allowances which go with fostering they would not have been able to look after the child. Yet inconsistencies with payments and other forms of support were evident. Some network carers were particularly assertive in their desire to be treated the same in every way as other foster carers, but financial equity was something for which there was almost universal agreement.

Some carers we interviewed expressed the desire to go on to foster other children. Two had not been approved for stranger care and from the interviews it seemed that they did not have a full understanding of the way the approval system operates. In particular they were surprised to find that whilst they might meet the criteria for one form of care, this did not give them automatic suitability to care for other children. On the other hand, some relative/friend carers do move on to a 'career' as foster carers for other children, with local authority support. For such people progressive training opportunities should be available.

Care Management

A dominant issue which is reflected in the carers' experiences, was the lack of consistency in the policies and practice used with this broad group of carers. This includes their legal status as 'foster carers'. Whilst not an explicit question in the interviews, the issue of legal status frequently arose in relation to carers' experiences of accessing financial entitlements, going to court, intrusion into family privacy and clarification of parental responsibilities. Some social workers felt that court orders had sometimes been used inappropriately because the decisions were resource-led rather than needs-led. One carer was clearly aware of this tension when she said, *'The caring part has to take second priority to their budgeting and that's what its all about.'* This was confirmed by a social worker:

> I felt it was awful, I felt the department was actually saving money at the expense of the child and only through the people, the relative carer's good nature were we able to keep these children in placement. I think that's wrong. I think we're actually playing on people's goodwill.

By contrast one adoption and fostering manager had ideas which might make it very difficult for staff involved to follow procedures:

> There are particular challenges with culture and social circumstances, particularly with the Black community – the community I'm part of. My experience of growing up is that if your mother or father, whoever can't look after you for whatever reasons, it's an automatic thing that your aunt, your uncle whoever takes over. It's nothing to do with the State. Grandparents or other relatives should not be paid.

This assumption that the family would 'look after its own' was also reflected in the responses regarding children of Asian origin. Staff also experienced difficulties regarding placements of mixed-race children, where the friend or relative was of a different racial background: *'If [the carer] wasn't of the same origin exactly where do we stand ... trying to make a same-race placement versus placement with a relative and where does that fit in with the Children Act philosophy?'* On the other hand, the carers semed to espouse the ethos that 'blood is thicker than water'.

As noted earlier, for many carers the need for formal involvement with a local authority was often only driven by the need to access financial support in order to maintain the same family lifestyle with one or more additional children for whom to care. For these families the focus of local authority involvement should be on using the strengths and values of the extended family, and how allowances support the continuation of family stability.

The strengths and shared histories of relative/friend carers and the children they cared for clearly provided a strong basis for managing the difficulties of the placements. The intimacy of the relationships place considerable demands upon them, particularly in matters of parental access and care plans. One social worker commented:

> Contact with parents varies from case to case but it's very difficult to manage. It's a very sensitive issue that certainly requires a lot of careful monitoring. There are no guidelines on this. This would be a good thing to put in some training for carers and professionals.

Interestingly most of the carers interviewed were involved in long-term care for the child. For some there were genuine and valid reasons for this, and the plan was well thought-out. However, some carers had just been left to get on with things and because no crisis had arisen, structured reviews were infrequent. A significant factor in this seemed to be the piecemeal information given to carers about what to expect concerning the management of the child's care and the responsibilities of the local authority in that process.

Policies and procedures were in place to varying degrees in all three departments. However, the professionals seemed not to be aware of them – or to use them:

> 'Many of these placements are made "on the hoof" for expediency and cheapness'
> 'I don't know of any policy decisions in this area. That's not to say we haven't got any, it's just that I've never unearthed it or worked with it.'

One manager summed up the whole question of policy and practice:

[These placements] have tended to evolve, rather than being thought through and it is time now to sit and think about ... how we're going to deal with them in the future, because as I say, I think there is going to be far more of them.

Experience of Training

We have already pointed out that assessment procedures usually happened after the child was placed. This is very different to the normal pattern of recruitment and assessment for 'stranger' foster carers where attendance on a training programme is usually a prerequisite for approval, situating training at the heart of the selection process. Not only is the status of the training raised, but also the training contributes to a process of self-selection. Many interested people may drop out during the training, because they realise they are unable to make the commitment, or because in other ways the training may provide an opportunity to reflect more closely on their decision to seek approval as foster carers.

For the relative or friend already looking after a child, the decision to offer care has already been made, with differing degrees of willingness. It is difficult for them to see the training as a priority activity to fit into their routines and the extra demands created by the presence of an additional family member.

Social workers also conveyed the difficulties of their position in balancing agency expectations and carers' needs. One summed up her dilemma:

If you've got nothing to dangle before them, there's no reason. Certainly I can't imagine either of this couple would ever have dreamed of coming on training. They would say 'Why have we got to go on training when we've brought up our own kids and she's been with us 12 months and you've not bothered then?'.

There were very mixed reactions from carers about the provision of training, as the following views show. One carer who had not been offered any training or support groups felt *'It would be helpful to be able to ring somebody up and get all your problems out of the way...'*. Another carer would have welcomed training but felt she was not asked because the child she was looking after was settled in and had not got any difficulties.

One carer felt the special circumstances of relative/friend care needed a specific training response:

I definitely think there should be new training. They should have the same training as people who want to become foster parents and perhaps slightly more because they have them without wanting to. Because it really has been thrown on to them.

Another carer who had attended training felt *'more informative stuff perhaps would have been more helpful than trying to play out roles. More like a lecture.'* Yet another carer felt differently again, that written information would be much less useful than a videotape. One carer summed up the views of many grandparent carers: *'If we wanted to go for training we could do but we didn't feel we needed it really. We had brought up three children so we thought we could go without it really. But we were offered it.'*

Training needs

The translation of the issues highlighted above into training needs for carers occurred through explicit questions and interpretation of the carers' experiences. The range of carers' motives also presents special challenges for the provision of generic training. This reality does not question the need for training; rather it dictates a more liberal and creative approach to its design and delivery. For example it is unlikely that the training response to the needs of a bereaved older grandmother would be the same as that of a family friend looking after a young person experiencing relationship problems with parents. The training needs to emerge from this wide range of perspectives have been clustered below into complementary groups. We will first outline the training needs as outlined by the carers themselves.

Information

One carer, aware of the limits of the information she had been given, said:

> I don't think we had enough information really because when x had been in the [unrelated] foster home she had been given all this information in a book about what you can and cannot do, whereas we were given nothing ... I thought 'Do the same rules apply for us?' because we're family and she (the social worker) said 'We'll look it up', but nobody ever got back to us.

The type of information needed by carers covered a range of events and processes. For many, contact with Social Services and the courts was an alienating experience and made them feel disempowered. One carer felt very angry about his failed attempts to get the information he needed: *'... feel like I'm kept in the dark. They don't ring me back ... I'm just angry cos they weren't listening to me.'*

It also became evident that carers needed to know the kinds of questions to ask at different stages of the placement. An early opportunity to think through the implications of different types of court orders affecting children and carers' roles would have helped many carers.

Many carers conveyed explicitly and implicitly the problems they encountered in coping with unfamiliar procedures and legislation. The decisions of the courts were particularly difficult to understand fully, as were decisions affecting both the carer's and child's financial entitlements, State benefits and allowances, and financial support for education and training. Two age groups that raised special questions were children moving towards 16 years of age and those aged 16–18.

Raising awareness of what foster carers are allowed to do – for example, relating to parental responsibility, medical treatment, holidays, smacking and discipline, and baby-sitting – would have lessened some of the potential for conflict with Social Services and ensured the needs of the child being looked after were the main priority.

Child care and contact

There was a range of needs in this area consistent with the complexities of managing a range of changing family relationships. There were the usual matters arising with child-rearing such as schooling, though one grandparent said she felt her parenting role was easier than when she brought up her own children: *'Things are a bit different now, there are more facilities and lots of things to do with him.'*

Carers also had to deal with their own emotional needs, for example taking on the caring role for a grandchild whilst grieving for the loss of their adult child.

They also talked about the demands of coping with the emotions of the child they were looking after, wondering how to explain different situations to them such as the absence of, or only sporadic visits by, parents. One carer explained how this affected the child she was looking after:

> He wants to speak to or hear from his dad all the time. He has gone through a lot and needs close connection, needs someone all the time. I know his trick. You can look at it and say why – his feelings for his parents. If he was in a foster home it would be difficult, there would be a great frustration. I think they would find him demanding.

The period following contact visits seemed to be a difficult time for many of them, both children and carers.

Support

The general impression across the interviews was how pragmatic and accepting the carers were in coping with the very demanding situations in which they found themselves. It was also clear that the local authority support was in general focused upon the needs of the child and that too often the carers' needs remained unmet. One carer noticed the shift in emphasis which came with a change in social worker for the child for whom she was caring:

> 'She has a completely different outlook, she was concerned about me I think. She knew x was well looked after and I think she was more concerned that I had some time for myself ... and my welfare.'

The impression was that training with an overlapping support function could go a long way towards validating carers' experiences and allowing them to acknowledge that fulfilling a family duty could be difficult and stressful. Carers felt that recognising the demands involved for them did not in any way lessen the feelings they had for the child or their parents.

Possibly one of the most uniquely challenging aspects of managing family relationships was with the adult parent of the child they were looking after. Putting the needs of the child before the adult in very intimate relationships, and setting new boundaries for behaviour and communication, asks a lot of carers without help and support to maintain these relationships.

Training needs as perceived by social workers

The social workers' perceptions of carers' training needs are summarised below. They highlight how priorities are similar and yet different from the carers' priorities:

- Rights as foster carer including financial entitlements
- Coping with family relationships; emotional ties and conflicts; letting go
- Religious and cultural issues; maintaining the identity of the child and carer
- Long-term effects on child, siblings, carers, extended families
- Explaining what is going on to all the children involved, fostered or 'homegrown'
- The behaviour of the child who has had a disrupted life and broader issues of bringing up children
- Coping with the emotional side of caring
- Children who have been abused – understanding; reasons for, and implementation of, prevention of contact or adhering to supervised contact

- Family allegiances and relationships
- Raising anti-discriminatory issues in an accessible way
- Help and guidance on parent wanting child back, including divided loyalties of carer and the child.

Social workers' training needs

The second part of this research was to identify the training needs of the social workers as seen by both the carers and the social workers. This chapter does not explore these needs, but many of the difficulties expressed by the carers might have been ameliorated had the social workers been specifically trained to deal with this particular group of carers. It is suggested that some training should be carried out jointly to enable each to understand better the role and difficulties of the other.

The Format and Content of Training Materials

A striking feature of our research findings is the diversity of situations and familial relationships which characterise friends and family foster care. Diversity is also reflected in the attitudinal perspectives of carers and social workers, which provide a significant backdrop to the caring tasks. Whilst the need for information and support was almost universal, the specific needs of this group of individual adult learners are extremely varied, making it much more difficult to promote a generic training response. Carers indicated that there were particular issues with which they struggled but the prominent conclusion was that carers were managing well with a life-changing situation which they had often not anticipated. Thus the orientation of any training should be one which validates a carer's changing experience, promotes strengths and leads people to identify their own learning needs without telling them what they should know.

Any training response needs to be respectful of the different ways people might wish to access a training resource. In general, it seems that an interactive and enabling approach involving the agency, caseworker and carer is viewed as the most productive. This means a resource that carers and workers can dip into, using part or all of the material. Our proposal is that the best model may be a pack of materials containing a number of stand-alone components. The components should be designed for use in a number of ways including delivery one-to-one by social workers so the emphasis would be on trainer notes for the social worker. The term 'trainer' might be replaced by the term 'mentor' to imply a more enabling role. Alternatively local authorities might train experienced carers to mentor new carers, possibly displacing some of the issues of power and authority inherent in the professional social work role. Some of the training components of the pack should include:

- An orientation handbook for the new carer
- Easy-to-read information sheets, for example, on types of court orders
- Scenarios from other carers with lively, decorated text
- Workshop activities
- Signposting to existing written or video material
- Lists of helping organisations.

It would also be important to explore the extent to which material from NFCA's training pack *Choosing to Foster – The Challenge to Care* (NFCA 1994a and b) was relevant or adaptable for this group of carers. *Choosing to Foster* is used extensively in the UK and in several other countries to prepare 'stranger' carers for their role and tasks.

Conclusion

The views of carers and social work staff revealed the need for a fundamental debate about the status of relative/friend carers and how far policy should seek to define the nature of the relationship between the child, the carer and the State as represented by the local authority. There is a need to continue the debate about how an essentially private relationship between the child, their family and the carers can be helped to work effectively and be properly resourced without compromising the qualities of intimacy which in best practice underpin this type of care. To judge effectiveness in terms of the welfare of a child inevitably means some form of intrusion. Should this intrusion in relation to training be of the same order as for 'stranger' foster care? The importance of this question is reinforced by the resentment some carers felt towards the intimate nature of many questions asked in the assessment process.

Clearly this form of care has expanded in recent years and is likely to continue to expand. Before adequate and appropriate training is provided for carers, policy decisions and guidelines need to be published nationally. Social workers need to be given help and guidance in all aspects of their work with friends and family who are carers to ensure consistency and comparability. A concerted pattern of training for both the kinship carers and their social workers would make a significant contribution to this process.

References

NFCA (1994a), *Choosing to Foster – The Challenge to Care: Leader's Guide*, London: National Foster Care Association.

NFCA (1994b), *Choosing to Foster – The Challenge to Care: Workbook*, London: National Foster Care Association.

Waterhouse, S. (1997) *The Organisation of Fostering Services: A Study of the Arrangements for the Delivery of Fostering Services in England*, London: National Foster Care Association.

Part III

Race, Gender and Welfare

10 Kinship Foster Care in New York State – An African-American Perspective

Joan M. Williams
USA

Introduction

Kinship foster care has always, whether formally or informally, been considered as one option for child welfare placements. However, discussions on the merit of this particular component of family preservation endeavours are replete with controversy.

Within the context of this chapter, the historical development of kinship foster care in New York State will be examined, as well as the demographics of the kinship foster care population and their relative caretakers. The major issues, needs and possibilities of kinship foster care will also be addressed. Finally, we will meet some of the youngsters who have had the experience of living with relative caretakers and hear their perspective on the subject.

A historical and cultural perspective

Kinship and communal networks are essential cultural components of African and African-American heritage. The practice of relatives caring for children is not new amongst those of African-American descent. It is a consuetude which has its roots in pre-slavery Africa:

> In West Africa, the concept of family is not limited to the biological parents. It includes the parents, grandparents, children, grandchildren, uncles, aunts, cousins, and the rest of the relatives both living and dead. This type of family gives security to all – young and old. In such a society, there is no need for

153

orphanages for the young or homes for the aged. Care for all lies in the hands of the community. (King 1976: 155–67)

It is from this concept that the African proverb 'It takes a whole village to raise a child' is born.

Historically, kinship and communal networks have played a significant role in the survival of African-Americans. In Africa, they served to hold families and communities together. In America during slavery, they provided fragmented and disjointed families with the opportunity to feel a part of the larger African-American family. The disintegration of the family structure resulting from individual members being 'sold away' as slaves often necessitated that others stand in the gap and fulfil the role of caretaker to many children. In addition, those who were not necessarily related by blood, but for whom an affinity was felt, were considered part of the extended family.

All of these factors are still quite prevalent in the African-American family of today. It is not uncommon, therefore, to hear African-American children refer to others as 'Aunt' or 'Uncle' even though a blood tie may not exist. Robert Hill's study (1977) reported that when African-American children who are born out of wedlock need alternative care, 90 per cent are taken in or adopted by extended family members.

Today, kinship and communal networks provide an identity for families who have migrated to the north, moved for economic reasons, or lost their connection to the past. They also provide the best opportunity for children in protective custody to have continuity in family relationships while minimising the trauma of precipitous placements in unfamiliar settings. Traditionally, kinship networks have been more prevalent amongst people on lower socio-economic strata, in other words, poor people. Even in those instances in which kinship arrangements have been forced, the traditions and history of African-American people have transformed the experience into a positive one for all concerned. At this juncture in history, however, this networking phenomenon is being threatened by economic success. Geographical moves into more socially affluent neighbourhoods are common among those able to surmount the cycle of poverty, and ultimately impact upon established kinship support networks.

In light of these historical and cultural antecedents, it is not surprising that thousands of relatives, particularly in New York City, have come forth, within the last decade, to care for African-American children as kinship foster parents. A child welfare system which is sensitive to the needs, historical background and culture of its consumers would have anticipated the kinship population explosion of the late 1980s, especially since African-American children represent an extremely high percentage (45 per cent in

New York City) of children in foster care. Yet, it did not and was unprepared to meet the challenges presented by this population

The Growth in Kinship Foster Care

In 1979, the United States Supreme Court in *Miller* v. *Youakin* held that it was contrary to the intent of Congress to exclude relatives who care for their kin, from eligibility for foster care benefits providing the case met certain eligibility criteria. Subsequently, a nationally recognised practice of paying foster care board rates to relatives was established. Prior to the application of this decision, particularly in New York State, although relatives were providing care for a substantial percentage of children placed with the Commissioner of Social Services, only a few such relatives were ever formally licensed or certified as foster parents and provided with the associated benefits.

In 1982, a federal audit pointed out inconsistencies in New York State's treatment of children placed with relatives; there were no specific procedures set forth for their use. In 1985, the New York State Department of Social Services produced regulations specifying a process and criteria for approving relatives as foster parents. However, legal challenges followed in the form of *Eugene F.* v. *Gross* (1986), a class action suit initiated on behalf of youngsters removed from their homes by order of the New York Family Courts, placed with relatives, and not provided with the expected child welfare services and associated financial remuneration. The child welfare system's practices failed to reflect the fact that kinship families need a wide array of services in order to cope with and hopefully overcome multiple socio-economic stressors, for example racism, underemployment and unemployment, poverty, health factors and incarceration to name a few.

In 1987, the New York State Department of Social Services set out a regulatory procedure for the emergency approval of relatives' homes to provide care for children who are taken into protective custody on an emergency basis. In addition, the category of relatives who may 'receive, board or keep' children without being certified or licensed was legislatively expanded to include relatives within the third degree from the child's parent (that is the child's great-aunts, great-uncles, first cousins and great-grandparents). In 1989, the Family Court judges were required by law to direct the Commissioner of Social Services to locate relatives as possible carers for a child who is remanded or placed pursuant to child protective proceedings. Likewise, in accepting a voluntary placement of a child, the Commissioner of Social Services was legally required to locate and evaluate relatives to care for the child.

Almost simultaneously, New York City's foster care system was experiencing a tremendous growth. During the period between 1986 and 1990, the number of children in the city's foster care population nearly tripled, from 16,000 to an astonishing 45,000, the tragic consequence of a crack epidemic plaguing the city, and an increase in abuse and neglect allegations which followed. The kinship programme's census rose from 1,000 in 1986 to 24,000 in 1992 (CWLA 1993). By that time, kinship placements accounted for almost 50 per cent of all foster care placements, up from only 6 per cent in 1986.

Nationally the picture was not much different. In 23 states that supplied information to the Department of Health and Human Resources, children placed with relatives grew from 18 per cent to 31 per cent of the foster care caseload from 1986 through 1990 (CWLA 1993).

In Illinois, 46 per cent (8,387 of 18,125) of the children in out-of-home care in 1992 were placed in kinship care (State of Illinois, Home of Relative Licence Report 1992, cited in CWLA 1993). Maryland likewise has experienced significant increases in kinship care. In 1986, there were approximately 154 children in kinship care, and almost 3,200 children in foster care with unrelated caregivers. By 1993, the number of children in unrelated foster care had stabilised, but the number of children in kinship care had grown to over 2,800 (Maryland Department of Human Resources 1993, cited in CWLA 1993). Although exact numbers are often difficult to obtain, it appears that protective placement of children with related caregivers has become a national trend.

It is also important to note that a shortage of unrelated caregivers has had a marked impact on the increase in kinship care. In the years between 1985 and 1990, the number of volunteer, unrelated caregivers declined by 27 per cent, while the number of children in out-of-home care increased by 47 per cent (National Foster Parent Association 1991). In 1991, the National Foster Parent Association (NFPA) reported an annual attrition rate of 29 per cent of all foster families.

Kinship foster care population and caretaker demographics

Research on the demographics of the kinship foster care population cohort is somewhat limited, and the data generated thereby tends to focus on specific geographical localities, communities or even smaller samples. None the less, important information can be gleaned about children in kinship care and about the kin who care for them.

Various studies conducted throughout the United States have concluded that children in kinship care are more likely to be African-American than children placed with non-related foster parents. Although the percentages vary in ways that are directly correlated to the composition of the localities' overall foster care population, the fact remains that kinship care seems to be the placement of choice for the majority of African-American children placed in foster care. A review of the literature further concludes that the health and educational statuses of children in kinship care as compared to those in non-relative foster care were similar, yet raised concern. The children were typically behind in school by at least one, often two or more, grade levels. They were also the recipients of educational services resulting from cognitive and language delays, as well as behavioural difficulties. Physical health factors were often related to prenatal drug exposure and fetal alcohol syndrome.

Certain trends among kinship carers are also ascertainable from literature reviews. Kinship carers are, for the most part, grandmothers or other close relatives. A study conducted in Baltimore, Maryland revealed that approximately half of the relatives who cared for kinship children were grandmothers; almost one-third were aunts, and the remaining caregivers were primarily older siblings, uncles or grandfathers (Dubowitz 1990). A study of a small sample of kinship caregivers in New York City yielded similar results. Grandmothers represented 60 per cent of that group of kinship caregivers and 30 per cent were aunts (Thornton 1991). In almost half of these cases, the caregivers were 51 years of age and older.

As the children placed in kinship care are predominantly people of colour, particularly those of African-American heritage, so are those responsible for their care. The kinship caregivers also tend to have limited incomes, significantly lower than that of unrelated foster parents – this is the case even when foster care payments are taken into account. Additionally, kinship caregivers are typically the recipients of some form of governmental financial remuneration. Kinship caregivers also tend to have less formal education than their unrelated foster parent counterparts, often not having completed their high school education.

Major issues and concerns

Having laid a foundation which places kinship foster care in a historical and cultural context, as well as identifying those most affected by this child welfare placement option, we can now explore the controversial issues related to the provision of kinship foster care services in the child welfare arena in the United States.

At every point, however, we must be mindful that we cannot separate the issues and concerns from those affected by them. We must make a conscious and concerted effort to avoid social service models and interventions which promote transculturation as opposed to enculturation (Black Task Force on Child Abuse and Neglect 1992) as their approach to working with families and children. Enculturation implies a process of service provision in which the cultural perspective of the consumer serves as the fundamental frame of reference. On the other hand, the transcultural perspective has an inherent expectation that the consumer should adhere to the expectations of the 'dominant' culture.

It is important, when designing services for African-Americans, to do so within a framework which recognises and appreciates their historical, cultural and racial identity, and economic development. A transcultural conceptual framework diminishes and dilutes the relevance of slavery and racial, cultural and economic oppression in favour of more stereotypical viewpoints, which portray African Americans as less intelligent, primitive, childlike and their families as dysfunctional and deficient. Unfortunately, these negative viewpoints permeate American society and have been institutionalised.

An approach rooted in enculturation, however, promotes a culturally relevant and non-deficit perspective in the design and delivery of the service. Consequently, a model of kinship service provision, and child welfare services as a whole, can be constructed in such a manner that it respects the culture of its consumers and considers any adverse environmental experiences and effects. Interventions can be built upon the consumer's cultural values in order to assist them toward further growth and fulfilment. Such an approach is essential to re-establishing self-esteem, health and the preservation of families for children. In addition, it is within this conceptual framework that practitioners can effectively tackle issues related to the quality and operation of the kinship home – permanency, discipline, parental access to the child and visitation, and fiscal implications.

Quality and Supervision of the Kinship Home

Are children who are placed with relatives safer than if they had remained with their parents? One of the most frequent reservations expressed about kinship care is often couched in the expression: 'The apple doesn't fall far from the tree.' The inference is that certain difficulties such as drug abuse or physical abuse are intergenerational and/or the resultants of poor parenting. Subsequently, the assessment of relatives' homes as kinship placements, as well as the supervision of the home thereafter, are conducted within the context of a value-laden approach. Such an approach presupposes that the lifestyles of relatives and other extended family members are similar to that of the child's birth parents and that placement in such an environment will only serve to perpetuate the problem. As a result, the interaction between child welfare workers and kinship placement resources is tainted and often adversarial.

As child welfare professionals, it behoves us to conduct an introspective examination of our personal attitudes, practices and standards to ensure that they are culturally relevant and competent, as opposed to being rooted in and further promoting procrasteanism (the obsession with trying to make other people fit our mould). We often espouse ethical principles such as the right of consumers to self-determination within the context of a helping relationship which values the dignity and worth of the person. Yet, our practices, policies and procedures inherently set forth a mould into which the child and their families are expected to fit.

In the United States kinship foster care placements are developed, managed and supervised in accordance with laws and policies promulgated for use with unrelated foster parents. In other words, the kinship foster parent is viewed as just another derivation of the standard model of a foster parent, as opposed to being seen as offering a distinctive pattern of care. Such a perspective negates a true appreciation for the historical roots of kinship networks in the African-American community.

Permanency

Children in kinship care, like all children, need safe, nurturing relationships which are intended to last a lifetime. The basic premise of permanency planning is founded upon the notion that children not only need safe, nurturing relationships, but that such relationships should be legally recognised. Additionally, it is suggested that the child welfare system should focus on this central goal from its first contact with a child and that this principle should be actively incorporated into every stage of planning, treatment and service. Finally, time limits should be set on the process of achieving the goals of permanency planning.

However, there are marked differences in permanency planning for children in kinship care as opposed to permanency planning in unrelated family foster care. These differences are attributed to a number of factors: the relationship between kinship carers and birth parents, the nature and the quality of the relationship between the kinship carers and the child welfare agency, and the child welfare system's response to kinship arrangements as less urgent and requiring less attention than 'regular' foster care. As a result, the permanency planning goals currently available under law for children in foster care – discharge to parents, discharge to adoption, independent living and adult residential care – do not sufficiently address the needs and relationship patterns of many kinship families.

Typically, the children placed with kin remain in care for longer periods of time than those in the care of unrelated families. Most kin are willing to make long-term commitments to care for their relative children. They typically prefer to do so without the supervision and services associated with foster care but find it financially impossible. In addition, they view adoption as unnecessary and superfluous, as they and the children are already related by blood.

A comparative study of 95 active kinship care cases in New York City revealed that children in kinship care more often had a goal of 'discharge to independent living' and very seldom had a goal of either return to parent or adoption (Thornton 1991). An awareness of the availability of adoption subsidies does not serve as an incentive for these families to pursue adoption. This factor dilutes the arguments of those who contend that kinship care is solely an avenue by which kinship care providers seek to supplement their income. The concern that familial relationships be maintained and not be subjected to the pain associated with termination of parental rights proceedings is viewed as far more important compared to any monetary support.

However, the questions still remain. Is it better to allow children to grow up in legally temporary homes, albeit with the reassurance that contact with the extended family provides, or to adhere strictly to the law and require adoption planning to ensure legal security? Should we urge kinship parents to adopt regardless of the tensions which may result with birth parents? Should we remove children from kinship placements to have them adopted by non-relatives? It may be pivotal to consider the necessity for additional legal options for permanency within the kinship context in order to ensure that the dual needs for permanence and financial support are met.

Ongoing debates speak to the need for a re-examination of our views on this issue. Such discussions must take place within a context which recognises the unique features of the kinship relationship, demonstrates an awareness and acceptance of human differences and respects the roles which cultural and environmental dynamics play in motivating human behaviour. An ability and willingness to build upon a cultural knowledge base must also be in evidence and an ability to engage in a culturally responsive practice rooted in enculturation.

Discipline

This particular component of child-rearing practices is both personal and quite controversial in and of itself. This is even more the case when discipline is thought of within the context of foster or kinship parenting.

Much has been written about the hazards of harsh, oppressive and punitive discipline. Although these warnings are valid and should be heeded, many use the consequences of oppressive discipline as a justification for failing to establish parental guidance and set boundaries within the context of the parent–child relationship. Child welfare regulations which have been predicated upon a need to protect children from excessive corporal punishment have been utilised by parents and child welfare professionals alike as an excuse for not addressing wilful and haughty acts of disobedience. Children use the same regulations as a manipulative ploy against being held accountable for their unacceptable behaviour.

None the less, whatever one's stance may be on the topic, the fact remains that to fully appreciate the role which discipline plays in the child-rearing practices of any group of people, one must fully appreciate the complexities associated with the socialisation and psychosocial development of that group's children, child-rearing practices in that group's families, as well as preferred teaching styles, communication styles and control strategies. To be specific, this understanding must be the basis for all interventions with African-American families in order to maximise the outcomes. The tendency to classify what we do not understand or that which is different as 'patho-logical deviation from the normal social order' must be resisted at all costs.

Parental access to the child and visitation

The New York State Office of Children and Family Services regulations about supervision of parental visitation apply to kinship foster homes just as they do to traditional foster homes. Should that be the case? What is the inference about the relative's ability to safeguard the child(ren)'s well-being during the parent's visit to their home? If the caseworker is unable to be present during a visit due to other obligations, should the parent's visit to the home of a relative be curtailed? How can we effectively monitor the extent of parental visitation when caseworkers do not feel that this aspect deserves much attention when compared to the other crises of the day? In cases where parents may be estranged from their families because of excessive drug use, what measures can be undertaken to prevent the disruption and/or failure of the kinship placement?

As with many aspects of kinship foster care, this one has many different facets. And of course, there are no answers which are germane to every case. However, these issues must be worked on within a context which appreciates the cultural features distinctive to the social organisation of African-American families.

Fiscal equity and implications

The question of fairness in the rates paid to foster parents, whether they are relatives or not, is raised continually. Often, there is a preconception amongst cynics that families who are involved in providing kinship care are 'in it for the money'. This contention is usually upheld without due analysis of the financial variables and different funding streams available to families.

Current policy and practice differentiates between kinship parents in a variety of ways. The financial support available to children being cared for by kin is contingent upon factors such as:

- The state where the child and kin live
- The child's eligibility for benefits
- Whether a state approves or licenses kinship homes
- Whether kinship parents can meet state licensing standards or other criteria applied to kinship care.

Poverty is often one of the antecedents to a family's involvement with the child welfare system. Amongst our nation's poor, African-American families are disproportionately represented. Yet, the financial assistance available to poor parents raising their own children is marginal when compared with the basic foster care rate, as is the AFDC (Aid to Families with Dependent Children) payment to the kinship family who takes in a relative's child outside the auspices of the foster care system. In New York City, if one person is added to a two-person family on AFDC, the monthly grant is increased by $108.50. The basic monthly foster care payment for a child 0–5 years old is $371 (plus an annual clothing allowance of $285, a monthly nappy allowance for children ages 0–3 of $44 per month, and baby-sitting funds for working foster parents). The funds involved have tremendous implications for the permanency planning aspects of these cases.

Personal reflections

As we re-examine the issues relative to kinship foster care and move to address issues from an encultural perspective, it is essential that we listen to the voices of those most affected by system – the children. What follows are the reflections of two young people who spent several years of their life in kinship foster care placements. While their experiences differ, practitioners and policymakers alike can learn from what they have to say.

Randy Taylor (a pseudonym), now 15 years old, entered kinship foster care placement when she was 5 years old. She was placed in foster care due to her pregnant mother's and father's crack abuse. At the time of placement, she was separated from her sibling and they were placed with separate foster families. No one had looked for family members at the time of placement. It was at Randy's request that her caseworker attempted to locate her paternal grandmother. She had two failed foster home placements before being placed in her paternal grandmother's home. The other sibling also experienced disrupted foster home placements and arrived in the paternal grandmother's home two weeks after Randy did. Randy's mother had two more children who were placed in the kinship home at different times within the next two years. Randy, in speaking about her experiences, said it was 'better to live with family'. Although young at the time, she recalls being uncomfortable living with people she didn't know, and that this only served to compound the sadness she was already experiencing as a result of being removed from her parents' care. Randy verbalised fond memories of a Guyanese caseworker named Patrick. She described him as very helpful and commented on his frequent visits to the kinship home, as well as twice-weekly trips to McDonald's. When asked if the race of her caseworker was important, Randy said it wasn't a major factor for her at the time. Her main dissatisfaction with the casework services was that during the eight years in which she lived in kinship foster care placement, she had five caseworkers. She recalls frequent visits by her mother to the kinship home on birthdays, holidays and other special occasions, although 'she wasn't supposed to visit us there'. She expressed the initial pain she experienced seeing her mother leave after those visits, but said that once her relatives helped her to understand, the anxiety was relieved. When asked if she had any advice for child welfare practitioners, Randy had this to say, 'Don't separate siblings. All we have is each other in times like those. If my siblings had been somewhere else for all of those years, I don't know what I would have done.' Also, 'try to reduce the number of caseworkers. It's upsetting when every time we get comfortable with someone, they leave.'

Although the next scenario presents an experience in kinship foster care placement which is not as positive as the former one, it serves to highlight some of the cultural differences that exist within African-American families. Additionally, it points out the need for the child welfare service practitioner to fully empower and equip the family with the necessary strategies to positively adjust to the changes in a household brought on by the entry of a new person, albeit a family member.

Anthony Hinton (his real name) is now 24 years old, and lives in his own apartment in New York City. At the age of 13 and after having suffered a severe beating at the hands of his mother, Anthony went to school and requested to be removed from his home. His mother was abusing drugs and alcohol and often physically abused him. His natural father was not involved, as he claimed Anthony was not his son. Despite this contention, Anthony's paternal grandmother was an active part of his life. Anthony recalls spending weekends at her home during a very difficult time in his life. It was with this paternal grandmother that he wanted to live, or so he thought. Anthony thought it would be better being placed with kin, but once there he didn't feel like he belonged. He felt that his cousin, who had been living in the home since birth, received preferential treatment. He and his cousin fought all the time. He described the 'culture' in the home as being different from what he was accustomed to. He cited differences in food, religious practices, dress code and expectations of him as an adolescent. Anthony hardly remembers ever seeing his caseworker. When she did come around and Anthony told her how he was feeling, all she would do is tell him he was in 'the best place for him'. Anthony says, 'She didn't understand that it was tearing me down inside, and making me depressed.' After a year, Anthony was removed from his paternal grandmother's home, at her request, and placed in a succession of two failed congregate care placements. The latter of the two group care placements was so anxious to 'get rid of me', that Anthony was sent home to his mother who, although she had been sober and drug-free for four years, had not been a significant part of her son's life during his placement in foster care. Parent/child conflict was inevitable, and Anthony's mother responded by withholding necessities. As a result, Anthony started selling drugs, and was arrested seven days before his 15th birthday. He was released back into the care of his paternal grandmother, who actively sought additional services to assist her in coping with Anthony's behavioural difficulties. One year later, Anthony attempted suicide. Again, he was released to his paternal grandmother after a brief hospitalisation. This happened despite Anthony making his caseworker aware that he was not happy in his paternal grandmother's home. None the less, he remained there for two more years until he facilitated his own placement into another group care programme at the recommendation of a friend who said it was 'a good place'. He recalls being listened to by the two people who helped him through the intake process. 'For the first time in my life someone heard me, and acted upon what I said,' says Anthony. Anthony's advice to child welfare practitioners is 'always listen to what your clients tell you, and act on that.' He believes that while living with family is not always better, it definitely should be explored before foster care placement into the home of an unrelated person. Anthony also advocates strongly for more participation on the part of the child welfare agency in assisting family members in dealing with adolescent issues. He believes it would have made the difference in his own kinship placement, and on the whole, could minimise the trauma of being moved to a new home environment, whether it is familiar to the young person or not.

Conclusion

While still evolving as a part of the child welfare system, kinship care is an indispensable child welfare service option. When children cannot remain with their parents, it has the potential, when appropriate assessment, planning, regulation and support is available, to afford children with love, care, protection and nurturance within the context of their kinship network.

The dramatic rise in the number of kinship homes reflects an expeditious, short-term, reaction to a systemic crisis brought on by crack addiction, AIDS and poverty. The existing foster and child welfare systems were manipulated and applied to meet an emergent need. However, this dramatic growth in the use of kinship foster homes has thrust on the child welfare system an obligation to re-examine policies and procedures. Such an undertaking must be embraced in an effort to ensure that the system is adequately responding to the unique needs and issues of these children and their families.

Child welfare practitioners, as well as state and local executive and legislative branches, must commit themselves to ensuring that the children and families involved in kinship placement are afforded the same protections and services as families in traditional foster care. They also need a context for service provision which recognises and values historical, cultural and social distinctions. No longer can we be found guilty of failing to adequately and definitively grapple with and address issues of race, ethnicity, spirituality, poverty and cultural diversity as they impact upon the children and families we have committed to serve. Enculturation is the order of the day. We must adjust accordingly.

References

Black Task Force on Child Abuse and Neglect (1992) Position Paper on Kinship

Foster Care, New York: Black Task Force on Child Abuse and Neglect.

CWLA (Child Welfare League of America) (1993) *Kinship Care: A Natural Bridge*, Washington, DC: CWLA Press.

Dubowitz, H. (1990), The Physical and Mental Health and Educational Status of Children Placed with Relatives, Baltimore: University of Maryland.

Hill, R.B. (1977), *Informal Adoptions Among Black Families*, Washington, DC: National Urban League Research Department.

King, J. (1976), 'African Survival in the Black American Family: Key Factors in Stability', *Journal of Afro-American Issues*, 4(1).

Thornton, J.L. (1991), 'Permanency Planning for Children in Kinship Foster Homes', *Child Welfare*, LXX(5).

11 Fostering in a Minority Community – Travellers in Ireland

Deirdre Pemberton
Ireland

This chapter reviews the establishing of the Shared Rearing Service, a foster care service to enable Traveller children to be placed with Traveller families. This was a major development in the history of child care provision in Ireland. To understand why, one needs to understand the attitudes towards Travellers, and the ambivalence held by those in the majority community (the 'settled' community) as to the origins and place of Travellers in Irish society.

For generations, Travellers have been viewed in a variety of different ways by the 'settled' majority – as descendants of royalty, as drop-outs from society, as constituting a particular sub-culture of poverty, and as 'fake', not 'real' Gypsies. In turn, these attitudes have fed into the policies which have affected the Traveller community over the years. For instance, in the late 1960s, the 'Itinerant Settlement Committees' set about trying to locate housing in the mainstream community for Traveller families. This was based on a set of beliefs that Travellers are drop-outs from mainstream society, or 'displaced people', and that relocating them within the larger society will break down what is really a culture of poverty. In essence the committees were attempting to integrate – or assimilate – the Traveller community. There is change, however, and since the mid-1980s, the state has been struggling to recognise 'the distinctiveness of the Traveller culture and lifestyle, without disregarding their rights and their obligations to the wider society'.

Who are the Travellers?

Irish Travellers are an indigenous nomadic people; they do not include new age Travellers and although they share some common characteristics, they are not a sub-group of the European gypsy.

The census of population does not include a section on the ethnic status of an individual, and available statistics are based on the annual count by the Department of the Environment. This count is conducted by local authorities who base their figures on Travellers known to them in relation to accommodation. Those families who do not seek local authority accommodation are unlikely to be included in this count. According to this count, at the end of 1994 there were 4,179 Traveller families in Ireland (Dept of Environment 1995).

The origins of the Irish Traveller appear to be 'lost in the mists of time'. Stories in Irish mythology mention the existence of people who had an identity and culture which was distinct from mainstream society. In the twelfth century the word 'tinker' appears in written documents relating to a group of Travelling craft workers. The language used by the Travellers is very close to 'old Irish' which was in general use prior to 1200.

In 1562, a law was passed making it illegal to be a 'counterfeit Egyptian', the term 'Egyptian' being used at that time to describe gypsies. The 'counterfeit Egyptians' were people who were similar in their clothing, patterns of work and lifestyle, and had similar patterns of marriage and family groupings, but were not 'Egyptian'. These people are now assumed to be Travellers.

During the great famine of the 1840s, thousands of people lost their land and lived on the roadside. However, within this group the Travellers were still easily identified, living as large extended families with several generations together. While many of the famine-displaced families moved back onto the land as soon as possible, the Travellers did not.

Despite the long-standing suspicions of Travellers, they filled a particular role in Irish rural society. As tinsmiths, peddlers, horse traders and migrant farm labourers, they contributed to the life of rural communities. After the Second World War, and with increasing speed after the 1960s, industrialisation wiped out the need for the services provided by the Travellers. They have become economically dependant and have become marginalised even further from the majority of Irish society. This change has had a dramatic impact on the well-being of the individual Traveller, and many of them feel that whilst the way of life changes for everyone, usually at a gradual pace, Travellers have been catapulted into change faster than they have been able to cope with over the last three decades.

Increasingly, Travellers have been subjected to more and more racist reactions. The local and national papers regularly carry articles which allege widespread drunkenness and idleness, and point out the negative characteristics of the Travellers. Local communities vigorously campaign to prevent Traveller halting sites being provided in their area, and shops and pubs have refused to serve Travellers. Recent anti-discriminatory laws are aimed at tackling this. Rottman (1984) showed that of all itinerant peoples, including those from Holland, Sweden and Czechoslovakia, the Irish Travellers are the least assimilated in or accepted by mainstream society.

From this evidence it is clear that the Travelling community have always been recognised as 'different', yet the step towards acknowledging them as an ethnic group is still being debated. In their briefing document on Irish Travellers, the Dublin Travellers Education and Development Group, now Pavee Point, summarise the answer to the question 'who are the Travellers?': 'The Travellers are an ethnic group. They are a people with a separate identity, culture and history though they are of Irish origin.'

They suggest that an ethnic group has been defined as 'a group that sees itself and is seen by others as being distinct as a result of having five key characteristics:

- a long shared history;
- a shared set of customs and traditions;
- common ancestry;
- distinct language ['gammon'],
- and an experience of oppression and discrimination as a minority group.'

They suggest that while the customs and traditions of the Travellers are largely related to nomadism, nomadism alone does not define the Traveller culture. Culture is something more intangible, encompassing the beliefs, values and lifestyle of a people. They point out that one is born a Traveller (membership of the group through shared ancestry) and to the gammon as a distinctive language. (Dublin Travellers Education and Development Group 1993)

Background to the project: Traveller children in Care

Within this wider picture, social work has had to look at its practices towards Traveller children in care. Statistics in relation to Traveller children in care are not maintained by the Department of Health. As with the census of population, there is no category which enables quantification. A study of Traveller children in care in one Health Board area (O'Higgins 1993) showed that Traveller children are 'over represented' among children placed in substitute care – the risk of their being admitted to care is much greater than for other children. The study also showed that 'almost 90 per cent of the

Traveller children in care had spent a year or more in care, compared with 83 per cent of the other children in the care population. Both of these proportions are extremely high.' This should not perhaps be surprising as there are many studies which show that there are disproportionate numbers of children from black and other ethnic minority groups in local authority care. An analysis of why this is so suggests that there is a lack of understanding of what constitutes 'normal' family life for an ethnic minority.

Traveller children in care were found three main types of placement: in a specialist residential unit which catered solely for Travellers and carried a nationwide brief; in local residential units; or with foster families from the settled community. It is worth noting that although the specialist unit was specifically for Traveller children, until recently all the staff in the unit were non-Travellers. Thus all three options involved Traveller children being cared for by non-Travellers, and were esentially assimilationist, removing children from their family and community towards a new identity.

There is a dearth of research into the success of placements of Traveller children in local residential or foster care, but numerous informal discussions with social workers have suggested that a number of these children have a serious identity crisis as they go through adolescence. The children are reared within a 'settled' culture with its different values and expectations. Their only contact with Travellers is with their own parents who are frequently angry and powerless at the dominant culture which has 'taken' their children. Under these circumstances a positive experience of Traveller family life is frequently lost to these children. When they attempt to establish an independent life, they have been prepared for a 'settled' way of life, and have little positive sense of themselves as Travellers, but find themselves ostracised by the settled community and treated as Travellers and outsiders. This 'limbo' existence easily leads to isolation, alienation and a drift into a culture of alcohol, drugs and offending.

In 1989 the management committee of the specialist unit, aware of some of the difficulties facing Traveller children leaving care, reviewed their knowledge of how those who had left the boys' unit between 1981 and 1988 had fared. Of the 56 boys who had left care, less than ten appeared to have managed the transition from institutional to independent living with a degree of success. Thirty-five had spent periods of time in jail in Ireland and Britain, their offences often involving serious alcohol abuse, violence to others and robbery, with or without violence. The agency believed that one important factor contributing to this was the lack of any significant connection between the agency and the Travelling community. From this discussion the idea of a specific fostering service for Traveller children began to take shape.

Setting up the Project

During 1990 and 1991, meetings were held with groups of Travellers around the country to stimulate interest in the needs of their children in care. When asked if they were willing to help, the response was an overwhelming 'yes'. At these meetings Travellers expressed many of the same anxieties as settled foster parents: 'I couldn't do short-term, it would break my heart when they go,' 'What do I do if the parents want their child back?' and 'What will I do if the parents turn up to visit and are drunk?'

Some dilemmas were more specific to the Traveller community. The first of these concerns revolved around the placement of children from other families where there was a history of conflict between the two families. Within this community, where differences arise between individuals this tends to develop into a disagreement between the two extended families. Traditionally when trouble arose, families would physically move away from one another and find a new campground. A consequence of this was that the underlying issue was frequently not resolved and so flared up into further trouble when the families met again. Conflicts could go back generations and extend to include cousins. Time and again it was said that the problem would not be with the individual child, but rather with their family.

Because of this complexity, when placements were being considered, the social worker had to discuss the child's origins with the shared-rearing family in much greater detail than when placing within the majority community. Confidentiality becomes an issue in these circumstances, and in sharing a particular child's need for placement, the worker had to take an extremely careful approach in order to avoid the risk of fuelling any existing conflict by revealing that a particular family was experiencing difficulties. Since the social worker was a member of the settled community, she could not know the complexity of relationships among the Travellers and therefore the responsibility for making decisions about placements had to be shared more fully with the foster families. Often the foster family already knew a great deal about the difficulties in the family of origin, but where they were being given fresh information, they frequently concluded for themselves that they should treat those new details as strictly confidential. This is sometimes particularly important because the boundary between the extended family and the Traveller community at large is not clear-cut, so once information is shared within the family it can easily become very public very quickly.

Travellers tend to be nomadic within a clearly defined area. Families in the south of the country appeared to have little or no involvement with or knowledge of those in the north. Recruiting families on a national basis gave some flexibility to avoid placements where conflicts would occur, by placing the child further afield. The case for placing a child so far from their own family of origin had to be carefully balanced against the costs for the child of lost contact with her own family. In practice shared rearing placements involving large distances happened more frequently due to a lack of any approved families in an area rather than because of conflict.

A second major issue was that the idea of working constructively in partnership with the statutory authorities was unheard of among Travellers. When Travellers had contact with the authorities it was almost always when they needed to request accommodation or welfare payments. The percentage of Travellers in trouble with the law is higher than for the majority community and so many of them had undergone bad experiences of the police, courts and the prison system.

Historically, none of these state agencies would consult with Travellers about their wishes, or how best to develop services which would fit their culture and lifestyle. This is now changing with an increasing understanding of the need to take cultural factors into account, but for many individual Travellers it would be a new experience.

Travellers feared that the child care agencies would not listen to them. They feared too that these agencies might not like what Travellers had to say and would ignore their comments. This proved to be a difficult fear to allay. It was relatively simple for the individual worker, as part of a small team, to assure families that the purpose of the project was to value their input and to use it in the best interests of the children. However, the project is only a small part of a very much larger, bureaucratic organisation. Where practice developed in the project could have implications for the larger agency, there could be no such guarantees that Traveller input would be valued.

Education

The commitment to valuing Traveller input was particularly tested on the issue of education. Traditionally, the formal educational system has had little to offer Travellers. Although Traveller parents saw the value of education for their children, and would have wanted them to go to school, the powerful forces of a society which labelled their children as backward and so in need of a 'special' class, and made no effort to consult with Travellers about the appropriateness of the system to their children, resulted in parents feeling powerless. Many children attended their local primary school for just enough time to make their first communion and then again for confirmation. By the age of 12 they were deemed by their parents to have acquired as much schooling as they would ever have use for. Children's education in life skills was continued at home, with the boys working with the men, and the girls keeping house and caring for the younger children.

During the 1990s, this has changed and Traveller groups have come together with the Department of Education to devise more appropriate programmes. However, attitudes change more slowly and it will be some time yet before positive strategies for Traveller education are implemented nationwide. In the meantime, all children are expected by the law to attend school regularly until they are 15.

For a minority of families involved in shared rearing, 'schooling' would cease, or had ceased, for children over twelve, and with the exception of the first communion and confirmation classes, attendance is sporadic. The families were very clearly able to state their reasons for not sending their children to school. In theory, if it accepted their argument, the Health Board would be in conflict with the law. If it insisted that families must at least send the foster child to school, they would be isolating that child within the family by comparison with the other children. If they refused to accept such families as foster parents, they were in danger of shaping Traveller families into an 'acceptable' mould which might not be very different to some of our settled foster parents. Furthermore, the majority of the families from which the children for placement came would rank formal education very low on their list of essential requirements for their child.

The debate goes on, with the Health Board struggling to keep a balance while working with the educational authorities to provide a satisfactory resolution as soon as possible. In the meantime no family has been turned down as a foster-parent on the basis of their attitude to education alone.

Respect and Consultation

Other challenges faced by the agency in accepting the diversity of lifestyle include a return to the traditional, stereotypical roles for men and women. The conflict here is very complex. Families still try to maintain the traditional male/female roles, while struggling to acknowledge that life is changing. More and more Traveller women are doing job training courses and are becoming the breadwinner, while the men continue to adjust to life claiming unemployment assistance. Still, the stated ideal is to return to the old ways. The agency has had to accept this conflict, while at times frustrated at what it sees as a lack of ambition for the children and a disappointing lack of desire to improve life for them.

As the assessment and training of families progressed, and as placements were made, the challenges of understanding the Travellers became greater and greater. As a non-Traveller worker for an agency which did not employ any Travellers, where was guidance to be found? In practice, it was informal networks which provided insights and debate. Travellers employed as youth and community workers in voluntary agencies, and voluntary organisations who worked with Traveller groups were very helpful, and frequently, open discussions with groups of Travellers in their homes, proved invaluable. The disadvantage of this was that in informing policy, it was the project worker who made the impact at a policy level, and frequently the impact of the Travellers' contribution was lost. More and more it became apparent that there was a need for a 'cultural adviser' who was a member of the Travelling community. When this was proposed at the start of the project, the shared-rearing parents were reluctant to consider it. Five years later, they were very keen to encourage the idea, and there was no shortage of volunteers for such a position. By then, the Travellers were convinced of the value of the project, and could therefore see the point of taking up a place in its policy-making process. Perhaps, too, there was an initial belief that ideas might be misunderstood or misused; later they had hopefully learned that the worker could be trusted to be genuine. I hope that this is a small reflection of the empowerment which families experienced as a result of their involvement in shared rearing.

Extended Families

The project was set up to recruit Traveller families, with an assumption that this meant 'stranger' Traveller families, that is, non-relatives. In the discussions about shared rearing, Travellers asked why the agency was not more actively seeking the involvement of the child's extended family when alternative care was needed. Within Traveller culture, it is the extended family who care for children when parents are in difficulty. We considered this to be important, and attempted to establish a system whereby extended family could be identified wherever possible. This meant asking Travellers to work with us, making contact with social workers when they were aware of family members being taken into care, or where they felt they had something to offer.

In a number of cases a child was placed with non-relatives, and a year or 18 months later the extended family located the child. Though they could have resumed care, they agreed that it would be best for the placement to continue, provided the child would now be linked with her extended family and know her history. Additionally, the Child Care Act 1991 now recommends that children should be maintained within their family of origin in preference to alternative families.

One reason why Traveller children were coming into care, was because the family had become isolated from their own extended family, for such reasons as an inappropriate marriage, excessive drinking or violence, or where a wider extended family were all isolated from the Travelling community as they were perceived to be 'trouble'. However even in these cases, relatives, sometimes distant relatives, frequently did exist and proved to be in a position to care for the children. Of the children referred to the project for placement, one-third were subsequently placed with their extended family, either formally or informally.

One difficult area to arise was where the potential foster carers were themselves a member of a dysfunctional extended family but appeared to have made a break and succeeded in putting the past behind them. These individuals had generally moved physically some distance away from their family of origin. They made new links with their spouse's family and carefully controlled the contact with their own family. They may have already sought out counselling or other help in dealing with some of their childhood experiences such as family violence and alcohol abuse.

When children from the family of origin needed placement, couples were often motivated by a desire to remove the children from the cycle of dysfunction and to give them the chance that they were already benefiting from. For some the reality was very difficult. Where issues from their own past had not been as fully addressed as they had hoped, the arrival of the foster child evoked very painful memories and experiences. They found themselves revisiting the reasons for their break from their own family, and the painful family history involved.

In addition, whereas they may have tightly controlled their own contact with their family, the pattern of contact between the birth family and the child was often less possible to control. One family spoke of the terrible dilemma posed for them when the child's parents arrived very drunk to see the child and sat on the front wall of the garden, hurling abuse when they were refused admission. In the past the relatives were never encouraged to visit and, as they had no reason to call and knew they were unwelcome anyway, no incidents like this had occurred. The couple's very finely balanced relationship with their settled neighbours took a serious blow, and only gradually re-established itself.

Experiences such as this highlighted the need for a thorough assessment of the extended family and the intensive support needed if placements were to succeed in the long term. Debate has gone on for years over the type of assessment which should be conducted for extended family applicants. A number of social workers favour a quicker method of assessment, while others insist that it is essential to follow the routine format for assessing 'standard' foster carers (for instance, BAAF form F). In the case of assessing extended families, at least for the Travelling community, a comprehensive exploration of the family dynamics, the management of difficulties in the past and the anticipated management of placements of a young relative, should form the focus of the assessment.

Evaluation – the Strengths of Shared Rearing

In mid-1996, eleven Traveller families had been approved by the Health Board as carers. The first placements were made in March 1993 and a total of 34 children benefited from placements up to July 1996. The children ranged in age from birth to 16, and placements included day care, emergency, respite, short-term, long-term, and in the case of adolescents in residential care, holiday and weekend contact. A number of non-relative applications were being processed by the project and in addition an increasing number of extended family applicants were making direct contact with area teams for specific children. A number of important strengths can now be identified in shared-rearing placements.

In one extended family, seven out of 13 brothers and sisters (and their partners) were approved carers and this proved to have its useful dynamic. First, it was possible to place a number of siblings from one family in a number of related households. Secondly, because of naturally occurring contact within the family, where one household was experiencing difficulties with a placement, initially they gained support from their own extended family: when necessary, they rearranged a placement among themselves if one member felt that a child was better suited to their household. Although on the one hand this was a relief to the child's social worker, to know that she didn't have to find an alternative placement, it was also interesting how out of control the social worker felt when Travellers discussed and made these decisions before informing the agency. As time went on I became more comfortable in accepting that this way of working could be successful. Settled workers' concerns that a child was being handed around like a parcel within the extended family were not understood by Travellers. They saw the child remaining within the wider family, gaining something from everyone, while the couple who maintained the focus and overall direction for the child were the identified carers. The children who were the subjects of these arrangements appeared to do well and, like their carers, had little difficulty in accepting the changes. This is not a pattern which is easily replicated amongst the settled community.

Access arrangements tended to work better with Traveller placements. The arrival of a number of members of the extended family raised few eyebrows for Travellers, yet invariably threw settled foster families and frequently social workers into a panic. Again this is a feature of the Traveller lifestyle. A number of family members might decide to visit a relative and would all make the journey together. Access visits did sometimes take place in health centres with supervision. Depending on the resources of the centre, this could be as difficult for the shared-rearing family as it was for the child's family. Larger rooms would be needed for larger groups of visitors, while contact facilities tended to be set up assuming just a parent or two would be involved. Alternative, more Traveller-friendly resources must be sought out.

Although most of the shared-rearing families lived in standard housing, they had regular contact with other family members who lived on halting sites and in trailers. Many of the carers had been brought up 'on the road' and understood the way of life and the hardships. This had a twofold advantage for the children.

First, they continued to see Travellers living in trailers and to accept it as a normal way of life – a choice rather than something abnormal and in some way deviant from the rest of society. Speech patterns, dialects and the occasional use of gammon, the Traveller language, were understood by carers and children, resulting in a quicker adjustment time for children in new placements. The Travellers' ability to identify family networks and so locate an individual within the community created an additional bond with the children placed. Even where families had indicated at the pre-placement stage that they were not aware of the child's family origin, they frequently identified common links in their families when a child was placed. These links, however distant, became very significant for the children, enabling them to claim the new family as in some way their own.

Secondly, the carers could understand the children's behaviour: they were able to interpret it in the context of what is 'normal' for a child living in a trailer or on the road and only of concern where it didn't fit the expected pattern. This meant far fewer discussions in an attempt to deal with behavioural problems and more relevent debate when necessary. One example would be the way that children would raise their voices and shout to one another routinely, even around the house, 'roaring' across the kitchen. Settled foster parents would say how loud the children were, and how wearing this behaviour was to live with. By contrast, Traveller carers recognised the pattern as normal behaviour when living much of life in the open. A second example was the tendency of Traveller children to greet any newcomer with a series of personal questions: 'who are you?' 'where are you from?' and 'who are you related to?' For settled carers this could be unsettling and embarrassing, particularly if some distant relative came in for the treatment! For Travellers, this is an essential part of their culture, as locating the background of a new acquaintance and establishing any links is fundamental to forming a relationship.

Of enormous value, especially for adolescents in placement, was the

Travellers' experience in knowing how to handle discriminatory actions. During the assessment process the families looked at discrimination and what it meant to them in their own lives. They looked at how they managed it and how the Travelling community as a whole handled the issue. All of the families attempted to tackle discrimination in a non-aggressive manner, realising that violence and anger frequently reinforced the stereotypes held by the majority community. All talked of the shame and humiliation of being refused service in a shop or pub, or the hurtful insults they occasionally heard on the street. Some dealt with it by quietly turning away while others confronted it as calmly as possible; this obviously depended on the circumstances and the personality of the individual. The adolescents had no belief that settled carers would or could understand the Traveller experience of discrimination; they felt that this exposure to a model of managing it was enormously useful for them. Finally young Travellers in care were exposed to positive experiences of Traveller lifestyle and so began to develop a pride in their identity. Their growing sense of identity as individuals was not broken as it would have been by placement with non-Travellers and their sense of their own place within the community was encouraged.

Conclusions

First, the project has shown workers not of the same cultural or ethnic group as the community they are working with, how important it is for them to listen, and to be genuinely open to hear what they are being told by the community. The worker must be willing to be led by the community and to find herself operating in different and perhaps uncomfortable ways – especially if they work! Although the project promoted the idea of having cultural advisers from the community, there is no doubt that the best model would ideally be to have workers who are of the same ethnicity as the community. In recruiting either workers or cultural advisers, care needs to be taken that unnecessary blocks are not in place in the form of irrelevant qualification requirements – a classic way of excluding minorities.

A second lesson is that the assessment process should be sufficiently flexible to encompass the extended family, not just one household. In one example, the worker went to interview a fostering applicant who was separated from her husband. In the caravan, waiting for the worker were not only the applicant, but various sisters and sisters-in-law, all a vital part of her support network. They proceeded to interview the worker, and to explain to her how they – all of them – would cope with the child in question – and when the placement was made, that was how it worked.

Thirdly, the project demonstrated how this sort of work must be long term and patient: the worker must acknowledge that she is entering a new group with a new idea. In this case it could be argued that more time on groundwork would have paid dividends. In fact, the project went ahead recruiting unrelated foster carers, only subsequently learning that extended families were more crucial than had been thought. What had happened was that the project had been too set on transferring a model from the mainstream rather than doing a radical rethink.

Finally, the project showed the need to link to the mainstream organisations, and to seek to change the way they work. Initially, carers approved under the project were not used by mainstream social workers, who had not taken on board the existence of a new group of foster carers and a new policy argument about meeting Traveller children's needs. Without information and lobbying, institutions will continue to run on in exactly the same way as always. On more than one occasion, the worker found comfort in the saying that 'it is easier to ask forgiveness than to ask permission!'

The challenge of more sympathetic work with Travellers raised all sorts of issues for the individual social worker. Ireland is only recently having to face issues raised by being a multi-cultural, multiracial society, and then only really in urban areas. As already noted, the issue of respect for the Travellers' culture has long been a problem and Travellers are often devalued in the eyes of the majority. Workers were now being faced with deeply personal issues which they were forced to confront if they were to consider Travellers as carers. The sense of encouragement which a family received would be influenced by the workers' ability to recognise and to deal with these issues. One consequence of this was the increased demand from social workers for information and training sessions, and the development of open group supervision sessions for social workers working with Travellers. The project revealed that some social workers were genuinely able to value and respect Travellers, some honestly acknowledged that they found it difficult to work with them; some tried to be 'colourblind', some believed that integration would be best and some were frankly prejudiced.

The future

Shared rearing is at an early stage and, although much has been learnt, much still remains to explore. It appears that the way forward is to develop the placement of children within their extended family and as a second option, within the wider Travelling community. In drawing up policy and guidelines to do this, the agency must include Travellers on its advisory bodies. A sense of trust has to develop between Travellers and the Health

Board in order that Traveller solutions can be seriously considered and adopted even when different to the solutions used by the settled community. Until there are Traveller social workers, we will have to listen to Traveller youth and community workers, childcare workers, and other Traveller spokespeople, who may not have professional social work skills but who know, better than us, what solutions will and will not work for their own people.

Developing shared rearing has been a challenge to Travellers and settled alike. By continuing to challenge and debate together, we can aim to provide an appropiate Traveller child care service.

References

Department of Environment (1996), *Housing Statistics Bulletin*, Dublin: Government Publications (March).

Dublin Traveller Education and Development Group (1993), *Briefing Document on Irish Travellers*, Dublin.

Madden, T., Griffin, F. and Kellegher, T. (1996), 'Social Work with Travellers in a Local Authority. The Dublin Corporation Experience', *Irish Social Worker*, 14(2).

O'Higgins, K. (1993), 'Surviving Separation: Traveller Child in Substitute Care' in Ferguson, H., Gilligan, R. and Tarode, R. (eds), *Surviving Childhood Adversity – Issues for Policy and Practice*, Dublin: Trinity College Dublin Social Studies Press.

Rottman, David B. (1984), 'Irish Travellers', *Irish Social Worker*, 3, quoted in O'Higgins, K. (1993).

12 Kinship Care in New Zealand – Cultural Sensitivity or Economic Expediency?

Jill Worrall
New Zealand

Originally, the eldest and the two youngest came to me, and the second eldest went to one of my sisters. Then the youngest went to my brother and sister-in-law. When things got tough, the youngest was shared between them and my mother. Then the youngest came back to me. Then the second eldest went to his paternal grandmother for a bit. Then they all ended back with me. Then the second eldest went back to my sister. (Maryanne)

Introduction

Since 1989, child welfare policy and practice in New Zealand has been guided by the 1989 Children, Young Persons and Their Families Act. This Act, while being hailed as progressive, culturally sensitive and empowering, represents a significant value shift from State responsibility for children in need of care and protection to family responsibility. Section 13 of the Act makes it clear that the primary responsibility for children and young persons in need of care and protection lies with the family, *whanau, hapu, iwi* and family group, who should be given all assistance to do this. *Whanau* refers to the family/extended family group, *hapu* to the sub-tribe, and *iwi* to the tribe. Children are only placed out of the family either as an interim measure until suitable family members are found or as a last-resort permanency placement. The underlying philosophy of the Act is one of family empowerment rather than judgmentalism.

This chapter identifies the contributing factors that fashioned the Act and describes the experiences of five families who are caring for abused and/or neglected kin children.

The History of Child Protection Law in New Zealand

New Zealand is a South Pacific island nation of 3.6 million people. The Maori people, or *'Tangata Whenua'* ('people of the land'), suffered colonisation by the English in the nineteenth century, a process that wreaked havoc with their well-being. Maori people currently comprise approximately 15.10 per cent of the population, 74.8 per cent are *pakeha*, or of European descent, approximately 5 per cent identify as Pacific Islanders (Samoan, Tongan, Rarotongan, Nuiean and Fijian) and Asians account for 4.64 per cent.

The role of the state in the provision of care for dependent and neglected children has reflected, until recently, the European monocultural philosophy undergirding the law and welfare services in New Zealand. At no time were Maori people involved in the establishment of the child welfare system, and in no way were the cultural values or social needs of Maori respected (Walker, 1990: 67). There was a failure to recognise social systems and institutions that were integral to the structure of Maori society. Based on the organic solidarity of kinship and tribal autonomy, the *whanau* was the most basic of kinship levels and was responsible for the support, education and rearing of its members. A child was seen not as the child of its biological parents, but as a child of the *whanau* – a communal responsibility (Ministerial Advisory Committee 1986). It can be evidenced that Maori children were removed from their families and placed both in institutional care and foster care with *pakeha* from the beginning of state intervention and were disenfranchised from all that was familiar to them (Walker 1990: 71–2). Child protection law was seen by Maori as part of the assimilation process. Judgmental attitudes and misguided principles of client self-determination and confidentiality led to a disregard of kin as caregivers. Both the 1925 Child Welfare Act and the 1974 Children and Young Persons Act had protection of children and not preservation of the family unit as the main emphasis (Cockburn 1994: 87).

Towards a new Act

Research undertaken both overseas and in New Zealand in the mid-1970s began to show large deficits in a system designed to provide safety and security for children in need of care and protection (Prasad 1975, 1988a). Longitudinal research on outcomes for New Zealand State Wards over a five-year period, published in 1981, showed a most concerning picture. Fifty-three per cent of children in care were Maori, when Maori represented only 12.3 per cent of the population of 0–14-year-olds, and they were predominantly placed with *pakeha* families. There was a high level of placement breakdown for the total foster care population and the children in the sample had an average of 6.5 placements over the five-year period of the study. Children, originally seen as needing only short-term care, were separated from their families for years. There was a lack of planning and little reunification work (McKay 1981). For many children, removal from home did not provide stability or security and was, in fact, a miserable and psychologically abusive experience.

While the findings of research were contributory, the development of the 1989 Act was influenced by a complexity of interrelated factors. First and foremost, Maori leaders called for a Maori perspective in the institutional arrangements of New Zealand, the return of Maori children to their *whanau*/family systems and observation of the principles of *whakapapa* (genealogy) (Bradley 1994: 187). There was also an emerging willingness for policy makers to listen, as Maori concerns were simultaneously voiced in regard to health, justice and unemployment.

A factor that is less likely to be noted, but highly influential, is the impact of the 1984 Labour government's process of economic and social reform, carried on by successive governments since then. This has led to a downsizing of the welfare state and a shift from state responsibility to family responsibility, not only in care and protection matters, but also in health and education. Previous care and protection responses were expensive and the government was most receptive to any cost-cutting measure. It is economically expedient to pay respect to the wider Maori definition of family that embraces kith and kin when transferring financial responsibility. It must also be noted that the Public Finance Act was passed in the same year as the Children, Young Persons and Their Families [CYPF] Act, and this has had an undeniable influence on its operation. The annual number of children in state guardianship has decreased by two-thirds since a decade ago, in spite of a significant increase in child abuse notifications during the same period.

Family responsibility – concepts and constructs of the 1989 Children, Young Persons and Their Families Act

In simple terms, the Act seeks to find family solutions to family problems (Mason et al. 1992: 4). Any intervention into family life should be the minimum necessary to ensure a child or young person's safety. The first response, where a child is deemed to be in need of care and protection, must be to provide, where practicable, the necessary assistance and support to enable that child to remain within her own family/*whanau*. A child should only be removed from her family/*whanau* if there is serious risk of harm, and all efforts must be made to return the child as soon as possible, after ensuring the environment is safe. When the child's immediate family/ *whanau, hapu, iwi* cannot offer permanent care, any care arrangements must be in the same locality in order that family links can be maintained. Any decisions made must take into account both the welfare of the child, and the stability of the family group.

A central feature of the 1989 CYPF Act is the emphasis it places on the role of kin in making decisions for children. This is effected through the process of a Family Group Conference. It is believed that given the resources, the information and the power, a family group will make safe and appropriate decisions for their kin children and will be collectively responsible. Under-pinning this belief is a recognition that whilst, paradoxically, most abuse of children is intra-familial, families will also protect children when charged with doing so (Ryburn 1993). The State rarely exercises its statutory powers to disagree with the family plan because of concern about the safety of the child or young person (Angus 1991). Those cases that go to court usually do so because either the family cannot agree as to who should have custody, or cannot provide care and protection from within family/*whanau* resources.

Section 6 of the CYPF Act originally stated that where there was perceived conflict between the rights of the child and the rights of the family, the rights of the child must be paramount. In response to a stated concern that the best interests of the child were not given due weight in practice (Mason et al. 1992), an amendment to the Act was passed in November 1994, which clearly states the interests of the child to be paramount, before the interests of the *whanau* or tribe. This centrality accorded the child is not in keeping with Maori tradition, where 'the child's interests are subsumed under the importance attached to the responsibility of the tribal group'. (Ministerial Advisory Committee 1986)

Apart from this retrenchment, the 1989 CYPF Act takes heed of recom-mendations of the Maori people. This represents a shift from British models of legislative authority to intervene in the lives of families, as contained in both the 1925 Child Welfare Act and the 1974 Children and Young Persons Act, to an indigenous cultural construct of family decision making. Now families/*whanau* have the chance to reclaim and nurture their own children. Cockburn (1994) described the Act as a legislative conceptual product of the cultural and social experiences of New Zealanders in the late 1980s.

Incidence of Kinship Care

The extent to which kinship care exists in New Zealand is unknown. Very little quantitative or qualitative research exists and data about Family Group

Conference outcomes has not been systematically collected. While the more serious care and protection notifications are responded to by holding a Family Group Conference, it should be noted that many cases are resolved and children placed with extended family through the more informal family/*whanau* meeting process. Additionally, many families resolve their own care and protection issues without state involvement. It can be estimated that, in New Zealand, approximately three times as many children are placed with kin as are under state guardianship, and considerably fewer children are now placed in the care system, either with stranger foster parents, in Family Group homes or in institutional care. The paucity of quantitative or qualitative research on kinship care keeps it 'invisible' and allows the particular needs of this group to remain unaddressed.

Hearing the Voices

I have undertaken a qualitative study of the experiences of five *pakeha* (the Maori term for those of European ethnicity) families who have cared for a total of 14 kin children who were abused and/or neglected by their parents. The transitions occurring in kinship care for the children and their families have been affected by the gendered, economic and political environment in New Zealand. My study showed that the task of caring for a kin child who has suffered abuse and neglect is taxing on both caregivers and the whole caregiving family and not made easier by virtue of a biological relationship. The 14 children in the study had high levels of physical, emotional and educational difficulties. Children placed with extended family and children placed in foster care with strangers are treated as two distinct populations in terms of both practice and policy, kinship care families being considerably under-resourced. Such a dichotomy is not justifiable and the personal consequences for the caregiving families have been significant. I wished to test ideologies of family and assumptions of family strength inherent in the Act. I also focused on the role of women in supporting the operation of the Act, looking at the life changes caregiving provoked and the social estimation of their economic worth. There is a social expectation that women will assume the caregiving role, sometimes of children related only by marriage, without consideration given to the effect that this has on their lives.

My aim, as researcher, was to make visible the true nature of the task of caring for an abused kin child and the effect on the whole extended family ecosystem. I wished to test several assumptions held in regard to kinship care, namely, that it provides greater placement stability, a greater likelihood of biological parent and sibling contact and that the family, knowing themselves and making the custody decision, do not need assessing, preparation or support to the extent that unrelated caregivers do. The stories the kin caregivers shared with me brought the reality of the task into sharp contrast to some of the idealistic notions of family strength held by policy makers and inherent in the Act.

Kinship care cannot be abstracted from the social world that produces it. Most commentators would now subscribe to a multi-factorial explanation of social phenomena (Parker et al. 1993), child abuse and placement within extended family being the case in point. Ecological child welfare practice identifies these factors and attends to, nourishes and supports the biological family, and kinship ties (Laird 1981: 98). The use of an ecological multi-level framework for data analysis brought to light both positive and negative connections and influences, that may otherwise have gone unnoticed.

Starting with the innermost setting, the micro- and meso-levels, I looked at the extended family, their roles and relationships, the factors that precipitated the need for care, and the family decision-making process about who should provide care.

The Role of the Extended Family Prior to Care

A theme of concern for other extended family members, especially the weak and vulnerable, runs through this collection of family stories. In all five families, there was concern for the welfare of the kin children long before they were assessed as needing alternative care. Support had been given in terms of food, clothing and respite care, the extended family at times removing the children from their parents in order to ensure their well-being. For most, the fact that their kin children needed care came as no surprise:

> My sister spent all the holidays with Mum and Dad, not only holidays, but many weekends – it was more the norm than the exception that she spent time at Mum and Dad's. They and my other sister used to take food through to feed them, that was for really bad situations. We breathed a sigh of relief when the marriage split up. I don't know which was worst. (Maryanne)

The activities, roles and relationships existing throughout the microsystem are highly influential in the developmental outcome of its members. When genuine reciprocal interaction between family members takes place, the risks to the well-being of the family unit are lessened (Prasad 1984). Even though the physical and emotional climate of the child's nuclear family may be deficient, other parts of the microsystem, in this case the extended family, can ameliorate this. When extended family members see it as their role to protect their most vulnerable members, and their activities are directed towards that end, the risks for the children are considerably lessened. When family links are numerous, strong, emotionally positive, have common goals, and information is shared, risk potential is minimised. Sometimes the extended families felt powerless to intervene directly in what they deemed to be dangerous situations for their kin children, and alerted the authorities. The families in the study had, in several instances, reported their concerns to the Children and Young Persons Service, the police, or both:

We started noticing things. He was hitting her, and then one day one of the little girls came out with all this big story, about him getting into bed with them, so that was it! The mother blamed the girls, and said they weren't having a Christmas. Well we weren't having that, so we got the girls and took them to the police station and the police pressed charges. So we got one of them, we had her over the holidays till her Mum calmed down a bit ... He lived in the house ... for another year before the mother persuaded us to take them ... All their stuff was dumped on the back lawn. And that was that. They stayed with us from then on. (Helen)

Making the Decision to Care

Being aware of the children's plight and alerting authorities is one thing, offering to take responsibility for care is another. While the 1989 CYPF Act encourages kin to take responsibility, there is no formal sanction, and whether they do or not is an individual matter. Ideologies about gender and the role of women as caregivers are very pervasive. I felt, however, that, although the women in the study all dearly loved the children for whom they cared, the decision was not always easily reached. There was a sense of duty mixed with the love, and a sense of conflict about what caring would mean in terms of life changes and opportunities. Feminists have emphasised the importance of understanding both the material and emotional aspects of care (Munford 1995), and that just because a woman cannot care 'for' it does not mean she does not care 'about' (Ungerson 1983; Graham 1983). When one woman was first asked to care for her grandchildren, she felt she could not. She explained,

'I didn't want the responsibility at that stage ... I was doing some training for myself! ... I was only on the DPB so I was pretty hard up ... I mean financially I couldn't and I had a son at school at the time.'

She was always interested in the children's welfare, however, regularly visiting them and taking gifts. When their foster placement broke down after four years, she agreed to take on the caregiving role.

The tragic death of a sister brought one family together to deal with the crisis. The police dropped the children off in the middle of the night to the nearest family member. The decision as to who should take the children was not easily reached:

> We were all in shock ... There was a bit of dissension in the ranks. I suppose you could put it, very bitter, as to who should have the children ... we all felt we should, and that sort of stuff. We needed more space to make the decision, we needed more options. The children needed to be in a safe place so we could think. The children weren't placed with the person they had the major psychological attachment to, there was too much risk. (Maryanne)

Some families felt a sense of pressure to make what was a very serious decision, and felt they needed more time to consider:

> 'Mind you, we didn't have enough time to think it through, only about a week. Suddenly, here we were, and we had to decide whether we wanted him. You don't think realistically in times of stress [Josie].'

Although, in each case in the study, the Children and Young Persons Service was involved at some point, the decision to offer care for the children came from the extended family itself without prompting from social workers. Both ecological and feminist theory contribute to an understanding of extended family dynamics and the motivation and decision to assume care of kin children. Historical roles, power relationships and expectations that exist within the kin family group affect the Family Group Conference process and care outcomes. Several families stated that the decision was made in an atmosphere of hostility and anger and there was not a great deal of choice as to who could take responsibility. One woman said she felt under pressure from her mother to take the children, in fact she felt the whole extended family expected it of her. She indicated that her husband felt some reluctance: 'He wasn't very fussed about having them here to start off with.'

Several of the caregivers expressed a sense of duty, an obligation to take responsibility for these kin children needing care. One explained 'Well, there was nobody else ... We didn't want these children split up' [Ngaire]. The families who were caring for more than one child all stated that they did not want the children separated, and this factor has also drawn comment from Minkler and Roe (1993), who give several examples of caregivers' desire to 'keep the family together'. All the caregivers said that, in hindsight, the whole family should have been part of the decision-making process, but, as would be expected, the children of the caregiving family were not present at the Family Group Conference when the decision was made.

Motivations to care were different to those expressed by stranger foster caregivers. The motivation to be a foster parent and the motivation to give care to a kin child are very different. To become a foster parent is a planned decision, based on altruism or the desire to extend one's family (Dinnage and Kelmer Pringle 1967). The families in this study did not plan to have more children, in fact they had completed their families. Although in some families there was a history of caring for relative children across generations, the decisions were made as a response to a caregiving crisis for kin children. In most cases, the effect it had on their own lives was of secondary consideration.

Profiles of the Children

All the children had suffered neglect and/or abuse. Several had lost a parent or significant other and had unresolved grief issues. One caregiver described her 15-year-old as *'emotionally a mess, academically a mess and very insecure'* (Josie). The caregivers described having to contend with severe soiling and wetting problems, faeces smearing, urinating under beds, public masturbation, extreme aggression, destructiveness, self-harm, promiscuity and extreme withdrawn behaviour. Chronic health conditions, namely, asthma, recurrent chest and ear infections, deafness, speech impediments, abdominal pain, encoporesis, diarrhoea and hyperactivity were also present. Some of these problems were still present seven years later and led to children moving about within the extended family itself, and for some, placement in standard foster care. One child came to his aunt after several 'stranger' foster care placements. Aged six, he showed acute attachment anxiety that would normally be expected of a child of a much younger age:

> *I couldn't go to the toilet and shut the door on him. He had to come too. He was just so insecure. I couldn't go out anywhere, he had to come too. We went out for our first wedding anniversary, and they had been with us six months then and he was so upset because I was going out at night. He didn't think I was going to come back – he thought I was going to leave him – and we were only out for about an hour and a half, we cut it short because he got so upset, and he had howled the whole time. When we got home he just threw himself at me screaming and then he spewed all over me!* (Helen)

It would appear, however, for the children in this study, that both the separation from birth parents and the trauma leading to care affected their sense of identity, their self-esteem, and both their physical and psychological states. The fact that the children were in the care of extended family members, who were known to them and totally committed, did not prevent severe behavioural and emotional problems. As I watched the caregivers interact with each other and with the children, I was impressed by their mutually caring relationships even though the behaviour of the children was, at times, extremely challenging.

Parental Contact and Caregiver–Biological Parent Relationships

Foster care research shows the importance of maintaining parental contact and that it is one of the key indicators for return home. Likelihood of return home is also enhanced when the relationship between caregivers and biological parents is positive (Prasad 1984). In each of these cases, there were relationship difficulties between the two parties. The children's contact with their parents was infrequent, even if they lived reasonably close. The kin caregivers stated that they felt unable to stop or limit access if they had concerns about the safety of the children or the effect of the contact. It appeared that knowledge of parents' violent behaviour in the past led to a reluctance to support contact, a fear of assault and fear for the children. This in turn led to lack of contact, and ensuing role and relationship confusion for the child, and a need for sensitive handling. Josie poignantly described the emotional confusion of her niece:

> She said 'I have tried the whole year to fit in with your family. I just want to be your daughter.' One of our children refers to her as 'my sister', and one as 'my cousin': I think she is a wee bit hurt. I just said to her 'we can't replace your Dad.' It's hard for all of us ... but I did say to her 'yes, you are part of us, we love you, we care for you, but,' I said,' you can't actually say that it is like you are our daughter you are our foster daughter and you are very special to us.' ... We ended up both crying.

In each case where reservations about contact were voiced, the caregivers said that they felt fine about the child returning to their parents if their safety and well-being could be guaranteed. Although the kinship care research indicates that children are more likely to sustain contact than in normal foster care, this was not the case for the children in the study. They tended not to see their parents and there were no plans for return home for any child. It is interesting to note that the adolescents in the study whose placements broke down returned to their parents, where this was possible, although in no instance was this sustained.

Sibling contact, on the other hand, was important and sustained, supporting the research evidence, which also shows that siblings are more likely to be placed together than in unrelated foster care. All the families in the sample, with one exception, were caring for several brothers and sisters. All had full or half-siblings living elsewhere. Some caregivers, however, did not think this was necessarily a good thing. Sibling abuse is likely to occur where children have had a severe abuse history, be it physical or sexual. The caregivers themselves stated the importance of the whole family unit being assessed prior to placement, in terms of sibling relationships and difficult behaviour. The caregiving family then needs assessing in terms of the vulnerability of individual family members and the ability to sustain care. This needs regular review. Caregiving families said, 'We didn't know what we were in for', 'The children should have been assessed before they came.' Careful planning, a collaborative approach and regular review are required in order to maintain sibling and extended family contact.

Schooling Difficulties

Several of the children had been suspended from school more than once, and some schools had refused to have the children back. They exhibited violent aggressive behaviour, were self-harming and consequently alienated from peers and teachers. The children in one of the families had witnessed marital violence from an early age, and had themselves suffered physical and sexual abuse. Still at primary school, they were suspended several times and eventually expelled for beating up other children and attacking teachers. Maryanne reflected:

> The hardest part is the schooling battles and struggles. I would say that has been the worst, that's made me choose between my job and the children. They attack the teachers, they attack the children, and me. It's inappropriate behaviour – when cornered they go crazy. The eldest one has had violence problems at school, but he's also been very bullied ... He used to soil everywhere at the end of the day. He doesn't talk much and is very withdrawn in comparison to the others.

The effect of this has not been resolved by counselling or time. Some caregivers went to great lengths to resocialise their children, taking positions of responsibility in Scout and Cub groups, coaching sports teams, and taking youth groups, in order that their grandchildren, nieces and nephews could join in.

Moving within the extended family

Several writers have claimed that kinship care offers a greater chance of placement stability than stranger foster care (Berridge and Cleaver 1987; Thornton 1991). However, moving about within the extended family is not addressed. It would appear from my small study and anecdotal evidence that moving around within the extended family is quite common. Families do not let on. Most of the children in the study had moved around within the extended family, and in all but one case, siblings of these children were being cared for by other family members:

> *We haven't got Suzie living with us now. A lot of things have happened over the years,*
> *and she's now living with my mother. The second youngest one has only just come to stay*
> *with us three or four months ago, because she wasn't getting on with my sister's daughter,*
> *because she is at puberty and wants her own space.*

While it could be argued that moving within the family is not as traumatic
as moving foster placements, it depends how this is seen by the child and
families concerned, and cultural concepts of family and family norms. If,
however, the child knows that the move derives from difficult behaviour
and another part of the family is having a go, then that may be different and
seen by the child as rejection. The new family may not have been assessed or
prepared to care for a traumatised, abused child. Family Group Conference
rules state that where there is a change from the plan, the coordinator needs
to be informed and a new plan drawn up. This does not necessarily happen.
In contrast, perhaps to stranger foster caregivers, families do not wish to
come to the attention of the Children and Young Persons Service again, and
try to deal with the problems within the family before seeking outside help.

Moving back to standard foster care

Any placement that disrupts just as the child is beginning to trust again may
destroy, with long-term effects, the child's ability to form and sustain
significant relationships. One young woman, who had experienced several
moves in foster care before moving to family, said, when her family
placement broke down, '*When a foster family chucks you out it's so what? but*
when your own family chucks you out, it's the pits, man!' Five out of the 14
placements had broken down and all but one placed in foster care with
strangers. Those kin families who were no longer able to sustain care of the
children suffered greatly. They felt a sense of acute grief, failure and guilt.
They each expressed how they had struggled to keep the children within the
family, each had called for help many times and not received it. The level of
behavioural difficulties shown by the children was extremely high, and, had
the children been in stranger foster care, the placement would very likely
have broken down much earlier.

Effect on the caregiving family

All the biological children of the caregiving families were independent, although one still lived at home. The women caregivers were in their forties and fifties and only one was employed and that was part time. The eldest husband was 66. Two husbands were employed full time, two had suffered long periods of unemployment and two were on benefits. One husband was a full-time caregiver, caring for four children and an invalid wife. All were uncles and aunts of the children, except for one set of grandparents, one of whom was a step-grandparent.

The caregivers all experienced an abrupt change in their everyday lifestyles and expected life courses. They had all moved through the caregiving phase and at mid-life had already experienced, or had been looking forward to, a taste of self-determination. Josie, in her early fifties, with children who were independent, again revisited the stresses of caring for a teenager.

> *I really was not prepared for what it's been like – and I'm not meaning that horribly, but it's been a hard adjustment. Suddenly we were free, and then suddenly we were not free ... To be honest, sometimes I have to think now if I had known all the pitfalls – why did I do it? Particularly when we have hassles – emotionally as you get older you don't cope with them as well as you did ... She was late home the other night – we were beside ourselves ... You've got more responsibility when it's not your child, so that started a row, because I just got worked up and he got worked up, quite agitated, and quite worried ... I have to say I don't cope as well as I would have. At times I think why did I do it? That sounds horrible! ... I think of my age and I think it's going to be at least another five years ... and also it's the financial strain I suppose.* (Josie)

The caregivers expressed feelings of ambivalence and worries about money; some felt socially isolated, and all told of health changes since the children had come to live with them:

> *My doctor keeps telling me – lower your stress levels, you've got to lower your stress levels. If I get an infection I just can't knock it. It took me a year to get rid of my infected sinuses ... There's just no comparison to how I was before the kids came. Some of that would be age [43], but I forget. I have always been known for my brilliant memory and I can't even remember names now. I just forget dates so I write everything down because I just can't remember ... I have spent years knowing I was pushed to the limits, wondering what I would do.* (Maryanne)

Commentators on care of the elderly have identified caregiver strain, and this syndrome seemed to exist for the caregivers, the women in particular. They complained of lowered immunity, tiredness and exhaustion. The grandmother, however, felt that she had a new lease of life. There was an inverse relationship between years of caring and levels of health. Those who had cared for the longest complained of feeling burnt out, and were emotionally traumatised, especially when the placement broke down.

The caregivers reported that feelings of jealousy and resentment were expressed by their own children, even if they had left home before the children came. One young man was heard to say, when he heard his cousin calling his mother 'Mum': *'You can't call her that! She's not your Mum! You've taken everything of mine, you are not taking my Mum.'* In some cases they were described as being oppositional and not supportive of their parents. In other families, some of the children were most supportive and offered to babysit so that their parents could go out occasionally. Several of the caregivers who had grown children felt that their children had left home sooner than they would have, had the kin children not moved in. All the married couples talked about strain on their relationships. Three out of the four couples stated that they had considered separation because of the stress of caring for such needy children. Anecdotal evidence gained in talking to kin caregivers who were not part of the study have also stated that this has been so, and some marriages have, in fact broken down. Whether they would have anyway cannot be surmised, but the couples themselves saw the stress factor of kinship care as being contributory.

Some of the women were undertaking intergenerational caregiving – being responsible for not only their nieces and nephews or grandchildren, but having to minister to their older parents as well. Women in the middle!

Support

The caregiving literature, whether discussing care of older people, the disabled, or children, shows support to be the most important variable in determining quality of care. Support comes from several places in the ecological milieu. The CYPF Act infers extended family strength and there is an inherent belief that any support needed should be sought from the extended family itself! The validity of this belief was one of the things I wished to test out in my research.

All the caregivers came from large extended families. Concepts of kin collectivity inherent in the Act were not visible for these families. Assistance from the extended family was not forthcoming in any form, be it weekends off, holidays, financial assistance or assistance of a material kind. This led to feelings of disappointment and resentment as help offered at the Family Group Conference was not forthcoming. Some caregivers described their relatives as full of self-interest, but others took a sympathetic view stating that they were struggling financially too and had suffered unemployment, illness or family troubles. Whatever the cause, it appeared that, for these *pakeha* families, relationships within the extended family changed after the kin children were placed. Brenda Smith (1991) identified judgements of good and bad mothers within the foster care milieu. In kinship care, judgements of good and bad mothers occur within the extended family itself and this affects family dynamics and relationships.

For several families, it was friends and neighbours who offered the most support. They took the children on outings, baby-sat, were there in an emergency, and provided a very necessary listening ear. For one woman it was her work colleagues who provided a lifeline in many ways, helping with food and clothing. Because of the extremely disordered behaviour of her children, one caregiver could not engage baby-sitters, and therefore was able to have little social life. The caregivers themselves, unsolicited, all stated the need for a self-help support group, saying that kinship care was not like foster care and particular problems set it apart.

Exosystem Influences

The economic reforms that have affected welfare service provision can offer kinship caregivers no hope of government support. In fact the families are penalised by being related to the children for whom they care. Kinship carers receive substantially less financial support than caregivers of unrelated foster children, especially when other ancillary payments, such as clothing allowances, education costs, medical costs, transport costs, Christmas and birthday present allowances and holiday costs received by stranger foster parents are taken into consideration. The foster care allowance paid to stranger foster parents is not seen as income by policy makers, but only part reimbursement for costs incurred. The current policy is grossly unfair to kinship caregivers, but is sustained by the belief that to be family is to be responsible. The costs incurred when caring for a disturbed child are high. The average annual income for the families was well below the New Zealand average, some of the families relying entirely on benefits. For the families in my study, it was mostly a case of placing the children of the poor with the poor. The families in the study have been drastically affected by recent economic policies, in particular benefit cuts, council housing 'fair' rents, and government department layoffs. Housing has caused considerable stress. Two of the families, at varying times, have had to resort to sleeping in the lounge and in caravans as they moved to smaller council houses that they could afford.

The Children and Young Persons Service was not seen by any of the families as being of assistance. The emotional trauma suffered by most of these children meant that they had ongoing counselling needs that were not being met. Some of the children had received initial counselling, but that was time limited and the families could not afford to pay for any themselves. With the current crisis in the Children and Young Person's Service, kinship care cannot be given high priority. Families told of not being able to access social workers and never having calls returned.

It appears that there is variable practice in regard to assessment and preparation of kinship caregivers. It is now policy that some form of kin family assessment is undertaken for those children who are the subject of a care and protection issue. This has not always been the case, owing to the belief that families know themselves and will make the right decisions for their kin children. The caregivers in the study did not all undergo assessment. They all stated, however, that they felt the whole caregiving family should have been assessed and prepared for what was a very difficult task. One mother stated that she wished they had been assisted to sit down as a family and discuss how taking the children would affect different family members. While police checks are done, that is a poor risk indicator and both risk and needs family assessments must be done.

All the families felt the need for training. One mother said '*I have qualifications in child development, but nothing could have prepared me for this! Specialised training for kinship caregivers is needed.*' While some of the needs of stranger foster parents and kin caregivers are the same, different issues arise because of the family dynamics that surround kinship care. Much research exists that suggests that abused children are at high risk of suffering further abuse in foster care. It is most essential that kinship caregivers are given training on how to care for the sexually and physically abused child. All foster parents are at risk of having an allegation of abuse laid against them, but kin carers are even more at risk as learned patterns of family interaction are re-enacted. Two of the families suffered allegations of abuse, one physical and one sexual, and although neither was substantiated, in each case the caregivers were left feeling burnt out, internalising and externalising blame. The families stated that help had been sought from the Children and Young Persons Service many times before the allegation but none was forthcoming. McFadden (1984) has identified that foster caregivers are at risk of caregiver burnout around the 6–7 year period. All the breakdowns in the study occurred after six years.

How closely the state should monitor a child who has been previously neglected or abused, when this wider definition of family exists and the child is replaced within it, is a question still open to debate. Unless it is clearly stated in the plan, extended family placements are not monitored automatically. Only if the family requests help, or another care and protection issue arises, will the state again intervene. In the past, family/*whanau* structures were considerably more intimate than they are today. In Polynesian cultures, the *whanau* lived, to all intent and purpose, under the same roof and therefore exerted a measure of authority and control over its members. Placing the child within an extended *pakeha* family usually means placing it into another nuclear family, where the extended family are not continually present, and where some of the same child-rearing norms and imperatives may exist.

Another issue worthy of more debate is legal status. Caregivers are asked to assume guardianship, either sole, or shared with the biological parents. The state has no intention of maintaining legal involvement once the family has taken custody. Guardianship is usually secured under the 1955 Guardianship Act, which has no review process, rather than the Children, Young Persons and their Families Act which has a statutory review period. All the caregivers stated that they felt pressured to take legal permanency and voiced concern that they had to meet high legal costs which they could not afford. They did feel, however, a need for legal protection from capricious parents who could uplift the children from their care. Those same parents can also challenge the guardianship order, qualifying for legal aid, while the kinship caregivers usually do not (Worrall 1993). Some of the caregivers also feared that once guardianship was taken, the total financial responsibility for the child would be theirs.

Conclusion

Behind every care and protection order lies a family story of pain, grief and struggle. While the Children, Young Persons and their Families Act gives a greater assurance that children will not be separated from their family structures, it is also based on assumptions about gender roles and how contemporary New Zealand families are structured and function. Such assumptions are the basis of service and resource provision to kin families. The high level of State intervention in family life and the suppression of family roles seen in previous decades were justified by narrow *pakeha* definitions of family and family 'failure'. Now that the State wishes to abdicate from that measure of responsibility, the definition is kin inclusive. Ryburn (1993) put it well when he claimed that 'family responsibility' does not mean letting families decide, it means letting families pay the cost, including the cost of failure, as this is decided by the State. The payment of an unsupported child allowance only ensures family income is not totally compromised by the arrival of another dependent. It does not recompense the caregiver for loss of earnings through taking on the caregiving responsibility. In *pakeha* families the burden of child care still lies predominantly with the mother, no matter whose child it is. My study showed that kin families and women in particular are economically and socially disadvantaged by assuming care. Whether families should care is not the issue, but rather that the task must be accorded the value it deserves.

The task asked of caregivers is not only invisible and undervalued, it is extremely difficult. Caring for an abused child is not made easier by virtue of being related. The network of extended family relationships and emotions often make it more difficult. The caregivers in this study felt invisible. They felt they were expected to care by the State, by the community, by the extended family and, paradoxically, they expected it of themselves. They all were totally committed to the children in their care, they wanted to care, but they wanted it to be qualitatively different. The stories of Maori caregivers also need telling and locating within their own *whanau* experiences of colonisation. For Maori, the experience of caring for kin children within the *whanau/hapu* will have different meanings and different interpretations. The structural issues that have affected the kin-families in this study will be likely to have also increased the already existing oppression experienced by Maori families. The best place for children who have suffered abuse and neglect and/or parental separation is with extended family who love them. If they are to recover from their trauma, their kin families need, at least, the same qualitative conditions as foster families caring for unrelated children. The challenge will be to make kinship care visible in order that the needs of the families and those for whom they care might be appreciated and addressed.

References

Angus, J. (1991), 'The Act: One Year On', *Social Work Review*, 3(4).

Berridge, D. and Cleaver, H. (1987), *Foster Home Breakdown*, Oxford: Basil Blackwell.

Bradley, J. (1994), 'Iwi and the Maatua Whangai Programme' in Munford and Nash (1994).

Cleaver, H. (1994), 'An Evaluation of the Frequency and Effects of Foster Home Breakdown' in McKenzie, B. (ed.), *Current Perspectives on Foster Family Care for Children and Youth*, Toronto: Wall and Emerson.

Cockburn, G. (1994), 'The Children, Young Persons and their Families Act' in Munford Nash (1994).

Dinnage, R. and Kelmer Pringle, M. (1967), *Foster Home Care: Facts and Fallacies*, London: Longman Green.

Finch, J. and Groves, D. (eds) (1983), *A Labour of Love: Women, Work and Caring*, London: Routledge and Kegan Paul.

Graham, H. (1983), 'Caring: A Labour of Love' in Finch and Groves 1983.

Kelsey, J. (1993), *Rolling Back the State: Privatisation of Power in Aotearoa/New Zealand*, Wellington: Bridget Williams Books.

Laird, J. (1981), 'An Ecological Approach to Child Welfare: Issues of Family Identity and Continuity' in Sinanoglu, P. and Maluccio, A. (eds), *Parents and Children in*

Placement: Perspectives and Programmes, Washington, DC: Child Welfare League of America.

Mason, K., Kirby, G. and Wray, R. (1992), *Review of the Children Young Persons and their Families Act 1989*, Report of the Ministerial Review Team to the Minister of Social Welfare (Mason Report), Wellington: Government Printer.

McFadden, E.J. (1984), *Preventing Abuse in Foster Care*, Ypsilanti, MI: Eastern Michigan University.

McKay, R.A. (1981), Children in Foster Care: An Examination of the Case Histories of a Sample of Children in Care, with particular emphasis on Children in Foster Homes, Wellington: Department of Social Welfare.

Miller, R. (ed.) (1997), *New Zealand Politics in Transition*, Auckland: Oxford University Press.

Ministerial Advisory Committee (1986), on a Maori Perspective to the Department of Social Welfare, Puao-Te-Ata-Tu (Daybreak), Wellington: Government Printer.

Minkler, M. and Roe, K. (1993), *Grandmothers as Caregivers: Raising Children of the Crack Cocaine Epidemic*, California: Sage.

Munford, R. (1995), 'The Gender Factor in Caregiving', paper presented at the Carers Association of Australia Conference: *Community Care ... The Next 20 Years*, Canberra, Australia, Published proceedings.

Munford, R. and Nash, M. (eds) (1994), *Social Work in Action*, Palmerston North: Dinmore Press.

Parker R., Ward, H., Jackson, S., Aldgate, J. and Wedge P. (1993), *Looking After Children: Assessing Outcomes in Child Care*, London: HMSO.

Prasad, R. (1975), 'Success and Failure in Foster Care in Auckland New Zealand', M.A. Thesis: Auckland University.

Prasad, R. (1984), 'A Journey into Foster Care', Palmerston North, New Zealand: Massey University.

Prasad, R. (1988a), *Foster Care Research – Emerging Practice Principles*, Virginia: Jacob Sprouse Jnr Publishers.

Roberts, C. (1995), 'The Right to Housing' in Rights and Responsibilities – Papers from the International Year of the Family Symposium on Rights and Responsibilities, Wellington, NZ: IYF Committee and Office of the Commissioner for Children.

Ryburn, M. (1993), 'A New Model for Family Decision Making in Child Care and Protection' in *Early Child Development and Care*, 86: 1–10.

Smith, B. (1991), 'Australian Women and Foster Care: A Feminist Perspective', *Child Welfare*, 70 (2): (Child Welfare League of America, New York).

Thornton, J.L. (1991), 'Permanency Planning for Children in Kinship Foster Homes', *Child Welfare*, 70 (5): 593–601 (CWLA New York).

Ungerson, C. (1983), 'Why do Women Care?' in Finch and Groves (1983).

Walker, P.J. (1990), 'Kin Group Care in the Department of Social Welfare: An Historical Perspective', unpublished Masters Thesis: Victoria University, Wellington.

Worrall, J.M. (1996), 'Because we're Family: A Study of Kinship Care of Children in New Zealand', unpublished Masters Thesis: Massey University, Palmerston North.

Worrall, J. (1993), 'Guardianship – A Viable Permanency Option?', *New Zealand Family and Foster Care Journal*, March 1989, Summer, 1993/94 (reprint).

Conclusion – Clear Policy and Good Practice in Kinship Foster Care

Roger Greeff

Perhaps the fundamental point of this book is to emphasise that kinship (or network) fostering is a significant part of the alternative care of children, but is often paid scant attention. Certainly in the US and western Europe, fostering by relatives is growing significantly as a proportion of all foster care (Williams, Brocklesby and Waterhouse). In eastern and central Europe the pattern is different: as Stelmaszuk has shown, relatives have continued to provide care for children through extensive upheavals in the overall political regime. The question here is whether the State is willing to recognise and support kinship caregivers. Whatever the social welfare ideology, relatives are offering care for children, and seeking some form of partnership with the state.

Policy

One key concern is the lack of clear policy in this area. Studies in the US and Britain have pointed out the ambivalence and uncertainty within policies, and in many cases the fact that they do not exist at all. The uncertainty starts at the level of national social policy and the unclear dividing line between the role and responsibility of the family on the one hand, and of the State on the other. The renegotiation of this dividing line has been a central theme of this book, from new social policy in Poland to the challenge of 'enculturation' in the United States, and most evidently in the new legal framework in New Zealand.

This analysis is reinforced by the findings of Waterhouse and Brocklesby, that in practice social workers often regard care by relatives as an alternative to public care, rather than a means of providing public care. This seems to imply that social workers regard the extended family as a source of support to the parents, rather than a source of partnership with the State. In the context of developing social policy in post-communist societies, it is interesting to observe a process where kinship care is moving from a position of invisibility to increasing recognition and support by the State and something approaching equality of status with other care alternatives (Stelmaszuk). Interestingly, the policy debate in Ireland has begun to address the question whether kinship foster care should be assimilated within 'foster care', or should be recognised as a similar, but distinct status. This is a key issue for policy makers: on the one hand, if kinship foster care is seen as 'different' from routine foster care, it risks second-class status, and a paucity of resources, support, training and planning. On the other hand, to regard kinship foster care as part of routine foster care risks overlooking its distinctive strengths and requirements.

O'Brien has observed that in Ireland the opportunity to establish a clear priority for kinship placements was not grasped during the passage of recent legislation. By contrast, in England and Wales, policy and guidance at a national level now does have a clear emphasis on looking first at the possibility of care by other family members when parents are unable to continue. Within agencies at local level however, Waterhouse and Brocklesby have identified that there is often little in the way of policy, with the result that actual practice is driven by practicalities and chance as to which social worker happens to make the placement decision. What is clear is that in this area national policy is not being translated into local agency policy with any clarity or consistency.

Finance

At the level of social policy, kinship fostering raises fundamental questions about the financial support of children and their carers. Is it right that different carers should receive different levels of funding to help them care for the same child? A foster carer may receive more than the parent, perhaps living in poverty – is this right? Grandparents may receive more than the parents for looking after a child of the family – is this right? Different grandparents (or other relatives) may receive different amounts for looking after their grandchild – from basic State support to residence allowances to fostering allowances – simply because of different legal arrangements.

Do we need a universal allowance for children – a recognition of children's rights – which is given to all children (or their carers!). This could be universally available, but possibly then taxed to ensure a redistributive element. Turning to foster care, it could be said that most foster carers are now being paid for the job they do and therefore allowances are more than simply literal costs of physical care of the child – should a similar basis apply to kinship carers? Is the test one of the degree of 'professionalism', or are we actually moving to financial recompense for the caring role?

More broadly, are social workers the right people to decide which kinship carers should get support and which should not – if so, how do they decide? Are there conditions attached, for instance, you will get support and we will get the right to supervise?

Should the provision of finance for children be tied in with some kind of test of moral obligation, that is, does this person deserve to have their caring financially supported and recognised? If they are under some sort of moral or legal obligation to provide care, does that forfeit their right to financial support in providing that care? Is it possible to distinguish the obligation to finance from the obligation to provide care? They are surely not necessarily the same thing. At its strongest, the duty here is that 'imperfect obligation' of (J.S. Mill's) – there is a level of obligation, but there is also some degree of choice.

Perhaps we are actually talking about a pattern of *negotiation* where there is no one rule or pattern of relationship that applies to all cases and where the relationship between a particular care network and the State is in the process of being negotiated. It is an individual matter depending upon particular elements of the situation – the financial situation of the family, their need for support as perceived on the one hand by the family themselves and on the other by the social worker; how far they define the situation as a family one and best dealt with internally, or how far the situation has already been defined as a public one in terms of child protection concerns, youth justice, etc.

Generally we perhaps need to separate the questions:

- Who understands this child best?
- Who should make decisions about what should happen to her?
- Who should be responsible for providing her with care?
- Who should pay for that care?

Assessment

Portengen and van der Neut have outlined a process for the social worker in assessing potential kinship foster carers. They argue that empowerment must lie at the heart of such a process: many of the potential difficulties which could arise later can be pre-empted if a genuinely participative partnership is achieved within the assessment. They urge that the assessment must openly and fully encompass the whole network, and not just focus on the people who may be offering care (an argument echoed by the kinship foster carers themelves in Worrall's study). Techniques such as genograms, ecograms and sociograms may also be helpful in locating possible carers where initially none was evident. Portengen and van der Neut also draw attention to the possibility that involving the wider family could lead directly to the sidelining of the parent, and that it is fundamental that the parent is fully involved in the assessment, and her appraisal of the potential carers is taken into account.

Several of the contributors emphasise how important it is to focus the assessment on the whole network, not on any particular household (Pemberton, Portengen and van der Neut). Pemberton makes the point that as well as assessing possible carers in the light of the overall dynamics within the network, we may also need to think ourselves into assessing the network as such. As she and Worrall point out, in some situations it may be the network itself that undertakes care of the child, and this may be shared between different households as the situation unfolds. This clearly represents a challenge to traditional thinking about fostering in that we are used to defining the critical unit as the household. Looking at kinship fostering forces us to question this assumption. Ironically, it could be argued that most of the children coming into public care do so precisely because the household in which they lived became detached for one reason or another from the wider support network which is so important in times of trouble.

The importance of family history is evidenced by Marchand, Portengen and van der Neut, and by Pemberton. Marchand and Meulenbergs in particular refer us to the possibility that agendas from previous generations' experience may have a very important influence on why these individuals are offering to care for the child – guilt, obligation, reparation and so on. That same history may have a crucial impact on the way that the placement unfolds. For instance, the child's behaviour may be attributed to a similarity to the parent or some other member of the family. Foulds also asks practitioners to be aware that in situations where there has been neglect or abuse by the parents, the assessment of the extended family or network should test out whether there is any denial or collusion about the abuse – and to be alert to the possibility that such abusive behaviours may be patterned into the whole (family) system.

Waldman and Wheal have drawn attention to the way that taking on the role of foster carer is a strange, complex and at times confusing experience for relatives. They may feel that it is almost contradictory to be caring for a child from within their family or network, but doing this in partnership with the State. Interestingly, this seems to mirror quite accurately the feelings of the social workers who are uncomfortable negotiating this particular boundary between the family and the State.

One of the themes in the book is the boundary of information. Simply by the fact of being involved, do social workers have the right to expect to be told everything about the family, its history and everything that is happening to the child? Or does the family retain the right to define, at least to some extent, the boundary of family privacy – even family secrecy – withholding information from the social worker unless they are convinced she really needs to know? Thus the key question is perhaps who decides whether there is a genuine need to know in the particular circumstances – the family or the social worker.

Both Pemberton and Williams have argued powerfully for an assessment process that acknowledges the particular culture and ethnicity of the family and is attuned to the values and perspectives of that community (encultura- tion'), rather than imposing the dominant culture's assumptions about good child care practice. Pemberton focuses on attitudes to education as an example of a real dilemma – minorities may have such poor experience of discrimination and disadvantage within the education system that they have minimal expectations of its ability to deliver. When we examine the care system from this perspective it may seem that the education system upholds a view of education which is either white and middle class, or naive!

Standards

It might also be suggested that a significant issue in the assessment of kinship foster carers is that social workers are not sure what is 'good enough'. The question is often asked, whether 'the standard' is the same for kinship carers as for 'regular' fostering? If it is not, are workers assuming that kinship placements are trouble-free? The clear message from this book is that this is not the case. If there is a difference, is it in material standards, in intellectual sophistication, in attitude to partnership with the agency, or what else? Is it that we are asking too much of regular foster care applicants? Have fostering standards drifted towards looking for 'professional' carers? Are the standards about safeguarding children, or about protecting the agency from criticism?

Assessing relatives as carers also highlights the question whether the assessment is positive or negative – in the end, is the worker looking for strengths to be developed, or warily undertaking a risk assessment? What, in the context of fostering, do we mean by the all-important phrase 'good enough'? Is that the test for fostering, or are we looking for something significantly more sophisticated? In turn, we are driven on to examine whether the process is about recruiting amateurs or professionals? There is an increasingly persuasive argument that mainstream foster carers are doing a sophisticated and demanding job based on a fundamental commitment to children, but going well beyond that. It may be, however, that kinship carers represent the older model, of spontaneous concern by people who see themselves as doing something 'natural', not a job. Such people do still acknowledge a need for financing, support and training (Waldman and Wheal), but also see themselves as doing something 'natural' rather than taking on a professional role. When assessing kinship foster carers, there are particular strengths and weaknesses as compared with 'regular' applicants. The obvious strength is that these carers will have some knowledge – and hopefully some understanding – of the child, and some existing commitment to her.

Support

Again, there is the question of priority: evidence from research in the US and Europe suggest that kinship foster carers receive a far lower level of support than regular foster carers. Waldman and Wheal's research suggests that while some carers resent the involvement of social workers, many do see a real need for support. Worrall finds that these children had significant needs in health, education and behavioural terms. She also points out that it may not be safe to assume that the kinship carers will themselves automatically receive support from an active kinship network: particularly in the white western European ethnic tradition, most of the network may operate as atomised nuclear households. The kinship foster carers to whom she spoke showed enthusiasm for the idea of self-help support groups for kinship carers.

When the social worker is offering support to kinship foster care placements, Marchand and Meulenbergs demonstrate how the worker may need to tune in to family history and mythology in order to make sense of some of the very complex dynamics between carers, parents and other members of the family. There may be many different sources of obligation and emotional indebtedness running through the generations of the family: some of these may be helpful, some may not, but many will be powerful. The worker will need skill in holding on to an overall view of the network, and its history and intergenerational themes.

As the placement develops, O'Brien offers a framework to help analyse and monitor the dynamics which develop between the parents, the carers and the agency. She suggests that the triangle of mutual cooperation between carers, parents and agency which represents the ideal of 'partnership' may be very elusive, and that even in 'cooperative' arrangements, it is likely that the carers are aligned primarily with either the parents or the agency, and that the third 'partner' will be marginalised. This analysis may help to explain why on the one hand the worker can feel like a 'spare part' at the edges of a family arrangement (the parents and carers are managing the situation without the need for social work help), or on the other, why longer-term kinship foster care correlates with a lower rate of children returning to their parents (the carers and the agency are excluding the parents).

O'Brien suggests that one of the key issues which can lead to conflict is who 'owns' the child and who is in control. Clearly, all three parties may feel a primary responsibility for the child, and all may therefore feel the need to have control. If they cannot find a way to share responsibility, conflict or exclusion are inevitable. Very importantly, she finds that the 'conflictual – distressed' networks were not necessarily identifiable at initial assessment. Often it is the changes in plans and difficulties in managing contact that lead to deterioration – and can lead to disruption of the placement. Again, the need for sustained professional involvement in monitoring and negotiation is clear. It is noteworthy that in Worrall's sample, placement disruptions occurred six years or more into the placement. O'Brien and Portengen and van der Neut propose that network meetings along the lines of family group conferences may be important in arriving at clear and agreed care plans for the child.

In the related area of training needs, Waldman and Wheal's research makes clear that kinship carers do recognise a need, and that this ranges from understanding the law and benefit system to how to explain to your own child why their cousin cannot go on living with her parents. The conclusion of that research is that what is needed is the ability to *customise* training to individual experience and identified need. Interestingly, this touches on a wider theme – that kinship foster care does not easily fit into one mould. This may explain part of its elusive quality for policy makers – it is not quite 'fostering' as routinely defined, and it includes a very wide range of particular circumstances.

Abused children

A similar theme about partnership, openness and exclusion occurs within Foulds' analysis of issues involved in protecting abused children. She suggests that the social worker will need to assess whether this is an open system, willing to work in partnership with the agency, and to acknowledge difficulties and stresses. It is critical to the management of risk to the child that the relative carers are able to acknowledge, not deny or minimise, the harm that has occurred. They must also be sufficiently comfortable with carrying a responsibility for monitoring the relationship between the child and her parents, and reporting to the agency. Once again the quality of the family's boundaries is crucial – are they permeable enough to allow a continuing relationship of trust with the social worker? Foulds quotes Reder et al. 'We understand closure to be primarily an issue about control ... and that outsiders were unwelcome intruders' (1993: 99).

She argues that in the case of child sexual abuse, the worker must be alert to the reasons why the child and other family members may be unable to reveal the full extent of the abuse. The abusers may retain effective control to silence their victims (who may include other family members as well as the child in question) through threats, bribery, and through projecting the blame and responsibility for the abuse onto their victims. Children trapped in an abusive situation may well have 'accommodated' to the situation. Equally, the worker must be aware that where abuse by one individual has been revealed, it is possible that a wider network of abuse is at work within the extended family and social network. A network meeting or family group conference could at times risk giving powerful but undisclosed abusers a dominant say in what happens to the child (Lupton 1998, referring to Atkin 1989 and Barbour 1991). Worrall points out that like other foster carers, kinship carers may find themselves subject to allegations of abuse, and that within a relatively familiar family context children may re-enact learned patterns of behaviour. Clearly, training and support in dealing with abused and emotionally disturbed children is essential for kinship foster carers too.

Permanency

One other factor here, and again one which questions a simple view of what we mean by 'permanency', is that sometimes patterns of kinship care may challenge the notion that permanency is to be achieved within a particular nuclear family unit. As Pemberton points out, various members of the extended family may at times support each other, and deal with difficulties presented by the child by sharing the care between different households. In the same way that the kinship foster carers may have offered respite care to the child's parents, so the wider family is able to offer respite care to the foster carers when pressures build. This flexibility is also supported by recent research which points to the usefulness, for teenagers in particular, of 'multiplex' placements:

> Social work placement plans may need to incorporate a number of stable 'known' contexts, all or mainly within the teenager's community, and include contingency arrangements ... Such a 'multiplex' placement plan would offer stability, allow

resources to be poolled, and encourage responsibility for and knowledge about the young person to be shared. (Department of Health 1996)

This description sounds just like network foster care at its best. What it also makes clear is that for teenagers at least, stability may be best achieved through flexible, complex arrangements, rather than by putting all the eggs into one basket. On the other hand, Worrall has pointed out that the child's perception of 'multiplex' placements can also be complex. Do the changes in living arrangements carry a message that here are a whole number of people who care about me – or is each move felt as a rejection?

Waldman and Wheal find that kinship foster carers do not want a changed legal status in relation to the child, though many of the children will remain long term. This does not fit with a simple 'permanence' model, but perhaps, as Williams suggests, we are learning a new model of permanence?

Children

Finally, but centrally, we return to a focus on the children. Kinship foster care can offer a placement in familiar surroundings, in the same community, allowing continuity of schooling, health care and relationship with friends. It can prevent the uprooting of children from their own (racial or ethnic) community and being exported and perhaps assimilated into a mainstream culture. Living with relatives can feel like somewhere the child naturally belongs without stigma, and she can feel that the offer to care is a statement of some commitment to her individually, not just a role. This, with an enhanced chance of maintaining contact with her parents and siblings, will enable a comfortable sense of security, which will help her to deal with the family tensions which may ensue:

> When a placement with a relative is appropriate and is well supported by the agency, it promotes an uninterrupted relationship for the child with the parent and relative, which is vital to a child's physical, social and emotional well being. (Barth et al. 1994)

All of this, we would argue needs careful policy making and skilled assessment and support from social workers. Wilson, commenting on informal caring in general, said

> The potential is evident in many agencies and programmes that the rediscovery of a basic fact of life - that people help each other – may represent a revolution in service delivery. It will require disciplined thought and action if the full potential of this discovery is to be realised. (Wilson 1986: 178–9)

References

Atkin, W.R. (1989), 'New Zealand: Children Versus Families – Is there a Conflict?, *Journal of Family Law*, 27(1).

Barbour, A. (1991), 'Family Group Conferences: Context and Consequences', *Social Work Review*, 3(40).

Barth, R., Berrick, J.D. and Gilbert, N. (eds) (1994), *Child Welfare Research Review*, Vol 1, New York: Columbia University Press.

Department of Health (1996), *Focus on Teenagers*, London: Department of Health.

Lupton, C. (1998), 'User Empowerment or Family Self-Reliance? The Family Group Conference Model', *British Journal of Social Work*, 28(1).

Redes, P., Duncan, S. and Gray, M. (1993), *Beyond Blame – Child Abuse Tragedies Revisited*, London: Routledge.

Wilson, P. (1986), 'Informal Care and Social Support: An Agenda for the Future', *British Journal of Social Work*, 16 (supplement): 173.

Index